Mastering Python Scripting for System Administrators

Write scripts and automate them for real-world administration tasks using Python

Ganesh Sanjiv Naik

BIRMINGHAM - MUMBAI

Mastering Python Scripting for System Administrators

Commissioning Editor: Vijin Boricha
Acquisition Editor: Shrilekha Inani
Content Development Editor: Sharon Raj
Technical Editor: Prashant Chaudhari
Copy Editor: Safis Editing
Project Coordinator: Drashti Panchal
Proofreader: Safis Editing
Indexer: Rekha Nair
Graphics: Tom Scaria
Production Coordinator: Jyoti Chauhan

First published: January 2019

Production reference: 1240119

Published by Packt Publishing Ltd.
Livery Place
35 Livery Street
Birmingham
B3 2PB, UK.

ISBN 978-1-78913-322-6

www.packtpub.com

I wish to dedicate this book to my Gurudev, His Holiness Dr. Jayant Balaji Athavale. I wish to express gratitude for his guidance on how to become a good human being, a good professional, and a seeker on the path of spiritual progress.

`mapt.io`

Mapt is an online digital library that gives you full access to over 5,000 books and videos, as well as industry leading tools to help you plan your personal development and advance your career. For more information, please visit our website.

Why subscribe?

- Spend less time learning and more time coding with practical eBooks and Videos from over 4,000 industry professionals

- Improve your learning with Skill Plans built especially for you

- Get a free eBook or video every month

- Mapt is fully searchable

- Copy and paste, print, and bookmark content

Packt.com

Did you know that Packt offers eBook versions of every book published, with PDF and ePub files available? You can upgrade to the eBook version at `www.packt.com` and as a print book customer, you are entitled to a discount on the eBook copy. Get in touch with us at `customercare@packtpub.com` for more details.

At `www.packt.com`, you can also read a collection of free technical articles, sign up for a range of free newsletters, and receive exclusive discounts and offers on Packt books and eBooks.

Contributors

About the author

Ganesh Sanjiv Naik is an author, consultant, and corporate trainer in the fields of AI, data science, machine learning, the **Internet of Things** (**IoT**), and embedded Linux in relation to product development. He has more than 20 years of professional experience in information technology. Ganesh has a passion and a deep desire for teaching. He has trained 2,000+ engineers in Linux and Android product development. He has worked as a corporate trainer for the ISRO, Intel, GE, Samsung, Motorola, Penang Skill Development Center (Malaysia), and various companies in Singapore, Malaysia, and India. He has started a company called Levana Technologies, which works in AI, machine learning, and data science, providing training, projects, and consultancy activities.

I want to thank my wife, Vishalakshi Naik, for providing valuable suggestions, support, and continuous motivation. I also want to thank my colleagues, Mansi Joshi and Kalpesh Patil, who helped me in editing and proofreading, and also provided feedback from a technical perspective.

Big thanks to the entire team at Packt, especially Shrilekha Inani, Priyanka Deshpande, and Sharon Raj, for providing me with motivating support throughout the book.

About the reviewers

Yogendra Sharma is a developer with experience in the architecture, design, and development of scalable and distributed applications, with a core interest in microservices and Spring. He is currently working as an IoT and cloud architect at Intelizign Engineering Services Pvt, Pune. He also has hands-on experience in technologies such as AWS Cloud, IoT, Python, J2SE, J2EE, Node.js, Angular, MongoDB, and Docker. He constantly explores technical novelties, and he is open-minded and eager to learn about new technologies and frameworks. He has reviewed several books and video courses published by Packt Publishing.

Abhijeet Mote has a master's degree in computer application (MCA) from University of Mumbai. He is an open source evangelist and works as a senior software engineer. He has worked in multiple domains, including education, media, and IoT. His hobbies involve work on open source projects, and he loves to give back to the open source community by spreading knowledge of Python and other open source stacks. He conducts training sessions for students, teachers, and enthusiastic developers, and he mentors students for their final year projects. He has been invited to conferences, such as FOSSASIA 2018, and PyGotham, for his contribution in teaching open source technology to enthusiastic developers and underrepresented groups.

Packt is searching for authors like you

If you're interested in becoming an author for Packt, please visit `authors.packtpub.com` and apply today. We have worked with thousands of developers and tech professionals, just like you, to help them share their insight with the global tech community. You can make a general application, apply for a specific hot topic that we are recruiting an author for, or submit your own idea.

Table of Contents

Preface

Python has evolved and extended its features toward every possible IT operation. This book will help you leverage the latest features of Python to write effective scripts and create command-line tools (for use when it comes to data types, loops, conditionals, functions, error handling, and more) to administer your environment. This book will revolve around the entire development process, from setup and planning to automated testing and building different command-line tools. This book gets you up and running with everything from basic scripting to using standard library packages. Finally, you will create a large scripting project where you will learn how to plan, implement, and distribute a project based on ideal resources.

Who this book is for

This book would be ideal for users with some basic understanding of Python programming who are interested in scaling their programming skills to command-line scripting and system administration.

Prior knowledge of Python is necessary.

What this book covers

Chapter 1, *Python Scripting Overview*, covers the installation procedures for Python as well as the use of the Python interpreter tool. You will learn how to assign values to variables and be introduced to variables and strings. You will study the sequence data types, including lists, tuples, sets, and dictionaries. Also, you will learn how to parse command-line options in scripts.

Chapter 2, *Debugging and Profiling Python Scripts*, teaches you how to debug Python programs using debugger tools. You will also learn how to handle errors, and explore the concepts of profiling and timing.

Chapter 3, *Unit Testing – Introduction to the Unit Testing Framework*, is about unit testing in Python. We will create unit tests to test programs.

Chapter 4, *Automating Regular Administrative Activities*, will teach you how to automate the regular administrative activities of the system administrator. You will learn about accepting inputs, handling passwords, the execution of external commands, reading config files, adding warning codes to scripts, implementing CPU limits, web browser launching, use of the os module, and taking backups.

Chapter 5, *Handling Files, Directories, and Data*, is where you will learn about using the os module for various activities. You will learn about the data and some methods applied to that data, such as copying, moving, merging, and comparing. You will also learn about the tarfile module and how to use it.

Chapter 6, *File Archiving, Encrypting, and Decrypting*, delves into file archiving, creating archives, and TAR and ZIP creation. You will also learn about unpacking the .tar and .zip files using applications.

Chapter 7, *Text Processing and Regular Expressions*, looks at text processing and regular expressions in Python. Python has a very powerful library of things called called regular expressions, which do tasks such as searching and extracting data. You will learn how to use regular expressions with files. You will also learn how to read and write to files.

Chapter 8, *Documentation and Reporting*, will teach you how to document and report information using Python. You will also learn how to take input using Python scripts and how to print the output. Using Python, you can write scripts for automated information gathering. Writing scripts for receiving emails is easier in Python. You will learn how to format information.

Chapter 9, *Working with Various Files*, will go into the issue of handling various files, such as PDF files, Excel files, and CSV files. You will learn how to open, edit, and get data from these files using Python.

Chapter 10, *Basic Networking – Socket Programming*, will first introduce the basics of networking; then you will learn about sockets such as TCP, UDP, and more. You will also learn about how to program sockets to communicate and get information of protocols such as HTTP and FTP.

Chapter 11, *Handling Emails Using Python Scripting*, explores how to compose and send emails using Python scripts. Sending emails is a very common task in any software program. We can use Python's smtplib module for sending emails in Python programs. In this chapter, you will also learn about the different protocols used for sending emails on different servers.

Chapter 12, *Remote Monitoring of Hosts Over Telnet and SSH*, shows you how to carry out basic configurations on a server with the SSH protocol. We will begin by using the Telnet module, after which we will implement the same configurations using the preferred method, SSH.

Chapter 13, *Building Graphical User Interface*, looks at graphical user interface creation with the PyQt module.

Chapter 14, *Working with Apache and Other Log Files*, explains how to work with Apache log files. You will also learn about log-parsing applications; that is, identifying the particular types of log messages. You will also learn how to parse these files and how to handle multiple files; detecting any exceptions, storing data, and producing reports.

Chapter 15, *SOAP and REST API Communication*, concerns the basics of SOAP and REST, and the differences between them. You will also get to know the SOAP API and how to use it using different libraries. We will also study the REST API and standard libraries.

Chapter 16, *Web Scraping – Extracting Useful Data from Websites*, will teach you about extracting data from a website using Python's libraries. You will also learn how to search for articles and source code using Python.

Chapter 17, *Statistics Gathering and Reporting*, is about advanced Python libraries that are used in scientific calculations. These libraries are NumPy, SciPy, and Matplotlib. You will learn about the concepts of data visualization and learn how to plot data.

Chapter 18, *MySQL and SQLite Database Administrations*, looks at database administration using MySQL and SQLite databases. You will learn about the requirements and design for this kind of administration, how to modify the plugin framework, and how to write producer and consumer code.

To get the most out of this book

We wrote this book to be as accessible as possible and to teach you many different approaches to programming with Python through several scripts. However, to get the most out of them, you need to do the following:

- Have a Linux system set up and configured for testing/debugging scripts
- Understand the created scripts
- Keep in mind what the components of each script are
- Check how the components could be reused or combined in new ways

This book assumes a certain level of Python knowledge to begin your journey; these basic skills will not be covered in this book. These skills include the following:

- How to set up and configure a Linux system
- How to install, access, and configure a specific Python IDE (although several are already included in most Linux distributions)
- Some basics about computing and programming (although we will do our best to provide a crash course)

Download the example code files

You can download the example code files for this book from your account at `www.packt.com`. If you purchased this book elsewhere, you can visit `www.packt.com/support` and register to have the files emailed directly to you.

You can download the code files by following these steps:

1. Log in or register at `www.packt.com`.
2. Select the **SUPPORT** tab.
3. Click on **Code Downloads & Errata**.
4. Enter the name of the book in the **Search** box and follow the onscreen instructions.

Once the file is downloaded, please make sure that you unzip or extract the folder using the latest version of:

- WinRAR/7-Zip for Windows
- Zipeg/iZip/UnRarX for Mac
- 7-Zip/PeaZip for Linux

The code bundle for the book is also hosted on GitHub `https://github.com/PacktPublishing/Mastering-Python-Scripting-for-System-Administrators-/`. In case there's an update to the code, it will be updated on the existing GitHub repository.

We also have other code bundles from our rich catalog of books and videos available at `https://github.com/PacktPublishing/`. Check them out!

Conventions used

There are a number of text conventions used throughout this book.

`CodeInText`: Indicates code words in text, database table names, folder names, filenames, file extensions, pathnames, dummy URLs, user input, and Twitter handles. Here is an example: " To unpack the archives `shutil` module has `unpack_archive()` function."

A block of code is set as follows:

```
>>> 3 * 'hi' + 'hello'
'hihihihello'
```

Any command-line input or output is written as follows:

```
sudo apt install python3-pip
```

Bold: Indicates a new term, an important word, or words that you see onscreen. Here is an example: " The **CSV** format, which stands for **Comma Separated Values** format."

Warnings or important notes appear like this.

Tips and tricks appear like this.

Get in touch

Feedback from our readers is always welcome.

General feedback: If you have questions about any aspect of this book, mention the book title in the subject of your message and email us at `customercare@packtpub.com`.

Errata: Although we have taken every care to ensure the accuracy of our content, mistakes do happen. If you have found a mistake in this book, we would be grateful if you would report this to us. Please visit `www.packt.com/submit-errata`, selecting your book, clicking on the Errata Submission Form link, and entering the details.

Piracy: If you come across any illegal copies of our works in any form on the Internet, we would be grateful if you would provide us with the location address or website name. Please contact us at `copyright@packt.com` with a link to the material.

If you are interested in becoming an author: If there is a topic that you have expertise in and you are interested in either writing or contributing to a book, please visit `authors.packtpub.com`.

Reviews

Please leave a review. Once you have read and used this book, why not leave a review on the site that you purchased it from? Potential readers can then see and use your unbiased opinion to make purchase decisions, we at Packt can understand what you think about our products, and our authors can see your feedback on their book. Thank you!

For more information about Packt, please visit `packt.com`

Python Scripting Overview

1

Python is a scripting language, created by Guido van Rossum in 1991, which is used in various applications, such as game development, GIS programming, software development, web development, data analytics, machine learning, and system scripting.

Python is an object-oriented, high-level programming language with dynamic semantics. Mainly, Python is an interpreted language. Python is used for rapid application development, as it has all of the advanced features for development.

Python is simple and easy to learn, as its syntax makes programs more readable. Hence, the program maintenance cost is low.

Python has one more important feature of importing modules and packages. This feature allows for code reuse. The Python interpreter is easy to understand. We can write the complete code one by one in it and, as Python is an interpreted language, the code gets executed line by line. Python also has a wide range of libraries for advanced functionality.

This chapter will cover the following topics:

- Python scripting
- Installing and using Python and various tools
- Variables, numbers, and strings
- Python supported data structures and how to use all of these concepts in a script
- Decision making; that is, the `if` statement
- Looping statements; that is, the `for` and `while` loops
- Functions
- Modules

Technical requirements

Before you start reading this book, you should know the basics of Python programming, such as the basic syntax, variable types, tuple data type, list dictionary, functions, strings, and methods. Two versions, 3.7.2 and 2.7.15, are available at `python.org/downloads/`. In this book we'll work with version 3.7 for code examples and package installing.

Examples and source code for this chapter are available in the GitHub repository: `https://github.com/PacktPublishing/Mastering-Python-Scripting-for-System-Administrators-`.

Why Python?

Python has a wide range of libraries for open source data analysis tools, web frameworks, testing, and so on. Python is a programming language that can be used on different platforms (Windows, Mac, Linux, and embedded Linux H/W platforms, such as Raspberry Pi). It's used to develop desktop as well as web applications.

Developers can write programs with fewer lines if they use Python. Prototyping is very quick, as Python runs on an interpreter system. Python can be treated in an object-oriented, a procedural, or a functional way.

Python can do various tasks, such as creating web applications. It is used with the software to create workflows; it connects to database systems, handles files, handles big data, and performs complex mathematics.

Python syntax compared to other programming languages

The code written in Python is highly readable because it's similar to the English language. To complete a command, Python uses new lines.

Python has a great feature: indentation. Using indentations, we can define the scope for decision-making statements, loops such as `for` and `while` loops, functions, and classes.

Python installation

In this section, we will be learning about the installation of Python on different platforms, such as Linux and Windows.

Installation on the Linux platform

Most Linux distributions have Python 2 in their default installations. Some of them also have Python 3 included.

To install `python3` on Debian-based Linux, run the following command in the Terminal:

```
sudo apt install python3
```

To install `python3` on `centos`, run the following command in the Terminal:

```
sudo yum install python3
```

If you are unable to install Python using the preceding commands, download Python from `https://www.python.org/downloads/` and follow the instructions.

Installation on the Windows platform

For installing Python in Microsoft Windows, you'll have to download the executable from `python.org` and install it. Download `python.exe` from `https://www.python.org/downloads/` and choose the Python version that you want install on your PC. Then, double-click on the downloaded `exe` and install Python. On the installation wizard, there's checkbox that says **Add Python to the path**. Check this checkbox and then follow the instructions to install `python3`.

Installing and using pip to install packages

In Linux, install `pip` as follows:

```
sudo apt install python-pip --- This will install pip for python 2.
sudo apt install python3-pip --- This will install pip for python 3.
```

In Windows, install `pip` as follows:

```
python -m pip install pip
```

Installation on Mac

To install `python3`, first we must have `brew` installed on our system. To install `brew` on your system, run the following command:

```
/usr/bin/ruby -e "$(curl -fsSL
https://raw.githubusercontent.com/Homebrew/install/master/install)"
```

By running the preceding command. `brew` will get installed. Now we will install `python3` using `brew`:

```
brew install python3
```

Installing Jupyter notebook

For installing the Jupyter Notebook, download Anaconda.

Install the downloaded version of Anaconda and follow the instructions on the wizard.

Install Jupyter using `pip`:

```
pip install jupyter
```

In Linux, `pip install jupyter` will install Jupyter for `python 2`. If you want to install `jupyter` for `python 3`, run the following command:

```
pip3 install jupyter
```

Installing and using the virtual environment

Now we will see how to install the virtual environment and how to activate it.

To install the virtual environment on Linux, perform the following steps:

1. First check whether `pip` is installed or not. We are going to install `pip` for `python3`:

   ```
   sudo apt install python3-pip
   ```

2. Install the virtual environment using `pip3`:

   ```
   sudo pip3 install virtualenv
   ```

3. Now we will create the virtual environment. You can give it any name; I have called it `pythonenv`:

   `virtualenv pythonenv`

4. Activate your virtual environment:

   `source venv/bin/activate`

5. After your work is done, you can deactivate `virtualenv` by using following command:

   `deactivate`

In Windows, run the `pip install virtualenv` command to install the virtual environment. The steps for installing `virtualenv` are same as with Linux.

Installing Geany and PyCharm

Download Geany from `https://www.geany.org/download/releases` and download the required binaries. Follow the instructions while installing.

Download PyCharm from `https://www.jetbrains.com/pycharm/download/#section=windows` and follow the instructions.

Python interpreter

Python is an interpreted language. It has an interactive console called the Python interpreter or Python shell. This shell provides a way to execute your program line by line without creating a script.

You can access all of Python's built-in functions and libraries, installed modules, and command history in the Python interactive console. This console gives you the opportunity to to explore Python. You're able to paste code into scripts when you are ready.

The difference between Python and Bash scripting

In this section, we're going to learn about the difference between Python and Bash scripting. The differences are as follows:

- Python is a scripting language, whereas Bash is a shell used for entering and executing commands
- Dealing with larger programs is easier with Python
- In Python, you can do most things just by calling a one-line function from imported modules

Starting the interactive console

We can access Python's interactive console from any computer that has Python already installed. Run the following command to start Python's interactive console:

```
$ python
```

This will start the default Python interactive console.

In Linux, if we write Python in the Terminal, the python2.7 console starts. If you want to start the python3 console, then enter python3 in the Terminal and press *Enter*.

In Windows, when you enter Python in Command Prompt, it will start the console of the downloaded Python version.

Writing scripts with the Python interactive console

The Python interactive console starts from >>> prefix. This console will accept the Python commands, which you'll write after >>> prefix. Refer to the following screenshot:

```
student@ubuntu:~$ python3
Python 3.5.2 (default, Nov 23 2017, 16:37:01)
[GCC 5.4.0 20160609] on linux
Type "help", "copyright", "credits" or "license" for more information.
>>>
```

Now, we will see how to assign values to the variable, as in the following example:

```
>>> name = John
```

Here, we've assigned a character value of John to the name variable. We pressed *Enter* and received a new line with >>> prefix:

```
>>> name = John
```

Now, we will see an example of assigning values to variables and then we will perform a math operation to get the values:

```
>>> num1 = 5000
>>> num2 = 3500
>>> num3 = num1 + num2
>>> print (num3)
8500
>>> num4 = num3 - 2575
>>> print (num4)
5925
>>>
```

Here, we assigned values to variables, added two variables, stored the result in a third variable, and printed the result on to the Terminal. Next, we subtracted one variable from the result variable, and the output will get stored in the fourth variable. Then, we printed the result on to the Terminal. So this tells us that we can also use the Python interpreter as a calculator:

```
>>> 509 / 22
23.136363636363637
>>>
```

Here, we performed a division operation. We divided 509 by 22 and the result we got is 23.136363636363637.

Multiple lines

When we write multiple lines of code in the Python interpreter (for example, the If statement and for and while loop functions), then the interpreter uses three dots (...) as a secondary prompt for line continuation. To come out of these lines, you have to press the *Enter* key twice. Now we will look at the following example:

```
>>> val1 = 2500
>>> val2 = 2400
>>> if val1 > val2:
```

```
... print("val1 is greater than val2")
... else:
... print("val2 is greater than val1")
...
val1 is greater than val2
>>>
```

In this example, we've assigned integer values to two variables, val1 and val2, and we're checking whether val1 is greater than val2 or not. In this case, val1 is greater than val2, so the statement in the if block gets printed. Remember, statements in if and else blocks are indented. If you don't use indentation, you will get the following error:

```
>>> if val1 > val2:
... print("val1 is greater than val2")
File "<stdin>", line 2
print("val1 is greater than val2")
^
IndentationError: expected an indented block
>>>
```

Importing modules through the Python interpreter

If you are importing any module, then the Python interpreter checks if that module is available or not. You can do this by using the import statement. If that module is available, then you will see the >>> prefix after pressing the *Enter* key. This indicates that the execution was successful. If that module doesn't exist, the Python interpreter will show an error:

```
>>> import time
>>>
```

After importing the time module, we get the >>> prefix. This means that the module exists and this command gets executed successfully:

```
>>> import matplotlib
```

If the module doesn't exist, then you will get Traceback error:

```
File "<stdin>", line 1, in <module>
ImportError: No module named 'matplotlib'
```

So here, matplotlib isn't available, so it gives an error: ImportError: No module named 'matplotlib'.

To solve this error, we will have to install `matplotlib` and then again try to import `matplotlib`. After installing `matplotlib`, you should be able to import the module, as follows:

```
>>> import matplotlib
>>>
```

Exiting the Python console

We can come out of the Python console in two ways:

- The keyboard shortcut: *Ctrl + D*
- Using the `quit()` or `exit()` functions

The keyboard shortcut

The keyboard shortcut, *Ctrl + D,* will give you the following code:

```
>>> val1 = 5000
>>> val2 = 2500
>>>
>>> val3 = val1 - val2
>>> print (val3)
2500
>>>
student@ubuntu:~$
```

Using the quit() or exit() functions

`quit()` will take you out of Python's interactive console. It will also take you to the original Terminal you were previously in:

```
>>> Lion = 'Simba'
>>> quit()
student@ubuntu$
```

Indentation and tabs

Indentation is a must when writing block code in Python. Indentation is useful when you are writing functions, decision-making statements, looping statements, and classes. This makes it easy to read your Python programs.

We use indentation to indicate the block of code in Python programs. To indent a block of code, you can use spaces or tabs. Refer to the following example:

```
if val1 > val2:
    print ("val1 is greater than val2")
print("This part is not indented")
```

In the preceding example, we indented the `print` statement because it comes under the `if` block. The next print statement doesn't come under the `if` block and that's why we didn't indent it.

Variables

Like other programming languages, there's no need to declare your variables first. In Python, just think of any name to give your variable and assign it a value. You can use that variable in your program. So, in Python, you can declare variables whenever you need them.

In Python, the value of a variable may change during the program execution, as well as the type. In the following line of code, we assign the value `100` to a variable:

```
n = 100
Here are assigning 100 to the variable n. Now, we are going to increase the
value of n by 1:
>>> n = n + 1
>>> print (n)
101
>>>
```

The following is an example of a type of variable that can change during execution:

```
a = 50 # data type is implicitly set to integer
a = 50 + 9.50 # data type is changed to float
a = "Seventy" # and now it will be a string
```

Python takes care of the representation for the different data types; that is, each type of value gets stored in different memory locations. A variable will be a name to which we're going to assign a value:

```
>>> msg = 'And now for something completely different'
>>> a = 20
>>> pi = 3.1415926535897932
```

This example makes three assignments. The first assignment is a string assignment to the variable named `msg`. The second assignment is an integer assignment to the variable named `a` and the last assignment is a `pi` value assignment.

The type of a variable is the type of the value it refers to. Look at the following code:

```
>>> type(msg)
<type 'str'>
>>> type(a)
<type 'int'>
>>> type(pi)
<type 'float'>
```

Creating and assigning values to variables

In Python, variables don't need to be declared explicitly to reserve memory space. So, the declaration is done automatically whenever you assign a value to the variable. In Python, the equal sign = is used to assign values to variables.

Consider the following example:

```
#!/usr/bin/python3
name = 'John'
age = 25
address = 'USA'
percentage = 85.5
print(name)
print(age)
print(address)
print(percentage)

Output:
John
25
USA
85.5
```

In the preceding example, we assigned `John` to the `name` variable, `25` to the `age` variable, `USA` to the `address` variable, and `85.5` to the `percentage` variable.

We don't have to declare them first as we do in other languages. So, looking at the value interpreter will get the type of that variable. In the preceding example, `name` and `address` are `strings`, `age` is an integer, and `percentage` is a floating type.

Multiple assignments for the same value can be done as follows:

```
x = y = z = 1
```

In the preceding example, we created three variables and assigned an integer value 1 to them, and all of these three variables will be assigned to the same memory location.

In Python, we can assign multiple values to multiple variables in a single line:

```
x, y, z = 10, 'John', 80
```

Here, we declared one string variable, y, and assigned the value John to it and two integer variables, x and z, and assigned values 10 and 80 to them, respectively.

Numbers

The Python interpreter can also act as a calculator. You just have to type an expression and it will return the value. Parentheses ( ) are used to do the grouping, as shown in the following example:

```
>>> 5 + 5
10
>>> 100 - 5*5
75
>>> (100 - 5*5) / 15
5.0
>>> 8 / 5
1.6
```

The integer numbers are of the int type and a fractional part is of the float type.

 In Python, the division (/) operation always returns a float value. The floor division (//) gets an integer result. The % operator is used to calculate the remainder.

Consider the following example:

```
>>> 14/3
4.666666666666667
>>>
>>> 14//3
4
>>>
>>> 14%3
```

```
2
>>> 4*3+2
14
>>>
```

To calculate powers, Python has the ** operator, as shown in the following example:

```
>>> 8**3
512
>>> 5**7
78125
>>>
```

The equal sign (=) is used for assigning a value to a variable:

```
>>> m = 50
>>> n = 8 * 8
>>> m * n
3200
```

If a variable does not have any value and we still try to use it, then the interpreter will show an error:

```
>>> k
Traceback (most recent call last):
File "<stdin>", line 1, in <module>
NameError: name 'k' is not defined
>>>
```

If the operators have mixed types of operands, then the value we get will be of a floating point:

```
>>> 5 * 4.75 - 1
22.75
```

In the Python interactive console, _ contains the last printed expression value, as shown in the following example:

```
>>> a = 18.5/100
>>> b = 150.50
>>> a * b
27.8425
>>> b + _
178.3425
>>> round(_, 2)
178.34
>>>
```

Number data types store numeric values, which are immutable data types. If we do this, Python will allocate a new object for the changed data type.

We can create number objects just by assigning a value to them, as shown in the following example:

```
num1 = 50
num2 = 25
```

The `del` statement is used to delete single or multiple variables. Refer to the following example:

```
del num
del num_a, num_b
```

Number type conversion

In some situations, you need to convert a number explicitly from one type to another to satisfy some requirements. Python does this internally in an expression

- Type `int(a)` to convert a into an integer
- Type `float(a)` to convert a into a floating-point number
- Type `complex(a)` to convert a into a complex number with real part x and imaginary part `zero`
- Type `complex(a, b)` to convert a and b into a complex number with real part a and imaginary part b. a and b are numeric expressions

Strings

Like numbers, strings are also one of the data structures in Python. Python can manipulate strings. Strings can be expressed as follows:

- Enclosed in single quotes (' . . . ')
- Enclosed in double quotes (" . . . ")

See the following example:

```
>>> 'Hello Python'
'Hello Python'
>>> "Hello Python"
'Hello Python'
```

A string is a set of characters. We can access the characters one at a time, as follows:

```
>>> city = 'delhi'
>>> letter = city[1]
>>> letter = city[-3]
```

In the second statement, we are selecting the character number 1 from `city` and assigning it to `letter`. The number in those square brackets is an index. The index indicates which character you want to access. It starts from 0. So, in the preceding example, when you will execute `letter = city[1]`, you will get the following output:

```
city d e l h i
index 0 1 2 3 4
-5 -4 -3 -2 -1

Output:
e
l
```

Concatenation (+) and repetition (*)

Next, comes concatenation and repetition. Refer to the following code:

```
>>> 3 * 'hi' + 'hello'
'hihihihello'
```

In the preceding example, we are doing string concatenation and repetition. `3 * 'hi'` means `hi` gets printed 3 times and, using the + sign, we are joining the `hello` string next to `hi`.

We can automatically concatenate two strings just by writing them next to each other. These two strings must be enclosed between quotes, as shown here:

```
>>> 'he' 'llo'
'hello'
```

This feature is really helpful when you have long strings and you want to break them. Here is an example:

```
>>> str = ('Several strings'
... 'joining them together.')
>>> str
'Several strings joining them together.'
```

String slicing

Strings support slicing, which means getting characters by a specified range from your string. Let's take a look at the following example. Note that starting index value is always included and an end value is always excluded.

Consider a string, `str = "Programming"`:

```
>>> str[0:2]
'Pr'
>>> str[2:5]
'ogr'
```

Now, the default of an omitted first index is zero, as in the example:

```
>>> str[:2] + str[2:]
'Python'
>>> str[:4] + str[4:]
'Python'
>>> str[:2]
'Py'
>>> str[4:]
'on'
>>> str[-2:]
'on'
```

Accessing values in strings

We can access characters from strings using slicing by using square brackets. We can also access characters from strings between the specified range. Refer to the following example:

```
#!/usr/bin/python3
str1 = 'Hello Python!'
str2 = "Object Oriented Programming"
print ("str1[0]: ", str1[0])
print ("str2[1:5]: ", str2[1:5])

Output:
str1[0]: H
str2[1:5]: bjec
```

Updating strings

We can update a string by reassigning a new value to the specified index. Refer to the following example:

```
#!/usr/bin/python3
str1 = 'Hello Python!'
print ("Updated String: - ", str1 [:6] + 'John')

Output:
Updated String: - Hello John
```

Escape characters

Python supports escape characters that are non-printable and can be represented with a backslash notation. An escape character gets interpreted in both single and double quoted strings:

Notations	Hex characters	Description
a	0x07	Bell or alert
b	0x08	Backspace
cx		Control-x
n	0x0a	Newline
C-x		Control-x
e	0x1b	Escape
f	0x0c	Form feed
s	0x20	Space
M-C-x		Meta-control-x
x		Character x
nnn		Octal notation, where n is in the range 0.7
r	0x0d	Carriage return
xnn		Hexadecimal notation, where n is in the range 0.9, a.f, or A.F
t	0x09	Tab
v	0x0b	Vertical tab

Special string operators

The following table shows string's special operators. Consider a is `Hello` and b is `World`:

Operator	Description	Example
+	Concatenation: adds values on either side of the operator	a + b will give `HelloWorld`
[]	Slice: gives the character from the given index	a[7] will give r
[:]	Range slice: gives the characters from the given range	a[1:4] will give `ell`
*	Repetition: creates new strings, concatenating multiple copies of the same string	a*2 will give `HelloHello`
not in	Membership: returns `true` if a character does not exist in the given string	Z not in a `will` give 1
in	Membership: returns `true` if a character exists in the given string	H in a will give 1
%	Format: performs string formatting	

% string formatting operator

`%` is a string formatting operator in Python. Refer to the following example:

```
#!/usr/bin/python3
print ("Hello this is %s and my age is %d !" % ('John', 25))


Output:
Hello this is John and my age is 25 !
```

The following table shows a list of symbols used along with `%`:

S.No.	Format symbol and conversion
1	%c – character
2	%s – string conversion via str() prior to formatting
3	%i – signed decimal integer
4	%d – signed decimal integer
5	%u – unsigned decimal integer
6	%o – octal integer
7	%x – hexadecimal integer (lowercase letters)

8	%X – hexadecimal integer (uppercase letters)
9	%e – exponential notation (with lowercase e)
10	%E – exponential notation (with uppercase E)
11	%f – floating point real number

Triple quotes in Python

Python's triple quotes functionality for strings is used to span multiple lines, including newlines and tabs. The syntax for triple quotes consists of three consecutive single or double quotes. Refer to the following code:

```
#!/usr/bin/python3

para_str = """ Python is a scripting language which was created by
Guido van Rossum in 1991, t which is used in various sectors such as Game
Development, GIS Programming, Software Development, web development,
Data Analytics and Machine learning, System Scripting etc.
"""
print (para_str)
```

It produces the following output. Note the tabs and newlines:

```
Output:
Python is a scripting language which was created by
Guido van Rossum in 1991, which is used in various sectors such as
Game Development, GIS Programming, Software Development, web development,
Data Analytics and Machine learning, System Scripting etc.
```

Strings are immutable

Strings are immutable, meaning we can't change the values. Refer to the given example:

```
>>> welcome = 'Hello, John!'
>>> welcome[0] = 'Y'
TypeError: 'str' object does not support item assignment
```

As the strings are immutable; we cannot change an existing string. But we can create a new string that will be different from the original:

```
>>> str1 = 'Hello John'
>>> new_str = 'Welcome' + str1[5:]
>>> print(str1)
Hello John
>>> print(new_str)
```

```
Welcome John
>>>
```

Understanding lists

Python supports a data structure called `list`, which is a mutable and ordered sequence of elements. Each element in that list is called as item. Lists are defined by inserting values between square brackets `[ ]`. Each element of `list` is given a number, which we call as a position or index. The index starts from zero; that is, the first index is zero, the second index is 1, and so on. We can perform the following operations on lists: indexing, slicing, adding, multiplying, and checking for membership.

Python's built-in `length` function returns the length of that list. Python also has function for finding the largest and smallest item of `list`. Lists can be numbered lists, string lists, or mixed list.

The following is the code for creating a list:

```
l = list()
numbers = [10, 20, 30, 40]
animals = ['Dog', 'Tiger', 'Lion']
list1 = ['John', 5.5, 500, [110, 450]]
```

Here, we've created three lists: the first is `numbers`, the second is `animals`, and the third is `list1`. A list within another list is called as nested list. Our `list1` is a nested list. A list containing no elements is called an empty list; you can create one with empty brackets, `[]`.

As you might expect, you can assign list values to variables:

```
>>> cities = ['Mumbai', 'Pune', 'Chennai']
>>> numbers_list = [75, 857]
>>> empty_list = []
>>> print (cities, numbers_list, empty_list)
['Mumbai', 'Pune', 'Chennai'] [75, 857] []
```

Accessing values in lists

We can access the values from a list by using index values. We will specify the index number in `[` and `]`. Index starts from 0. Refer to the given example:

```
#!/usr/bin/python3
cities = ['Mumbai', 'Bangalore', 'Chennai', 'Pune']
```

```
numbers = [1, 2, 3, 4, 5, 6, 7 ]
print (cities[0])
print (numbers[1:5])
```

```
Output:
Mumbai
[2, 3, 4, 5]
```

Updating lists

You can update elements of lists, as shown in the following code:

```
#!/usr/bin/python3
cities = ['Mumbai', 'Bangalore', 'Chennai', 'Pune']
print ("Original Value: ", cities[3])
cities[3] = 'Delhi'
print ("New value: ", cities[3])
```

```
Output:
Original Value: Pune
New value: Delhi
```

Deleting list elements

To remove a list element, you can use either the `del` statement if you know exactly which element(s) you are deleting. You can use the `remove()` method if you do not know exactly which items to delete. Refer to the following example:

```
#!/usr/bin/python3
cities = ['Mumbai', 'Bangalore', 'Chennai', 'Pune']
print ("Before deleting: ", cities)
del cities[2]
print ("After deleting: ", cities)

Output:
Before deleting: ['Mumbai', 'Bangalore', 'Chennai', 'Pune']
After deleting: ['Mumbai', 'Bangalore', 'Pune']
```

Basic list operations

There are five basic list operations:

- Concatenation
- Repetition
- Length
- Membership
- Iteration

Description	Expression	Result
Concatenation	`[30, 50, 60] + ['Hello', 75, 66]`	`[30,50,60,'Hello',75,66]`
Membership	`45 in [45,58,99,65]`	`True`
Iteration	`for x in [45,58,99] : print (x,end = ' ')`	`45 58 99`
Repetition	`['Python'] * 3`	`['python', 'python', 'python']`
Length	`len([45, 58, 99, 65])`	`4`

List operations

In this section, we are going to learn about basic list operations: concatenation and repetition.

The + operator concatenates lists:

```
>>> a = [30, 50, 60]
>>> b = ['Hello', 75, 66 ]
>>> c = a + b
>>> print c
[30,50,60,'Hello',75,66]
```

Similarly, the * operator repeats a list a given number of times:

```
>>> [0] * 4
[0, 0, 0, 0]
>>> ['Python'] * 3
['python', 'python', 'python']
```

Indexing, slicing, and matrices

List indices work the same way as string indices. Values can be accessed using `index`. If you try to read or write an element that does not exist, you get `IndexError`. If an index has a negative value, it counts backward from the end of the list.

Now, we will create a list named `cities` and we will see the index operations:

```
cities = ['Mumbai', 'Bangalore', 'Chennai', 'Pune']
```

Description	Expression	Results
Index start at zero	cities[2]	'Chennai'
Slicing: getting sections	cities[1:]	['Bangalore', 'Chennai', 'Pune']
Negative: count from the right	cities[-3]	'Bangalore'

Tuples

Python's tuple data structure is immutable, meaning we cannot change the elements of the tuples. Basically, a tuple is a sequence of values that are separated by commas and are enclosed in parentheses `( )`. Like lists, tuples are an ordered sequence of elements:

```
>>> t1 = 'h', 'e', 'l', 'l', 'o'
```

Tuples are enclosed in parentheses `( )`:

```
>>> t1 = ('h', 'e', 'l', 'l', 'o')
```

You can also create a tuple with a single element. You just have to put a final comma in the tuple:

```
>>> t1 = 'h',
>>> type(t1)
<type 'tuple'>
```

A value in parentheses is not a tuple:

```
>>> t1 = ('a')
>>> type(t1)
<type 'str'>
```

We can create an empty tuple using the `tuple()` function:

```
>>> t1 = tuple()
>>> print (t1)
()
```

If the argument is a sequence (string, list, or tuple), the result is a tuple with the elements of the sequence:

```
>>> t = tuple('mumbai')
>>> print t
('m', 'u', 'm', 'b', 'a', 'i')
```

Tuples have values between parentheses ( ) separated by commas:

```
>>> t = ('a', 'b', 'c', 'd', 'e')
>>> print t[0]
'a'
```

The slice operator selects a range of elements.

```
>>> print t[1:3]
('b', 'c')
```

Accessing values in tuples

To access values in a tuple, use the square brackets for slicing along with the index or indices to obtain the value available at that index or indices, as shown in the following example:

```
#!/usr/bin/python3
cities = ('Mumbai', 'Bangalore', 'Chennai', 'Pune')
numbers = (1, 2, 3, 4, 5, 6, 7)
print (cities[3])
print (numbers[1:6])

Output:
Pune
(2, 3, 4, 5)
```

Updating tuples

Tuple updating is not possible in Python, as tuples are immutable. But you can create a new tuple with an existing tuple, as shown in the following example:

```
#!/usr/bin/python3
cities = ('Mumbai', 'Bangalore', 'Chennai', 'Pune')
numbers = (1,2,3,4,5,6,7)
tuple1 = cities + numbers
print(tuple1)

Output:
('Mumbai', 'Bangalore', 'Chennai', 'Pune', 1, 2, 3, 4, 5, 6, 7)
```

Deleting tuple elements

We cannot remove individual tuple elements. So, to remove an entire tuple explicitly, use the `del` statement. Refer to the following example:

```
#!/usr/bin/python3
cities = ('Mumbai', 'Bangalore', 'Chennai', 'Pune')
print ("Before deleting: ", cities)
del cities
print ("After deleting: ", cities)

Output:
Before deleting: ('Mumbai', 'Bangalore', 'Chennai', 'Pune')
Traceback (most recent call last):
File "01.py", line 5, in <module>
print ("After deleting: ", cities)
NameError: name 'cities' is not defined
```

Basic tuple operations

Like lists, there are five basic tuple operations:

- Concatenation
- Repetition
- Length

- Membership
- Iteration

Description	Expression	Results
Iteration	`for x in (45,58,99) :` `print (x,end = ' ')`	`45 58 99`
Repetition	`('Python') * 3`	`('python', 'python', 'python')`
Length	`len(45, 58, 99, 65)`	`4`
Concatenation	`(30, 50, 60) + ('Hello', 75, 66)`	`(30,50,60,'Hello',75,66)`
Membership	`45 in (45,58,99,65)`	`True`

Indexing, slicing, and matrices

Tuple indices work the same way as list indices. Values can be accessed using index. If you try to read or write an element that does not exist, you get `IndexError`. If an index has a negative value, it counts backward from the end of the list.

Now, we will create a tuple named `cities` and perform some index operations:

```
cities = ('Mumbai', 'Bangalore', 'Chennai', 'Pune')
```

Description	Expression	Results
Index starts at zero	`cities[2]`	`'Chennai'`
Slicing: getting sections	`cities[1:]`	`('Bangalore', 'Chennai', 'Pune')`
Negative: count from the right	`cities[-3]`	`'Bangalore'`

max() and min()

Using the `max()` and `min()` functions, we can find the highest and lowest values from the tuple. These functions allow us to find out information about quantitative data. Let's look at an example:

```
>>> numbers = (50, 80,98, 110.5, 75, 150.58)
>>> print(max(numbers))
150.58
>>>
```

Using `max()`, we will get the highest value in our tuple. Similarly, we can use the `min()` function:

```
>>> numbers = (50, 80,98, 110.5, 75, 150.58)
>>> print(min(numbers))
50
>>>
```

So, here we are getting the minimum value.

Sets

A set is an unordered collection of elements with no duplicates. The basic use of a set is to check membership testing and eliminate duplicate entries. These set objects support mathematical operations, such as union, intersection, difference, and symmetric difference. We can create a set using curly braces or the `set()` function. If you want create an empty set, then use `set()`, not `{}`.

Here is a brief demonstration:

```
>>> fruits = {'Mango', 'Apple', 'Mango', 'Watermelon', 'Apple', 'Orange'}
>>> print (fruits)
{'Orange', 'Mango', 'Apple', 'Watermelon'}
>>> 'Orange' in fruits
True
>>> 'Onion' in fruits
False
>>>
>>> a = set('abracadabra')
>>> b = set('alacazam')
>>> a
{'d', 'c', 'r', 'b', 'a'}
>>> a - b
{'r', 'd', 'b'}
>>> a | b
{'d', 'c', 'r', 'b', 'm', 'a', 'z', 'l'}
>>> a & b
{'a', 'c'}
>>> a ^ b
{'r', 'd', 'b', 'm', 'z', 'l'}
```

Set comprehensions are also supported in Python. Refer to the following code:

```
>>> a = {x for x in 'abracadabra' if x not in 'abc'}
>>> a
{'r', 'd'}
```

Dictionaries

A dictionary is a data type in Python, which consists of key value pairs and is enclosed in curly braces { }. Dictionaries are unordered and indexed by keys, where each key must be unique. These keys must be immutable type. Tuples can be used as keys if they contain only strings, numbers, or tuples.

Just a pair of braces creates an empty dictionary: { }. The main operations on a dictionary are storing a value with some key and extracting the value given to the key. It is also possible to delete a key value pair with del. If you store using a key that is already in use, the old value associated with that key is forgotten. It is an error to extract a value using a non-existent key. Here is a small example using a dictionary:

```
>>> student = {'Name':'John', 'Age':25}
>>> student['Address'] = 'Mumbai'
>>> student
student = {'Name':'John', 'Age':25, 'Address':'Mumbai'}
>>> student['Age']
25
>>> del student['Address']
>>> student
student = {'Name':'John', 'Age':25}
>>> list(student.keys())
['Name', 'Age']
>>> sorted(student.keys())
['Age', 'Name']
>>> 'Name' in student
True
>>> 'Age' not in student
False
```

Arbitrary key and value expressions along with dictionary comprehensions are used to create dictionaries:

```
>>> {x: x**2 for x in (4, 6, 8)}
{4: 16, 6: 36, 8: 64}
```

When the keys are simple strings, it is sometimes easier to specify pairs using keyword arguments:

```
>>> dict(John=25, Nick=27, Jack=28)
{'Nick': 27, 'John': 25, 'Jack': 28}
```

Parsing command-line arguments

In this section, we are going to learn about parsing arguments and the module used to parse arguments.

Command-line arguments in Python

We can start a program with additional arguments, in the command line. Python programs can start with command-line arguments. Let's look at an example:

```
$ python program_name.py img.jpg
```

Here, `program_name.py` and `img.jpg` are arguments.

Now, we are going to use modules to get the arguments:

Module	Use	Python version
optparse	Deprecated	< 2.7
sys	All arguments in `sys.argv` (basic)	All
argparse	Building a command-line interface	>= 2.3
fire	Automatically generating **Command-Line Interfaces (CLIs)**	All
docopt	Creating CLIs interfaces	>= 2.5

Sys.argv

The `sys` module is used to access command-line parameters. The `len(sys.argv)` function contains the number of arguments. To print all of the arguments, simply execute `str(sys.argv)`. Let's have a look at an example:

```
01.py
import sys
print('Number of arguments:', len(sys.argv))
print('Argument list:', str(sys.argv))
```

```
Output:
Python3 01.py img
Number of arguments 2
Arguments list: ['01.py', 'img']
```

Decision making

When we want to execute a code block when the condition is `true`, decision making comes to the rescue. The `if...elif...else` statement is used in Python for decision making.

Python if statement syntax

The following is the syntax for the `if` statement:

```
if test_expression:
    statement(s)
```

Here, the program evaluates the test expression and will execute `statement(s)` only if the text expression is `true`. If the text expression is `false`, `statement(s)` isn't executed.

In Python, the body of the `if` statement is indicated by the indentation. The body starts with an indentation and the first unindented line marks the end. Let's look at an example:

```
a = 10
if a > 0:
    print(a, "is a positive number.")
print("This statement is always printed.")

a = -10
if a > 0:
    print(a, "is a positive number.")

Output:
10 is a positive number.
This statement is always printed.
```

Python if...else statement syntax

In this section, we are going to learn about the if..else statement. The else block will get executed only when the if condition is false. Refer to the following syntax:

```
if test expression:
    if block
else:
    else block
```

The if..else statement evaluates the test expression and will execute the body of if only when the test condition is true. If the condition is false, the body of else is executed. Indentation is used to separate the blocks. Refer to the following example:

```
a = 10
if a > 0:
    print("Positive number")
else:
    print("Negative number")

Output:
Positive number
```

Python if...elif...else statement

The elif statement checks multiple statements for a true value. Whenever the value evaluates to true, that code block gets executed. Refer to the following syntax:

```
if test expression:
    if block statements
elif test expression:
    elif block statements
else:
    else block statements
```

elif is short for else if. It allows us to check for multiple expressions. If the condition written in the if statement is false, then it will check the condition of the next elif block, and so on. If all of the conditions are false, the body of else is executed.

Only one block among the several `if...elif...else` blocks is executed according to the condition. The `if` block can have only one else block. But it can have multiple `elif` blocks. Let's take a look at an example:

```python
a = 10
if a > 50:
 print("a is greater than 50")
elif a == 10:
 print("a is equal to 10")
else:
 print("a is negative")

Output:
a is equal to 10
```

Loops

To handle all of the looping requirements in your script, Python supports two loops:

- `for loop`
- `while loop`

Now, we are going to learn about `for loop` and `while loop`.

for loop

`for loop` iterates over each item of the sequence or any other iterable object and it will execute the statements in the for block each time. Refer to the following syntax:

```python
for i in sequence:
    for loop body
```

Here, `i` is the variable that takes the value of the item inside the sequence on each iteration. This loop continues until we reach the last item in the sequence. This is illustrated in the following diagram:

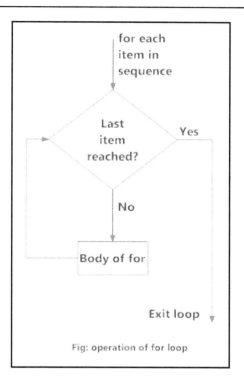

Fig: operation of for loop

Refer to the following example:

```
numbers = [6, 5, 3, 8, 4, 2, 5, 4, 11]
sum = 0
for i in numbers:
 sum = sum + i
 print("The sum is", sum)

Output:
The sum is 6
The sum is 11
The sum is 14
The sum is 22
The sum is 26
The sum is 28
The sum is 33
The sum is 37
The sum is 48
```

The range() function

The Python `range()` function will generate a sequence of numbers. For example, `range(10)` will generate numbers from 0 to 9 (10 numbers).

We can also define the start, stop, and step size as parameters and `range()` will be as follows:

```
range(start, stop, step size).
Step size defaults to 1 if not provided.
For loop example using range() function:
```

Let's take a look at an example:

```
for i in range(5):
 print("The number is", i)

Output:
The number is 0
The number is 1
The number is 2
The number is 3
The number is 4
```

while loop

`while` is a looping statement that will iterate over a block of code until the entered test expression is `true`. We use this loop when we don't know how many times the iterations will go on. Refer to the following syntax:

```
while test_expression:
    while body statements
```

In the while loop, first we will check the test expression. The `while` block will get executed only if the test expression is `true`. After one iteration, the expression will be checked again and this process continues until `test_expression` evaluates to `false`. This is illustrated in the following diagram:

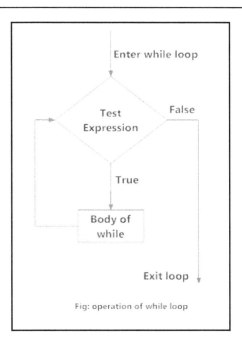

Fig: operation of while loop

The following is an example of the `while` loop:

```
a = 10
sum = 0
i = 1
while i <= a:
    sum = sum + i
    i = i + 1
    print("The sum is", sum)
```

```
Output:
The sum is 1
The sum is 3
The sum is 6
The sum is 10
The sum is 15
The sum is 21
The sum is 28
The sum is 36
The sum is 45
The sum is 55
```

Iterators

In Python, an iterator is an object that can be iterated upon. It is an object that will return data, one element at a time. Python's iterator object implements two methods, __iter__() and __next__(). Mostly, iterators are implemented within loops, generators, and comprehensions.

In the following example, we are using the next() function, which will iterate through all of the items. After reaching the end and there is no more data to be returned, it will raise StopIteration, as shown in the following example:

```
numbers = [10, 20, 30, 40]

numbers_iter = iter(numbers)

print(next(numbers_iter))
print(next(numbers_iter))
print(numbers_iter.__next__())
print(numbers_iter.__next__())

next(numbers_iter)

Output:
10
20
30
40
Traceback (most recent call last):
  File "sample.py", line 10, in <module>
    next(numbers_iter)
StopIteration
```

Generators

We can create iterators using Python generators. In Python, a generator is a function that returns an object that we can iterate over.

How to create a generator in Python?

Creating a generator is easy in Python. You can create a generator just by defining a function with a `yield` statement instead of a `return` statement. If a function contains at least one `yield` statement, it becomes a generator function. `yield` and `return` statements will return some value from a function. Here is an example:

```python
def my_gen():
    n = 1
    print('This is printed first')
    yield n
    n += 1
    print('This is printed second')
    yield n
    n += 1
    print('This is printed at last')
    yield n
    for item in my_gen():
        print(item)

Output:
This is printed first
1
This is printed second
2
This is printed at last
3
```

Functions

A function is a set of statements that perform a specific task. Using functions helps in breaking our program into smaller parts. Programs will be more organized if we use functions as it avoids repetition and makes code reusable. Look at the following syntax:

```python
def function_name(parameters):
    statement(s)
```

Refer to the following example:

```
def welcome(name):
    print("Hello " + name + ", Welcome to Python Programming !")

welcome("John")

Output:
Hello John, Welcome to Python Programming !
```

The return statement

The `return` statement is used to exit a function. Refer to the following syntax:

```
return [expression_list]
```

This statement may contain an expression where a value has to be returned. If there is no expression, then the function will return a None object, as shown in the following example:

```
def return_value(a):
    if a >= 0:
        return a
    else:
        return -a
print(return_value(2))
print(return_value(-4))

Output:
2
4
```

Lambda functions

In Python, an anonymous function is a function that is defined without a name and is called a `lambda` function, as it is defined using a keyword `lambda`. We use these functions whenever we require a function for a short period of time.

Lambda functions are used along with built-in functions, such as `filter()`, and `map()`.

The filter() function returns a list of elements and has only one iterable as input. The following shows an example using `filter()`:

```
numbers = [10, 25, 54, 86, 89, 11, 33, 22]
new_numbers = list(filter(lambda x: (x%2 == 0) , numbers))
```

```
print(new_numbers)

Output:
[10, 54, 86, 22]
```

In this example, the `filter()` function is taking a `lambda` function and a list as an argument.

The `map()` function returns a list of results after applying the specified function. Now, let's look at an example using `map()`:

```
my_list = [1, 5, 4, 6, 8, 11, 3, 12]
new_list = list(map(lambda x: x * 2 , my_list))
print(new_list)

Output:
[2, 10, 8, 12, 16, 22, 6, 24]
```

Here, the `map()` function is taking a `lambda` function and a list.

Modules

Modules are just files that contain Python statements and definitions. A file that contains Python code (for example, `sample.py`) is called a module and its module name would be `sample`. Using modules, we can break larger programs into small and organized ones. An important feature of a module is re-usability. Instead of copying the definitions of the most used functions in different programs, you can define them in the module and just import them whenever needed.

Let's create a module and import it. We will create two scripts: `sample.py` and `add.py`. We will import a sample module in our `add.py`. Now, save the following code as `sample.py`. Let's take a look with the following example:

```
sample.py
def addition(num1, num2):
    result = num1 + num2
    return result
```

Here, we have defined a `addition()` function inside a module named `sample`. The function takes in two numbers and returns their sum. Now we have created a module. You can import this in any Python program.

Importing modules

Now, after creating a module, we will learn how to import that module. In the previous example, we created a sample module. Now we will import the sample module in `add.py` script:

```
add.py
import sample
sum = sample.addition(10, 20)
print(sum)

Output:
30
```

Summary

In this chapter, we've given an overview of the Python scripting language. We have learned about how to install Python and various tools. We also learned about the Python interpreter and how to use it. We learned about Python-supported data types, variables, numbers and strings, decision-making statements, and looping statements in Python. We also learned about functions and how to use them in scripts and modules and how to create and import them.

In the next chapter, *Debugging and Profiling Python Scripts*, you will learn about Python debugging techniques, error handling (exception handling), debuggers tools, debugging basic program crashes, profiling and timing programs, and making programs run faster.

Questions

1. What are iterators and generators ?
2. Are lists mutable or immutable ?
3. What are the data structures in Python ?
4. How to access values in a list ?
5. What are modules ?

Further reading

All of the Python documentation is available on the following site: `www.python.org`.

You can also check the following books, *Learn Python Hard Way* and *Byte of Python*, to cover the basics of Python.

Debugging and Profiling Python Scripts

2

Debugging and profiling play an important role in Python development. The debugger helps programmers to analyze the complete code. The debugger sets the breakpoints whereas the profilers run our code and give us the details of the execution time. The profilers will identify the bottlenecks in your programs. In this chapter, we'll learn about the `pdb` Python debugger, `cProfile` module, and `timeit` module to time the execution of Python code.

In this chapter, you'll learn about the following:

- Python debugging techniques
- Error handling (exception handling)
- Debugger tools
- Debugging basic program crashes
- Profiling and timing programs
- Making programs run faster

What is debugging?

Debugging is a process that resolves the issues that occur in your code and prevent your software from running properly. In Python, debugging is very easy. The Python debugger sets conditional breakpoints and debugs the source code one line at a time. We'll debug our Python scripts using a `pdb` module that's present in the Python standard library.

Python debugging techniques

To better debug a Python program, various techniques are available. We're going to look at four techniques for Python debugging:

- `print()` statement: This is the simplest way of knowing what's exactly happening so you can check what has been executed.
- `logging`: This is like a `print` statement but with more contextual information so you can understand it fully.
- `pdb` debugger: This is a commonly used debugging technique. The advantage of using `pdb` is that you can use `pdb` from the command line, within an interpreter, and within a program.
- IDE debugger: IDE has an integrated debugger. It allows developers to execute their code and then the developer can inspect while the program executes.

Error handling (exception handling)

In this section, we're going to learn how Python handles exceptions. But first, what is an exception? An exception is an error that occurs during program execution. Whenever any error occurs, Python generates an exception that will be handled using a `try...except` block. Some exceptions can't be handled by programs so they result in error messages. Now, we are going to see some exception examples.

In your Terminal, start the `python3` interactive console and we will see some exception examples:

```
student@ubuntu:~$ python3
Python 3.5.2 (default, Nov 23 2017, 16:37:01)
[GCC 5.4.0 20160609] on linux
Type "help", "copyright", "credits" or "license" for more information.
>>>
>>> 50 / 0


Traceback (most recent call last):
  File "<stdin>", line 1, in <module>
ZeroDivisionError: division by zero
>>>
>>> 6 + abc*5
Traceback (most recent call last):
  File "<stdin>", line 1, in <module>
NameError: name 'abc' is not defined
```

```
>>>
>>> 'abc' + 2
Traceback (most recent call last):
  File "<stdin>", line 1, in <module>
TypeError: Can't convert 'int' object to str implicitly
>>>
>>> import abcd
Traceback (most recent call last):
  File "<stdin>", line 1, in <module>
ImportError: No module named 'abcd'
>>>
```

These are some examples of exceptions. Now, we will see how we can handle the exceptions.

Whenever errors occur in your Python program, exceptions are raised. We can also forcefully raise an exception using `raise` keyword.

Now we are going to see a `try...except` block that handles an exception. In the `try` block, we will write a code that may generate an exception. In the `except` block, we will write a solution for that exception.

The syntax for `try...except` is as follows:

```
try:
          statement(s)
except:
          statement(s)
```

A `try` block can have multiple except statements. We can handle specific exceptions also by entering the exception name after the `except` keyword. The syntax for handling a specific exception is as follows:

```
try:
          statement(s)
except exception_name:
          statement(s)
```

We are going to create an `exception_example.py` script to catch `ZeroDivisionError`. Write the following code in your script:

```
a = 35
b = 57
try:
          c = a + b
          print("The value of c is: ", c)
          d = b / 0
```

```
            print("The value of d is: ", d)

except:
            print("Division by zero is not possible")

print("Out of try...except block")
```

Run the script as follows and you will get the following output:

```
student@ubuntu:~$ python3 exception_example.py
The value of c is:  92
Division by zero is not possible
Out of try...except block
```

Debuggers tools

There are many debugging tools supported in Python:

- `winpdb`
- `pydev`
- `pydb`
- `pdb`
- `gdb`
- `pyDebug`

In this section, we are going to learn about `pdb` Python debugger. `pdb` module is a part of Python's standard library and is always available to use.

The pdb debugger

The `pdb` module is used to debug Python programs. Python programs use `pdb` interactive source code debugger to debug the programs. `pdb` sets breakpoints and inspects the stack frames, and lists the source code.

Now we will learn about how we can use the `pdb` debugger. There are three ways to use this debugger:

- Within an interpreter
- From a command line
- Within a Python script

We are going to create a `pdb_example.py` script and add the following content in that script:

```python
class Student:
        def __init__(self, std):
                self.count = std

        def print_std(self):
                for i in range(self.count):
                        print(i)
                return
if __name__ == '__main__':
        Student(5).print_std()
```

Using this script as an example to learn Python debugging, we will see how we can start the debugger in detail.

Within an interpreter

To start the debugger from the Python interactive console, we are using `run()` or `runeval()`.

Start your `python3` interactive console. Run the following command to start the console:

```
$ python3
```

Import our `pdb_example` script name and the `pdb` module. Now, we are going to use `run()` and we are passing a string expression as an argument to `run()` that will be evaluated by the Python interpreter itself:

```
student@ubuntu:~$ python3
Python 3.5.2 (default, Nov 23 2017, 16:37:01)
[GCC 5.4.0 20160609] on linux
Type "help", "copyright", "credits" or "license" for more information.
>>>
>>> import pdb_example
>>> import pdb
>>> pdb.run('pdb_example.Student(5).print_std()')
> <string>(1)<module>()
(Pdb)
```

To continue debugging, enter `continue` after the (Pdb) prompt and press *Enter*. If you want to know the options we can use in this, then after the (Pdb) prompt press the *Tab* key twice.

Now, after entering `continue`, we will get the output as follows:

```
student@ubuntu:~$ python3
Python 3.5.2 (default, Nov 23 2017, 16:37:01)
[GCC 5.4.0 20160609] on linux
Type "help", "copyright", "credits" or "license" for more information.
>>>
>>> import pdb_example
>>> import pdb
>>> pdb.run('pdb_example.Student(5).print_std()')
> <string>(1)<module>()
(Pdb) continue
0
1
2
3
4
>>>
```

From a command line

The simplest and most straightforward way to run a debugger is from a command line. Our program will act as input to the debugger. You can use the debugger from command line as follows:

```
$ python3 -m pdb pdb_example.py
```

When you run the debugger from the command line, source code will be loaded and it will stop the execution on the first line it finds. Enter `continue` to continue the debugging. Here's the output:

```
student@ubuntu:~$ python3 -m pdb pdb_example.py
> /home/student/pdb_example.py(1)<module>()
-> class Student:
(Pdb) continue
0
1
2
3
4
The program finished and will be restarted
> /home/student/pdb_example.py(1)<module>()
-> class Student:
(Pdb)
```

Within a Python script

The previous two techniques will start the debugger at the beginning of a Python program. But this third technique is best for long-running processes. To start the debugger within a script, use `set_trace()`.

Now, modify your `pdb_example.py` file as follows:

```
import pdb
class Student:
        def __init__(self, std):
                self.count = std

        def print_std(self):
                for i in range(self.count):
                        pdb.set_trace()
                        print(i)
                return

if __name__ == '__main__':
        Student(5).print_std()
```

Now, run the program as follows:

```
student@ubuntu:~$ python3 pdb_example.py
> /home/student/pdb_example.py(10)print_std()
-> print(i)
(Pdb) continue
0
> /home/student/pdb_example.py(9)print_std()
-> pdb.set_trace()
(Pdb)
```

`set_trace()` is a Python function, therefore you can call it at any point in your program.

So, these are the three ways by which you can start a debugger.

Debugging basic program crashes

In this section, we are going to see the trace module. The trace module helps in tracing the program execution. So, whenever your Python program crashes, we can understand where it crashes. We can use trace module by importing it into your script as well as from the command line.

Now, we will create a script named `trace_example.py` and write the following content in the script:

```
class Student:
            def __init__(self, std):
                        self.count = std

            def go(self):
                        for i in range(self.count):
                                    print(i)
                        return
if __name__ == '__main__':
            Student(5).go()
```

The output will be as follows:

```
student@ubuntu:~$ python3 -m trace --trace trace_example.py
 --- modulename: trace_example, funcname: <module>
trace_example.py(1): class Student:
 --- modulename: trace_example, funcname: Student
trace_example.py(1): class Student:
trace_example.py(2):    def __init__(self, std):
trace_example.py(5):    def go(self):
trace_example.py(10): if __name__ == '__main__':
trace_example.py(11):              Student(5).go()
 --- modulename: trace_example, funcname: init
trace_example.py(3):                self.count = std
 --- modulename: trace_example, funcname: go
trace_example.py(6):                   for i in range(self.count):
trace_example.py(7):                           print(i)
0
trace_example.py(6):                   for i in range(self.count):
trace_example.py(7):                           print(i)
1
trace_example.py(6):                   for i in range(self.count):
trace_example.py(7):                           print(i)
2
trace_example.py(6):                   for i in range(self.count):
trace_example.py(7):                           print(i)
3
trace_example.py(6):                   for i in range(self.count):
trace_example.py(7):                           print(i)
4
```

So, by using `trace --trace` at the command line, the developer can trace the program line-by-line. So, whenever the program crashes, the developer will know the instance where it crashes.

Profiling and timing programs

Profiling a Python program means measuring an execution time of a program. It measures the time spent in each function. Python's cProfile module is used for profiling a Python program.

The cProfile module

As discussed previously, profiling means measuring the execution time of a program. We are going to use the cProfile Python module for profiling a program.

Now, we will write a cprof_example.py script and write the following code in it:

```
mul_value = 0
def mul_numbers( num1, num2 ):
            mul_value = num1 * num2;
            print ("Local Value: ", mul_value)
            return mul_value
mul_numbers( 58, 77 )
print ("Global Value: ", mul_value)
```

Run the program and you will see the output as follows:

```
student@ubuntu:~$ python3 -m cProfile cprof_example.py
Local Value:   4466
Global Value:   0
         6 function calls in 0.000 seconds
   Ordered by: standard name

   ncalls  tottime  percall  cumtime  percall filename:lineno(function)
        1    0.000    0.000    0.000    0.000 cprof_example.py:1(<module>)
        1    0.000    0.000    0.000    0.000
cprof_example.py:2(mul_numbers)
        1    0.000    0.000    0.000    0.000 {built-in method
builtins.exec}
        2    0.000    0.000    0.000    0.000 {built-in method
builtins.print}
        1    0.000    0.000    0.000    0.000 {method 'disable' of
'_lsprof.Profiler' objects}
```

So, using `cProfile`, all functions that are called will get printed with the time spent on each function. Now, we will see what these column headings mean:

- `ncalls`: Number of calls
- `tottime`: Total time spent in the given function
- `percall`: Quotient of `tottime` divided by `ncalls`
- `cumtime`: Cumulative time spent in this and all `subfunctions`
- `percall`: Quotient of `cumtime` divided by primitive calls
- `filename:lineno(function)`: Provides the respective data of each function

timeit

`timeit` is a Python module used to time small parts of your Python script. You can call `timeit` from the command line as well as import the `timeit` module into your script. We are going to write a script to time a piece of code. Create a `timeit_example.py` script and write the following content into it:

```python
import timeit
prg_setup = "from math import sqrt"
prg_code = '''
def timeit_example():
            list1 = []
            for x in range(50):
                        list1.append(sqrt(x))
'''
# timeit statement
print(timeit.timeit(setup = prg_setup, stmt = prg_code, number = 10000))
```

Using `timeit`, we can decide what piece of code we want to measure the performance of. So, we can easily define the setup code as well as the code snippet on which we want to perform the test separately. The main code runs 1 million times, which is the default time, whereas the setup code runs only once.

Making programs run faster

There are various ways to make your Python programs run faster, such as the following:

- Profile your code so you can identify the bottlenecks
- Use built-in functions and libraries so the interpreter doesn't need to execute loops
- Avoid using globals as Python is very slow in accessing global variables
- Use existing packages

Summary

In this chapter, we learned about the importance of debugging and profiling programs. We learned what the different techniques available for debugging are. We learned about the `pdb` Python debugger and how to handle exceptions. We learned about how to use the `cProfile` and `timeit` modules of Python while profiling and timing our scripts. We also learned how to make your scripts run faster.

In the next chapter, we are going to learn about unit testing in Python. We are going to learn about creating and using unit tests.

Questions

1. To debug a program, which module is used?
2. Check how to use `ipython` along with all aliases and magic functions.
3. What is **Global interpreted lock (GIL)**?
4. What is the purpose of the `PYTHONSTARTUP`, `PYTHONCASEOK`, `PYTHONHOME`, and `PYTHONSTARTUP` environment variables?

5. What is the output of the following code? a) `[0]`, b) `[1]`, c) `[1, 0]`, d) `[0, 1]`.

```
def foo(k):
    k = [1]
q = [0]
foo(q)
print(q)
```

6. Which of the following is an invalid variable?
   a) `my_string_1`
   b) `1st_string`
   c) `foo`
   d) `_`

Further reading

- How to handle GIL problems in python: `https://realpython.com/python-gil/`
- Check how to use `pdb` module in command line: `https://fedoramagazine.org/getting-started-python-debugger/`

Unit Testing - Introduction to the Unit Testing Framework

3

Testing your project is an essential part of your software development. In this chapter, we are going to learn about unit testing in Python. Python has the module called `unittest`, which is a unit testing framework. We are going to learn about the `unittest` is framework in this chapter.

In this chapter, you will learn about the following topics:

- Introduction to unit testing framework
- Creating unit testing tasks

What is unittest?

The `unittest` is a unit testing framework in Python. It supports multiple tasks such as test fixtures, writing test cases, aggregating test cases into the test suites, and running tests.

`unittest` supports four main concepts, which are listed here:

- `test fixture`: This includes preparation and cleanup activities for performing one or more tests
- `test case`: This includes your individual unit test. By using the `TestCase` base class of `unittest`, we can create new test cases
- `test suite`: This includes a collection of test cases, test suites, or both. This is for executing test cases together
- `test runner`: This includes arranging the test executions and giving output to the users

Python has a `unittest` module that we will import in our script. The `unittest` module has `TestCase` class for creating test cases.

Individual test cases can be created as methods. These method names start with the word *test*. So, test runner will know which methods represent test cases.

Creating unit tests

In this section, we are going to create unit tests. To do this, we will create two scripts. One will be your normal script and the other will contain the code for testing.

First, create a script named `arithmetic.py` and write the following code in it:

```
# In this script, we are going to create a 4 functions: add_numbers,
sub_numbers, mul_numbers, div_numbers.
def add_numbers(x, y):
    return x + y

def sub_numbers(x, y):
    return x - y

def mul_numbers(x, y):
    return x * y

def div_numbers(x, y):
    return (x / y)
```

In the preceding script, we created four functions: `add_numbers`, `sub_numbers`, `mul_numbers`, and `div_numbers`. Now, we are going to write test cases for these functions. First, we will learn how we can write test cases for the `add_numbers` function. Create a `test_addition.py` script and write the following code in it:

```
import arithmetic
import unittest

# Testing add_numbers function from arithmetic.
class Test_addition(unittest.TestCase):
    # Testing Integers
    def test_add_numbers_int(self):
        sum = arithmetic.add_numbers(50, 50)
        self.assertEqual(sum, 100)
    # Testing Floats
    def test_add_numbers_float(self):
        sum = arithmetic.add_numbers(50.55, 78)
        self.assertEqual(sum, 128.55)
```

```
    # Testing Strings
    def test_add_numbers_strings(self):
        sum = arithmetic.add_numbers('hello','python')
        self.assertEqual(sum, 'hellopython')

if __name__ == '__main__':
    unittest.main()
```

In the preceding script, we have written the three test cases for the `add_numbers` function. The first is for testing integer numbers, the second is for testing float numbers, and the third is for testing strings. In strings, adding means concatenating two strings. Similarly, you can write the test cases for subtraction, multiplication, and division.

Now, we will run our `test_addition.py` test script and we will see what result we get after running this script.

Run the script as follows and you will get the following output:

```
student@ubuntu:~$ python3 test_addition.py
...
----------------------------------------------------------------------
Ran 3 tests in 0.000s

OK
```

Here, we get `OK` , which means our testing was successful.

Whenever you run your test script, you have three possible test results:

Result	Description
OK	Successful
FAIL	Test failed– raises an `AssertionError` exception
ERROR	Raises an exception other than `AssertionError`

Methods used in unit testing

Whenever we use `unittest`, there are some methods we use in our script. These methods are the following:

- `assertEqual()` and `assertNotEqual()`: This checks for an expected result
- `assertTrue()` and `assertFalse()`: This verifies a condition

- assertRaises(): This verifies that a specific exception gets raised
- setUp() and tearDown(): This defines instructions that are executed before and after each test method

You can use the unittest module from the command line as well. So, you can run the previous test script as follows:

```
student@ubuntu:~$ python3 -m unittest test_addition.py
...
--------------------------------------------------------------------
Ran 3 tests in 0.000s

OK
```

Now, we will see another example. We will create two scripts: if_example.py and test_if.py. if_example.py will be our normal script and test_if.py will contain test case. In this test, we are checking whether the entered number is equal to 100 or not. If it is equal to 100 then our test will be successful. If not, it must show a FAILED result.

Create a if_example.py script and write the following code in it:

```python
def check_if():
    a = int(input("Enter a number \n"))
    if (a == 100):
        print("a is equal to 100")
    else:
        print("a is not equal to 100")
    return a
```

Now, create a test_if.py test script and write following code in it:

```python
import if_example
import unittest

class Test_if(unittest.TestCase):
    def test_if(self):
        result = if_example.check_if()
        self.assertEqual(result, 100)

if __name__ == '__main__':
    unittest.main()
```

Run the test script as follows:

```
student@ubuntu:~/Desktop$ python3 -m unittest test_if.py
Enter a number
100
a is equal to 100
.
----------------------------------------------------------------------
Ran 1 test in 1.912s

OK
```

We run the script for a successful test result. Now, we will enter some value other than 100 and we must get a FAILED result. Run the script as follows:

```
student@ubuntu:~/Desktop$ python3 -m unittest test_if.py
Enter a number
50
a is not equal to 100
F
======================================================================
FAIL: test_if (test_if.Test_if)
----------------------------------------------------------------------
Traceback (most recent call last):
  File "/home/student/Desktop/test_if.py", line 7, in test_if
    self.assertEqual(result, 100)
AssertionError: 50 != 100

----------------------------------------------------------------------
Ran 1 test in 1.521s

FAILED (failures=1)
```

Summary

In this chapter, we have learned about the unittest, which is Python's unit testing framework. We also learned about how to create test cases and methods used in unit testing.

In the next chapter, we are going to learn how to automate the regular administrative activities of the system administrator. You will learn about accepting inputs, handling passwords, executing external commands, reading config files, adding warning codes to scripts, setting CPU limits, web-browser launching, using the `os` module, and taking backups.

Questions

1. What is unit testing, automation testing, and manual testing?
2. What are the alternative modules available apart from `unittest`?
3. What is the use of writing test cases?
4. What is PEP8 standards ?

Further reading

- Unit testing documentation: `https://docs.python.org/3/library/unittest.html`
- PEP8 coding standards in Python: `https://www.python.org/dev/peps/pep-0008/`

4
Automating Regular Administrative Activities

There are various administrative activities performed by system administrators. These activities may contain file handling, logging, administrating CPU and memory, password handling, and, most importantly, making backups. These activities need automation. In this chapter, we're going to learn about automating these activities using Python.

In this chapter, we will cover the following topics:

- Accepting input by redirection, pipe, and input files
- Handling passwords at runtime in scripts
- Executing external commands and getting their output
- Prompting for a password during runtime and validation
- Reading configuration files
- Adding logging and warning code to scripts
- Putting limits on CPU and memory usage
- Launching a web browser
- Using the `os` module for handling directory and files
- Making backups (with `rsync`)

Accepting input by redirection, pipe, and input files

In this section, we are going to learn about how users can accept input by redirection, pipe, and external input files.

For accepting input by redirection, we use `stdin`. `pipe` is another form of redirection. This concept means providing the output of one program as the input to another program. We can accept input by external files as well as by using Python.

Input by redirection

`stdin` and `stdout` are objects created by the `os` module. We're going to write a script in which we will use `stdin` and `stdout`.

Create a script called `redirection.py` and write the following code in it:

```python
import sys

class Redirection(object):
    def __init__(self, in_obj, out_obj):
        self.input = in_obj
        self.output = out_obj
    def read_line(self):
        res = self.input.readline()
        self.output.write(res)
        return res

if __name__ == '__main__':
    if not sys.stdin.isatty():
        sys.stdin = Redirection(in_obj=sys.stdin, out_obj=sys.stdout)
    a = input('Enter a string: ')
    b = input('Enter another string: ')
    print ('Entered strings are: ', repr(a), 'and', repr(b))
```

Run the preceding program as follows:

```
$ python3 redirection.py
```

We will receive the following output:

```
Output:
Enter a string: hello
Enter another string: python
Entered strings are:  'hello' and 'python'
```

Whenever the program runs in an interactive session, `stdin` is the keyboard input and `stdout` is the user's Terminal. The `input()` function is used to take input from the user, and `print()` is the way to write on the Terminal (`stdout`).

Input by pipe

Pipe is another form of redirection. This technique is used to pass information from one program to another. The | symbol denotes pipe. By using the pipe technique, we can use more than two commands in such a way that the output of one command acts as input to the next command.

Now, we are going to see how we can accept an input using pipe. For that, first we'll write a simple script that returns a `floor` division. Create a script called `accept_by_pipe.py` and write the following code in it:

```
import sys

for n in sys.stdin:
    print ( int(n.strip())//2 )
```

Run the script and you will get the following output:

```
$ echo 15 | python3 accept_by_pipe.py
Output:
7
```

In the preceding script, `stdin` is a keyboard input. We are performing a `floor` division on the number we enter at runtime. The floor division returns only the integer part of the quotient. When we run the program, we pass 15 followed by the pipe | symbol, and then our script name. So, we are providing 15 as input to our script. So the floor division is performed and we get the output as 7.

We can pass multiple input to our script. So, in the following execution, we have passed multiple input values as 15, 45, and 20. For handling multiple input values, we have written a `for` loop in our script. So, it will first take the input as 15, followed by 45, and then 20. The output will be printed on a new line for each input, as we have written \n between the input value. To enable this interpretation of a backslash, we passed the −e flag:

```
$ echo -e '15\n45\n20' | python3 accept_by_pipe.py
Output:
7
22
10
```

After running this, we got floor divisions for 15, 45 and 20 as 7, 22, and 10, respectively, on new lines.

Input by input file

In this section, we are going to learn about how we can take input from an input file. Taking input from an input file is easier in Python. We are going to look at an example for this. But first, we are going to create a simple text file called `sample.txt` and we'll write the following code in it:

`Sample.txt`:

```
Hello World
Hello Python
```

Now, create a script called `accept_by_input_file.py` and write the following code in it:

```
i = open('sample.txt','r')
o = open('sample_output.txt','w')

a = i.read()
o.write(a)
```

Run the program and you will get the following output:

```
$ python3 accept_by_input_file.py
$ cat sample_output.txt
Hello World
Hello Python
```

Handling passwords at runtime in scripts

In this section, we will look at a simple example for handling passwords in script. We will create a script called `handling_password.py` and write the following content in it:

```
import sys
import paramiko
import time

ip_address = "192.168.2.106"
username = "student"
password = "training"
ssh_client = paramiko.SSHClient()
ssh_client.set_missing_host_key_policy(paramiko.AutoAddPolicy())
ssh_client.load_system_host_keys()
ssh_client.connect(hostname=ip_address,\
                                    username=username, password=password)
print ("Successful connection", ip_address)
```

```
ssh_client.invoke_shell()
remote_connection = ssh_client.exec_command('cd Desktop; mkdir work\n')
remote_connection = ssh_client.exec_command('mkdir test_folder\n')
#print( remote_connection.read() )
ssh_client.close
```

Run the preceding script and you will receive the following output:

```
$ python3 handling_password.py

Output:
Successful connection 192.168.2.106
```

In the preceding script, we used the `paramiko` module. The `paramiko` module is a Python implementation of `ssh` that provides client-server functionality.

Install `paramiko` as follows:

```
pip3 install paramiko
```

In the preceding script, we are remotely connecting to the host, `192.168.2.106`. We have provided the host's username and password in our script.

After running this script, on the `192.168.2.106` desktop, you will find a `work` folder and `test_folder` can be found in the `home/` directory of `192.168.2.106`.

Executing external commands and getting their output

In this section, we are going to learn about Python's subprocess module. Using `subprocess`, it's easy to spawn new processes and get their return code, execute external commands, and start new applications.

We are going to see how we can execute external commands and get their output in Python by using the `subprocess` module. We will create a script called `execute_external_commands.py` and write the following code in it:

```
import subprocess
subprocess.call(["touch", "sample.txt"])
subprocess.call(["ls"])
print("Sample file created")
subprocess.call(["rm", "sample.txt"])
```

```
subprocess.call(["ls"])
print("Sample file deleted")
```

Run the program and you will get the following output:

```
$ python3 execute_external_commands.py
Output:
1.py        accept_by_pipe.py       sample_output.txt       sample.txt
accept_by_input_file.py             execute_external_commands.py
output.txt          sample.py
Sample.txt file created
1.py        accept_by_input_file.py         accept_by_pipe.py
execute_external_commands.py    output.txt              sample_output.txt
sample.py
Sample.txt file deleted
```

Capturing output using the subprocess module

In this section, we are going to learn about how we can capture output. We will pass PIPE for the stdout argument to capture the output. Write a script called capture_output.py and write the following code in it:

```
import subprocess
res = subprocess.run(['ls', '-1'], stdout=subprocess.PIPE,)
print('returncode:', res.returncode)
print(' {} bytes in stdout:\n{}'.format(len(res.stdout),
res.stdout.decode('utf-8')))
```

Execute the script as follows:

```
student@ubuntu:~$ python3 capture_output.py
```

On execution, we will receive the following output:

```
Output:
returncode: 0
191 bytes in stdout:
1.py
accept_by_input_file.py
accept_by_pipe.py
execute_external_commands.py
getpass_example.py
ouput.txt
output.txt
```

```
password_prompt_again.py
sample_output.txt
sample.py
capture_output.py
```

In the preceding script, we imported the subprocess module of Python, which helps in capturing the output. The subprocess module is used for creating new processes. It also helps in connecting input/output pipes and getting return code. `subprocess.run()` will run the command passed as an argument. `Returncode` will be the exit status of your child process. In the output, if you get return code as `0`, it indicates it ran successfully.

Prompting for passwords during runtime and validation

In this section, we are going learn about the `getpass module` to handle passwords at runtime. The `getpass()` module in Python prompts the user to enter a password without echoing. The `getpass` module is used to handle the password prompt whenever programs interact with a user through the Terminal.

We are going to see some examples of how to use the `getpass` module:

1. Create a script called `no_prompt.py` and write the following code in it:

```
import getpass
try:
            p = getpass.getpass()
except Exception as error:
            print('ERROR', error)
else:
            print('Password entered:', p)
```

In this script, a prompt is not provided for the user. So, by default, it is set to the `Password` prompt.

Run the script as follows:

```
$ python3 no_prompt.py
Output :
Password:
Password entered: abcd
```

2. We will provide a prompt for entering a password. So, create a script callled `with_prompt.py` and write the following code in it:

```python
import getpass
try:
        p = getpass.getpass("Enter your password: ")
except Exception as error:
        print('ERROR', error)
else:
        print('Password entered:', p)
```

Now, we have written a script that provides a prompt for a password. Run the program as follows:

```
$ python3 with_prompt.py
Output:
Enter your password:
Password entered: abcd
```

Here, we have provided the `Enter your password` prompt for the user.

Now, we will write a script where if we enter a wrong password, it will just print a simple message but it will not prompt again to enter a correct password.

3. Write a script called `getpass_example.py` and write the following code in it:

```python
import getpass
passwd = getpass.getpass(prompt='Enter your password: ')
if passwd.lower() == '#pythonworld':
        print('Welcome!!')
else:
        print('The password entered is incorrect!!')
```

Run the program as follows (here we are entering a correct password, that is, `#pythonworld`):

```
$ python3 getpass_example.py
Output:
Enter your password:
Welcome!!
```

Now, we will enter a wrong password and will check what message we receive:

```
$ python3 getpass_example.py
Output:
Enter your password:
The password entered is incorrect!!
```

Here, we have written a script that never asks again to enter a password if we write a wrong password.

Now, we will write a script that will ask to enter the correct password again when we provide a wrong password. To get the login name of the user, getuser() is used. The getuser() function will return the system logged-in user. Create a script called password_prompt_again.py and write the following code in it:

```
import getpass
user_name = getpass.getuser()
print ("User Name : %s" % user_name)
while True:
            passwd = getpass.getpass("Enter your Password : ")
            if passwd == '#pythonworld':
                        print ("Welcome!!!")
                        break
            else:
                        print ("The password you entered is incorrect.")
```

Run the program and you will get the following output:

```
student@ubuntu:~$ python3 password_prompt_again.py
User Name : student
Enter your Password :
The password you entered is incorrect.
Enter your Password :
Welcome!!!
```

Reading configuration files

In this section, we are going learn about the configparser module of Python. By using the configparser module, you can manage user-editable configuration files for the application.

The common use of these configuration files is that users or system administrators can edit the files using a simple text editor to set application defaults and then the application will read and, parse them and act based on the contents written in them.

To read a configuration file, configparser has the read() method. Now, we will write a simple script named read_config_file.py. Before that, create a .ini file named read_simple.ini and write the following content in it: read_simple.ini

```
[bug_tracker]
url = https://timesofindia.indiatimes.com/
```

Create `read_config_file.py` and enter the following content in it:

```
from configparser import ConfigParser
p = ConfigParser()
p.read('read_simple.ini')
print(p.get('bug_tracker', 'url'))
```

Run `read_config_file.py` and you will get the following output:

```
$ python3 read_config_file.py

Output:
https://timesofindia.indiatimes.com/
```

The `read()` method accepts more than one filename. Whenever each filename gets scanned and if that file exists, then it will be opened and read. Now, we will write a script for reading more than one filename. Create a script called `read_many_config_file.py` and write the following code in it:

```
from configparser import ConfigParser
import glob

p = ConfigParser()
files = ['hello.ini', 'bye.ini', 'read_simple.ini', 'welcome.ini']
files_found = p.read(files)
files_missing = set(files) - set(files_found)
print('Files found:  ', sorted(files_found))
print('Files missing:  ', sorted(files_missing))
```

Run the preceding script and you will get the following output:

```
$ python3 read_many_config_file.py

Output
Files found:    ['read_simple.ini']
Files missing:   ['bye.ini', 'hello.ini', 'welcome.ini']
```

In the preceding example, we used the `configparser` module of Python, which helps in managing configuration files. First, we created a list named `files`. The `read()` function will read the configuration files. In the example, we created a variable called `files_found`, which will store the names of the configuration files present in your directory. Next, we created another variable called `files_missing`, which will return filenames that aren't in your directory. And, lastly, we are printing the file names that are present and missing.

Adding logging and warning code to scripts

In this section, we will learn about the logging and warnings modules of Python. The logging module will keep a track of events occurring within a program. The warnings module warns the programmers about the changes made in the language as well as the libraries.

Now, we are going to see a simple logging example. We will write a script called `logging_example.py` and write the following code in it:

```python
import logging
LOG_FILENAME = 'log.txt'
logging.basicConfig(filename=LOG_FILENAME, level=logging.DEBUG,)
logging.debug('This message should go to the log file')
with open(LOG_FILENAME, 'rt') as f:
            prg = f.read()
print('FILE:')
print(prg)
```

Run the program as follows::

```
$ python3 logging_example.py
```

```
Output:
FILE:
DEBUG:root:This message should go to the log file
```

Check `hello.py` and you see the debug message printed in that script:

```
$ cat log.txt
```

```
Output:
DEBUG:root:This message should go to the log file
```

Now, we will write a script called `logging_warnings_codes.py` and write the following code in it:

```python
import logging
import warnings
logging.basicConfig(level=logging.INFO,)
warnings.warn('This warning is not sent to the logs')
logging.captureWarnings(True)
warnings.warn('This warning is sent to the logs')
```

Run the script as follows:

```
$ python3 logging_warnings_codes.py
```

```
Output:
logging_warnings_codes.py:6: UserWarning: This warning is not sent to the
logs
    warnings.warn('This warning is not sent to the logs')
WARNING:py.warnings:logging_warnings_codes.py:10: UserWarning: This warning
is sent to the logs
    warnings.warn('This warning is sent to the logs')
```

Generating warnings

warn() is used to generate the warnings. Now, we will see a simple example of generating warnings. Write a script called generate_warnings.py and write a following code in it:

```
import warnings
warnings.simplefilter('error', UserWarning)
print('Before')
warnings.warn('Write your warning message here')
print('After')
```

Run the script as follows:

```
$ python3 generate_warnings.py
```

```
Output:
Before:
Traceback (most recent call last):
  File "generate_warnings.py", line 6, in <module>
    warnings.warn('Write your warning message here')
UserWarning: Write your warning message here
```

In the preceding script, we passed a warning message through warn(). We used a simple filter so that your warning will get treated as an error and that error will get solved accordingly by the programmer.

Putting limits on CPU and memory usage

In this section, we will learn about how we can limit CPU and memory usage. First, we will write a script for putting a limit on CPU usage. Create a script called `put_cpu_limit.py` and write the following code in it:

```
import resource
import sys
import signal
import time
def time_expired(n, stack):
            print('EXPIRED :', time.ctime())
            raise SystemExit('(time ran out)')
signal.signal(signal.SIGXCPU, time_expired)
# Adjust the CPU time limit
soft, hard = resource.getrlimit(resource.RLIMIT_CPU)
print('Soft limit starts as   :', soft)
resource.setrlimit(resource.RLIMIT_CPU, (10, hard))
soft, hard = resource.getrlimit(resource.RLIMIT_CPU)
print('Soft limit changed to :', soft)
print()
# Consume some CPU time in a pointless exercise
print('Starting:', time.ctime())
for i in range(200000):
            for i in range(200000):
                        v = i * i
# We should never make it this far
print('Exiting :', time.ctime())
```

Run the preceding script as follows:

```
$ python3 put_cpu_limit.py

Output:
Soft limit starts as   : -1
Soft limit changed to : 10
Starting: Thu Sep  6 16:13:20 2018
EXPIRED : Thu Sep  6 16:13:31 2018
(time ran out)
```

In the preceding script, we used `setrlimit()` to limit the CPU usage. So, in our script, we have set the limit to 10 seconds.

Launching webbrowser

In this section, we will learn about the `webbrowser` module of Python. This module has functions to open URLs in browser applications. We will see a simple example. Create a script called `open_web.py` and write the following code in it:

```
import webbrowser
webbrowser.open('https://timesofindia.indiatimes.com/world')
```

Run the script as follows:

```
$ python3 open_web.py

Output:
Url mentioned in open() will be opened in your browser.
webbrowser - Command line interface
```

You can also use the `webbrowser` module of Python through the command line and can use all of it. To use `webbrowser` through the command line, run the following command:

```
$ python3 -m webbrowser -n https://www.google.com/
```

Here, `https://www.google.com/` will be opened in the browser window. You can use the following two options:

- `-n`: Open a new window
- `-t`: Open a new tab

Using the os module for handling directory and files

In this section, we will learn about the `os` module of Python. Python's `os` module helps in achieving operating system tasks. We need to import the `os` module if we want to perform operating system tasks.

We will look at some examples related to handling files and directories.

Creating and deleting the directory

In this section, we are going to create a script where we will see what functions we can use for working with the directories on your filesystem, which will include creating, listing, and removing the content. Create a script called `os_dir_example.py` and write the following code in it:

```
import os
directory_name = 'abcd'
print('Creating', directory_name)
os.makedirs(directory_name)
file_name = os.path.join(directory_name, 'sample_example.txt')
print('Creating', file_name)
with open(file_name, 'wt') as f:
            f.write('sample example file')
print('Cleaning up')
os.unlink(file_name)
os.rmdir(directory_name)         # Will delete the directory
```

Run the script as follows:

```
$ python3 os_dir_example.py

Output:
Creating abcd
Creating abcd/sample_example.txt
Cleaning up
```

When you create a directory using `mkdir()`, all of the parent directories must be already created. But, when you create a directory with `makedirs()`, it will create any directory, which is mentioned in a path that doesn't exist. `unlink()` will remove the file path and `rmdir()` will remove the directory path.

Examining the content of a filesystem

In this section, we will list all of the content of a directory using `listdir()`. Create a script called `list_dir.py` and write the following code in it:

```
import os
import sys
print(sorted(os.listdir(sys.argv[1])))
```

Run the script as follows:

```
$ python3 list_dir.py /home/student/

['.ICEauthority', '.bash_history', '.bash_logout', '.bashrc', '.cache',
'.config', '.gnupg', '.local', '.mozilla', '.pam_environment', '.profile',
'.python_history', '.ssh', '.sudo_as_admin_successful', '.viminfo', '1.sh',
'1.sh.x', '1.sh.x.c', 'Desktop', 'Documents', 'Downloads', 'Music',
'Pictures', 'Public', 'Templates', 'Videos', 'examples.desktop',
'execute_external_commands.py', 'log.txt', 'numbers.txt',
'python_learning', 'work']
```

So, by using `listdir()`, you can list of all the content of the folder.

Making backups (with rsync)

This is the most important work system administrators have to do. In this section, we will learn about making backups using `rsync`. The `rsync` command is used for copying files and directories locally, as well as remotely, and performing data backups using `rsync`. For that, we are going write a script called `take_backup.py` and write the following code in it:

```python
import os
import shutil
import time
from sh import rsync
def check_dir(os_dir):
        if not os.path.exists(os_dir):
                        print (os_dir, "does not exist.")
                        exit(1)
def ask_for_confirm():
        ans = input("Do you want to Continue? yes/no\n")
        global con_exit
        if ans == 'yes':
                con_exit = 0
                return con_exit
        elif ans == "no":
                con_exit = 1
                return con_exit
        else:1
                print ("Answer with yes or no.")
                ask_for_confirm()
def delete_files(ending):
        for r, d, f in os.walk(backup_dir):
                for files in f:
                                if files.endswith("." + ending):
```

```
                                            os.remove(os.path.join(r,
files))

backup_dir = input("Enter directory to backup\n")    # Enter directory name
check_dir(backup_dir)
print (backup_dir, "saved.")
time.sleep(3)
backup_to_dir= input("Where to backup?\n")
check_dir(backup_to_dir)
print ("Doing the backup now!")
ask_for_confirm()
if con_exit == 1:
            print ("Aborting the backup process!")
            exit(1)
rsync("-auhv", "--delete", "--exclude=lost+found", "--exclude=/sys", "--
exclude=/tmp", "--exclude=/proc",
"--exclude=/mnt", "--exclude=/dev", "--exclude=/backup", backup_dir,
backup_to_dir)
```

Run the script as follows:

```
student@ubuntu:~/work$ python3 take_backup.py

Output :
Enter directory to backup
/home/student/work
/home/student/work saved.
Where to backup?
/home/student/Desktop
Doing the backup now!
Do you want to Continue? yes/no
yes
```

Now, check Desktop/directory and you will see your work folder in that directory. There are a few options used with the rsync command, namely the following:

- -a: Archive
- -u: Update
- -h: Human-readable format
- -v: Verbose
- --delete: Deletes extraneous files from the receiving side
- --exclude: Exclude rule

Summary

In this chapter, we learned about how we can automate regular administration tasks. We learned about accepting input by various techniques, prompting for passwords at runtime, executing external commands, reading configuration files, adding warnings in your script, launching `webbrowser` through the script as well as the command line, using the `os` module to handle files and directories, and making backups.

In the next chapter, you will learn more about the `os` module and handling data. Also, you will learn about the `tarfile` module and how you can use it.

Questions

1. How to use `readline` module?
2. What are the Linux commands used for reading, creating the new file, deletion of the file, list the file in current directory?
3. To run the Linux/windows commands in python which packages are available?
4. How to read, or set new values in configuration `ini` file
5. List the libraries available for finding the `cpu` usage?
6. List the different methods to accept the input from the user?
7. What is the difference between sort and sorted?

Further reading

- Learn basic commands of linux: `https://maker.pro/linux/tutorial/basic-linux-commands-for-beginners`
- Selenium webdriver documentation: `https://selenium-python.readthedocs.io/index.html`

Handling Files, Directories, and Data

5

The system administrator performs tasks such as handling various files, directories, and data. In this chapter, we will learn about the os module. The os module provides the functionality to interact with the operating system. Python programmers can easily use this os module for performing file and directory operations. The os module provides tools for programmers that deal with files, paths, directories, and data.

In this chapter, you will learn about the following:

- Using the os module to work with directories
- Copying, moving, renaming, and deleting data
- Working with paths, directories, and files
- Comparing data
- Merging data
- Pattern matching files and directories
- Metadata: data about data
- Compressing and restoring
- Using a `tarfile` module to create TAR archives
- Using a `tarfile` module to examine the contents of TAR files

Using the os module to work with directories

A directory or folder is a collection of files and sub-directories. The os module provides various functions that allow us to interact with the operating system. In this section, we will learn about some functions that can be used while working with directories.

Get the working directory

To start working with directories, first, we will get the name of our current working directory. The os module has a getcwd() function, using which we can get the current working directory. Start the python3 console and enter the following commands to get the directory name:

```
$ python3
Python 3.6.5 (default, Apr  1 2018, 05:46:30)
[GCC 7.3.0] on linux
Type "help", "copyright", "credits" or "license" for more information.
>>> import os
>>> os.getcwd()
'/home/student'
>>
```

Changing the directory

Using the os module, we can change the current working directory. For that, the os module has the chdir() function, for example:

```
>>> os.chdir('/home/student/work')
>>> print(os.getcwd())
/home/student/work
>>>
```

Listing files and directories

Listing the directory contents is easy in Python. We are going to use the os module that has a function named listdir(), which will return the names of files and directories from your working directory:

```
>>> os.listdir()
['Public', 'python_learning', '.ICEauthority', '.python_history', 'work',
'.bashrc', 'Pictures', '.gnupg', '.cache', '.bash_logout',
'.sudo_as_admin_successful', '.bash_history', '.config', '.viminfo',
'Desktop', 'Documents', 'examples.desktop', 'Videos', '.ssh', 'Templates',
'.profile', 'dir', '.pam_environment', 'Downloads', '.local', '.dbus',
'Music', '.mozilla']
>>>
```

Renaming a directory

The os module in Python has a rename() function that helps in changing the name of the directory:

```
>>> os.rename('work', 'work1')
>>> os.listdir()
['Public', 'work1', 'python_learning', '.ICEauthority', '.python_history',
'.bashrc', 'Pictures', '.gnupg', '.cache', '.bash_logout',
'.sudo_as_admin_successful', '.bash_history', '.config', '.viminfo',
'Desktop', 'Documents', 'examples.desktop', 'Videos', '.ssh', 'Templates',
'.profile', 'dir', '.pam_environment', 'Downloads', '.local', '.dbus',
'Music', '.mozilla']
>>
```

Copying, moving, renaming, and deleting data

We will be learning about the four basic operations that system administrators perform on data, which are copy, move, rename, and delete. Python has a built-in module called shutil, which can perform these tasks. Using the shutil module, we can perform high-level operations on the data as well. To use the shutil module in your program, just write the import shutil import statement. The shutil module offers a few functions that support file copy and remove operations. Let's learn about these operations one by one.

Copying the data

In this section, we will see how we can copy files using the shutil module. For that, first, we will create a hello.py file and write some text in it.

hello.py:

```
print ("")
print ("Hello World\n")
print ("Hello Python\n")
```

Now, we will write the code for copying into the `shutil_copy_example.py` script. Write the following content in it:

```
import shutil
import os
shutil.copy('hello.py', 'welcome.py')
print("Copy Successful")
```

Run the script as follows:

```
$ python3 shutil_copy_example.py

Output:
Copy Successful
```

Check the presence of the `welcome.py` script and you will find the contents of `hello.py` are copied successfully in `welcome.py`.

Moving the data

Here, we will see how we can move the data. We will use `shutil.move()` for this purpose. `shutil.move(source, destination)` will move the file from source to destination. Now, we will create a `shutil_move_example.py` script and write the following content in it:

```
import shutil
shutil.move('/home/student/sample.txt', '/home/student/Desktop/.')
```

Run the script as follows:

```
$ python3 shutil_move_example.py
```

In this script, our file to move is `sample.txt`, which is in the `/home/student` directory. `/home/student` is our source folder and `/home/student/Desktop` is our destination folder. So, after running the script, `sample.txt` will be moved from `/home/student` to the `/home/student/Desktop` directory.

Renaming data

In the previous section, we learned how we can use shutil.move() to move files from source to destination. Using shutil.move(), files can be renamed. Create a shutil_rename_example.py script and write the following content in it:

```
import shutil
shutil.move('hello.py', 'hello_renamed.py')
```

Run the script as follows:

```
$ python3 shutil_rename_example.py
```

Output:

Now, check that your filename will be renamed hello_renamed.py.

Deleting data

We will learn how to delete files and folders using the os module in Python. The remove() method of the os module will delete a file. If you try to remove a directory using this method, it will give you an OSError. To remove directories, use rmdir().

Now, create a os_remove_file_directory.py script and write the following content in it:

```
import os
os.remove('sample.txt')
print("File removed successfully")
os.rmdir('work1')
print("Directory removed successfully")
```

Run the script as follows:

```
$ python3 os_remove_file_directory.py

Output:
File removed successfully
Directory removed successfully
```

Working with paths

Now, we are going to learn about `os.path()`. It is used for path manipulations. In this section, we will look at some of the functions that the `os` module offers for pathnames.

Start the `python3` console:

```
student@ubuntu:~$ python3
Python 3.6.6 (default, Sep 12 2018, 18:26:19)
[GCC 8.0.1 20180414 (experimental) [trunk revision 259383]] on linux
Type "help", "copyright", "credits" or "license" for more information.
>>
```

- `os.path.absname(path)`: Returns the absolute version of your pathname.

```
>>> import os
>>> os.path.abspath('sample.txt')
'/home/student/work/sample.txt'
```

- `os.path.dirname(path)`: Returns the directory name of your path.

```
>>> os.path.dirname('/home/student/work/sample.txt')
'/home/student/work'
```

- `os.path.basename(path)`: Returns the base name of your path.

```
>>> os.path.basename('/home/student/work/sample.txt')
'sample.txt'
```

- `os.path.exists(path)`: Returns `True` if path refers to the existing path.

```
>>> os.path.exists('/home/student/work/sample.txt')
True
```

- `os.path.getsize(path)`: Returns the size of the entered path in bytes.

```
>>> os.path.getsize('/home/student/work/sample.txt')
39
```

- `os.path.isfile(path)`: Checks whether the entered path is an existing file or not. Returns `True` if it is a file.

```
>>> os.path.isfile('/home/student/work/sample.txt')
True
```

- `os.path.isdir(path)`: Checks whether the entered path is an existing directory or not. Returns `True` if it is a directory.

```
>>> os.path.isdir('/home/student/work/sample.txt')
False
```

Comparing data

Here, we are going to learn about how to compare data in Python. We will use a `pandas` module for this purpose.

Pandas is an open source data analysis library that provides data structures and data analysis tools that are easy to use. It makes importing and analyzing data easier.

Before starting with the example, make sure you have `pandas` installed on your system. You can install pandas as follows:

```
pip3 install pandas      --- For Python3

or

pip install pandas       --- For python2
```

We will study an example of comparing data using pandas. Initially, we will create two `csv` files: `student1.csv` and `student2.csv`. We will compare the data of these two `csv` files and in output it should return the comparison. Create two `csv` files as follows:

Create the `student1.csv` file content as follows:

```
Id,Name,Gender,Age,Address
101,John,Male,20,New York
102,Mary,Female,18,London
103,Aditya,Male,22,Mumbai
104,Leo,Male,22,Chicago
105,Sam,Male,21,Paris
106,Tina,Female,23,Sydney
```

Create the `student2.csv` file content as follows:

```
Id,Name,Gender,Age,Address
101,John,Male,21,New York
102,Mary,Female,20,London
103,Aditya,Male,22,Mumbai
104,Leo,Male,23,Chicago
105,Sam,Male,21,Paris
106,Tina,Female,23,Sydney
```

Now, we will create a `compare_data.py` script and write the following content in it:

```python
import pandas as pd
df1 = pd.read_csv("student1.csv")
df2 = pd.read_csv("student2.csv")
s1 = set([ tuple(values) for values in df1.values.tolist()])
s2 = set([ tuple(values) for values in df2.values.tolist()])
s1.symmetric_difference(s2)
print (pd.DataFrame(list(s1.difference(s2))), '\n')
print (pd.DataFrame(list(s2.difference(s1))), '\n')
```

Run the script as follows:

```
$ python3 compare_data.py

Output:
      0     1       2   3         4
0   102  Mary  Female  18    London
1   104   Leo    Male  22   Chicago
2   101  John    Male  20  New York


      0     1       2   3         4
0   101  John    Male  21  New York
1   104   Leo    Male  23   Chicago
2   102  Mary  Female  20    London
```

In the preceding example, we are comparing the data between the two `csv` files: `student1.csv` and `student2.csv`. We first converted our dataframes (`df1`, `df2`) into sets (`s1`, `s2`). Then, we used the `symmetric_difference()` set. So, it will check the symmetric difference between `s1` and `s2` and then we will print the result.

Merging data

We are going to learn about how to merge data in Python. For that, we are going to use Python's pandas library. To merge the data, we are going to use two `csv` files that already created in the previous section, `student1.csv` and `student2.csv`.

Now, create a `merge_data.py` script and write the following code in it:

```python
import pandas as pd
df1 = pd.read_csv("student1.csv")
df2 = pd.read_csv("student2.csv")
result = pd.concat([df1, df2])
print(result)
```

Run the script as follows:

```
$ python3 merge_data.py
```

```
Output:
     Id    Name   Gender  Age   Address
0   101    John     Male   20   New York
1   102    Mary   Female   18    London
2   103  Aditya     Male   22    Mumbai
3   104     Leo     Male   22   Chicago
4   105     Sam     Male   21     Paris
5   106    Tina   Female   23    Sydney
0   101    John     Male   21   New York
1   102    Mary   Female   20    London
2   103  Aditya     Male   22    Mumbai
3   104     Leo     Male   23   Chicago
4   105     Sam     Male   21     Paris
5   106    Tina   Female   23    Sydney
```

Pattern matching files and directories

In this section, we will learn about pattern matching for files and directories. Python has the `glob` module, which is used to find the names of files and directories that match specific patterns.

Now, we will look at an example. First, create a `pattern_match.py` script and write the following content in it:

```python
import glob
file_match = glob.glob('*.txt')
print(file_match)
```

```
file_match = glob.glob('[0-9].txt')
print(file_match)
file_match = glob.glob('**/*.txt', recursive=True)
print(file_match)
file_match = glob.glob('**/', recursive=True)
print(file_match)
```

Run the script as follows:

```
$ python3 pattern_match.py

Output:
['file1.txt', 'filea.txt', 'fileb.txt', 'file2.txt', '2.txt', '1.txt',
'file.txt']
['2.txt', '1.txt']
['file1.txt', 'filea.txt', 'fileb.txt', 'file2.txt', '2.txt', '1.txt',
'file.txt', 'dir1/3.txt', 'dir1/4.txt']
['dir1/']
```

In the previous example, we used Python's `glob` module for pattern matching. `glob` (pathname) will return the list of names that matches with the pathname. In out script, we have passed three pathnames in three different `glob()` functions. In the first `glob()`, we passed the pathname as `*.txt`; this will return all the filenames with `.txt` extensions. In the second `glob()`, we passed `[0-9].txt`; this will return filenames that start with a digit. In the third `glob()`, we passed `**/*.txt`, which will return filenames as well as directory names. It will also return the filenames from those directories. In the fourth `glob()`, we passed `**/`, which will return directory names only.

Metadata: data about data

In this section, we are going learn about the `pyPdf` module, which helps in extracting the metadata from a `pdf` file. But first, what is metadata? Metadata is data about data. Metadata is structured information that describes primary data. Metadata is a summary of that data. It contains the basic information regarding your actual data. It helps in finding a particular instance of your data.

 Make sure you have the `pdf` file present in your directory from which you want to extract the information.

First, we have to install the `pyPdf` module, as follows:

```
pip install pyPdf
```

Now, we will write a `metadata_example.py` script and we will see how we get the metadata information from it. We are going to write this script in Python 2:

```python
import pyPdf
def main():
            file_name = '/home/student/sample_pdf.pdf'
            pdfFile = pyPdf.PdfFileReader(file(file_name,'rb'))
            pdf_data = pdfFile.getDocumentInfo()
            print ("----Metadata of the file----")
            for md in pdf_data:
                        print (md+ ":" +pdf_data[md])
if __name__ == '__main__':
            main()
```

Run the script as follows:

```
student@ubuntu:~$ python metadata_example.py
----Metadata of the file----
/Producer:Acrobat Distiller Command 3.0 for SunOS 4.1.3 and later (SPARC)
/CreationDate:D:19980930143358
```

In the preceding script, we used the `pyPdf` module of Python 2. First, we created a `file_name` variable that stores the path of our `pdf`. Using `PdfFileReader()`, data gets read. The `pdf_data` variable will hold the information about your `pdf`. Lastly, we wrote a for loop to get the metadata information.

Compressing and restoring

In this section, we are going to learn about the `make_archive()` function of the `shutil` module, which will compress an entire directory. For that, we are going to write a `compress_a_directory.py` script and write the following content in it:

```python
import shutil
shutil.make_archive('work', 'zip', 'work/')
```

Run the script as follows:

```
$ python3 compress_a_directory.py
```

In the preceding script, in `shutil.make_archive()` function, we passed the first argument as a name to our compressed file. `zip` will be our compression technique. And the, `work/` will be the name of the directory that we want to compress.

Now, to restore the data from the compressed file, we are going to use the `unpack_archive()` function from the `shutil` module. Create an `unzip_a_directory.py` script and write the following content in it:

```
import shutil
shutil.unpack_archive('work1.zip')
```

Run the script as follows:

```
$ python3 unzip_a_directory.py
```

Now, check your directory. You will get all the contents after unzipping the directory.

Using the tarfile module to create TAR archives

This section will help you to learn about how we can create tar archives using Python's `tarfile` module.

The `tarfile` module is used to read and write tar archives using `gzip`, `bz2` compression techniques. Make sure the necessary files and directories are present. Now, create a `tarfile_example.py` script and write the following content in it:

```
import tarfile
tar_file = tarfile.open("work.tar.gz", "w:gz")
for name in ["welcome.py", "hello.py", "hello.txt", "sample.txt",
"sample1.txt"]:
            tar_file.add(name)
tar_file.close()
```

Run the script as follows:

```
$ python3 tarfile_example.py
```

Now, check your present working directory; you will see `work.tar.gz` has been created.

Using a tarfile module to examine the contents of TAR files

In this section, we will learn about how we can examine the contents of a created tar archive without actually extracting that tar file. We will do it using Python's `tarfile` module.

Create a `examine_tar_file_content.py` script and write the following content in it:

```
import tarfile
tar_file = tarfile.open("work.tar.gz", "r:gz")
print(tar_file.getnames())
```

Run the script as follows:

```
$ python3 examine_tar_file_content.py

Output:
['welcome.py', 'hello.py', 'hello.txt', 'sample.txt', 'sample1.txt']
```

In previous example, we used the `tarfile` module to examine the contents of the created tar file. We used the `getnames()` function to read the data.

Summary

In this chapter, we learned about Python scripts for handling files and directories. We also learned how to use the `os` module to work with directories. We learned how to copy, move, rename, and delete files and directories. We also learned about the pandas module in Python, which is used in comparing and merging data. We learned about creating tar files and reading the contents of tar files using the `tarfile` module. We also did pattern matching while searching files and directories.

In the next chapter, we will learn about `tar` archives and ZIP creations.

Questions

1. How to deal with different path regardless of different OS (Windows, Llinux)?
2. What are different arguments available for `print()` in python?
3. What is the use of `dir()` keyword in python?
4. What is dataframe, series in `pandas` ?
5. What is list comprehension?
6. Can we do set comprehension and dictionary comprehension? If yes how?
7. How to print first/last N rows using pandas dataframe?
8. Write a program using list comprehension for printing the odd numbers
9. What is the type of `sys.argv`?
10. a) set
11. b) list
12. c) tuple
13. d) string

Further reading

- `pathlib` documentation: https://docs.python.org/3/library/pathlib.html
- `pandas` documentation: https://pandas.pydata.org/pandas-docs/stable/
- `os` module documentation: https://docs.python.org/3/library/os.html

File Archiving, Encrypting, and Decrypting

In the previous chapter, we learned about handling files, directories, and data. We also learned about the `tarfile` module. In this chapter, we'll learn about file archiving, encryption, and decryption. Archiving plays an important role in managing files, directories, and data. But first, what is archiving? Archiving is a process that stores the files and directories into a single file. Python has the `tarfile` module for creating such archive files.

In this chapter, we will cover the following topics:

- Creating and unpacking archives
- Tar archives
- ZIP creation
- File encryption and decryption

Creating and unpacking archives

In this section, we're going to learn about how we can create and unpack archives using the `shutil` module of Python. The `shutil` module has the `make_archive()` function, which creates a new archive file. Using `make_archive()`, we can archive the entire directory with its contents.

Creating archives

Now, we are going to write a script called `shutil_make_archive.py` and write the following content in it:

```python
import tarfile
import shutil
import sys

shutil.make_archive(
            'work_sample', 'gztar',
            root_dir='..',
            base_dir='work',
)
print('Archive contents:')
with tarfile.open('work_sample.tar.gz', 'r') as t_file:
  for names in t_file.getnames():
    print(names)
```

Run the program and you'll get the following output:

```
$ python3 shutil_make_archive.py
Archive contents:
work
work/bye.py
work/shutil_make_archive.py
work/welcome.py
work/hello.py
```

In the preceding example, to create an archive file, we used the `shutil` and `tarfile` modules of Python. In `shutil.make_archive()`, we specified `work_sample`, which will be the name of the archive file and will be in `gz` format. We've specified our work directory name in the base directory attribute. Finally, we printed the names of files that are archived.

Unpacking archives

To unpack the archives, the `shutil` module has the `unpack_archive()` function. Using this function, we can extract the archive files. We passed the archive filename and the directory where we want to extract the contents. If no directory name is passed, then it will extract the contents into your current working directory.

Now, create a script called `shutil_unpack_archive.py` and write the following code in it:

```
import pathlib
import shutil
import sys
import tempfile
with tempfile.TemporaryDirectory() as d:
  shutil.unpack_archive('work_sample.tar.gz',
extract_dir='/home/student/work',)
  prefix_len = len(d) + 1
  for extracted in pathlib.Path(d).rglob('*'):
  print(str(extracted)[prefix_len:])
```

Run the script as follows:

```
student@ubuntu:~/work$ python3 shutil_unpack_archive.py
```

Now, check your `work/` directory and you will find the `work/` folder in it, which will have the extracted files.

Tar archives

In this section, we are going to learn about the `tarfile` module. We'll also learn about testing the entered filename, assessing whether it's a valid archive filename or not. We'll look at how to add a new file into the already archived file, how we can read metadata using the `tarfile` module, and how to extract the files from an archive using the `extractall()` function.

First, we will test whether the entered filename is a valid archive file or not. To test this, the `tarfile` module has the `is_tarfile()` function, which returns a Boolean value.

Create a script called `check_archive_file.py` and write the following content in it:

```
import tarfile

for f_name in ['hello.py', 'work.tar.gz', 'welcome.py', 'nofile.tar',
'sample.tar.xz']:
  try:
    print('{:} {}'.format(f_name, tarfile.is_tarfile(f_name)))
  except IOError as err:
    print('{:} {}'.format(f_name, err))
```

Run the script and you will get the following output:

```
student@ubuntu:~/work$ python3 check_archive_file.py
hello.py          False
work.tar.gz       True
welcome.py        False
nofile.tar            [Errno 2] No such file or directory: 'nofile.tar'
sample.tar.xz     True
```

So, `tarfile.is_tarfile()` will check every filename mentioned in the list. The `hello.py`, `welcome.py` file are not tar files so we got a Boolean value, `False`. `work.tar.gz` and `sample.tar.xz` are tar files, so we got the Boolean value, `True`. And there is no such file as `nofile.tar` present in our directory, so we have got an exception, as we've written it in our script.

Now, we are going to add a new file into our already created archived file. Create a script called `add_to_archive.py` and write the following code in it:

```
import shutil
import os
import tarfile
print('creating archive')
shutil.make_archive('work', 'tar', root_dir='..', base_dir='work',)
print('\nArchive contents:')
with tarfile.open('work.tar', 'r') as t_file:
 for names in t_file.getnames():
 print(names)
os.system('touch sample.txt')
print('adding sample.txt')
with tarfile.open('work.tar', mode='a') as t:
 t.add('sample.txt')
print('contents:',)
with tarfile.open('work.tar', mode='r') as t:
 print([m.name for m in t.getmembers()])
```

Run the script and you will get the following output:

```
student@ubuntu:~/work$ python3 add_to_archive.py
Output :
creating archive
Archive contents:
work
work/bye.py
work/shutil_make_archive.py
work/check_archive_file.py
work/welcome.py
work/add_to_archive.py
```

```
work/shutil_unpack_archive.py
work/hello.py
adding sample.txt
contents:
['work', 'work/bye.py', 'work/shutil_make_archive.py',
'work/check_archive_file.py', 'work/welcome.py', 'work/add_to_archive.py',
'work/shutil_unpack_archive.py', 'work/hello.py', 'sample.txt']
```

In this example, first we created an archive file using `shutil.make_archive()` and then we printed the contents of the archived file. We then created a `sample.txt` file in the next statement. Now, we want to add that `sample.txt` in the already created `work.tar`. Here, we used the append mode, `a`. And next, we are again displaying the contents of the archived file.

Now, we will learn about how we can read the metadata from an archive file. The `getmembers()` function will load the metadata of the files. Create a script called `read_metadata.py` and write the following content in it:

```python
import tarfile
import time
with tarfile.open('work.tar', 'r') as t:
        for file_info in t.getmembers():
                    print(file_info.name)
                    print("Size    :", file_info.size, 'bytes')
                    print("Type    :", file_info.type)
                    print()
```

Run the script and you will get the following output:

```
student@ubuntu:~/work$ python3 read_metadata.py
Output:
work/bye.py
Size : 30 bytes
Type : b'0'
work/shutil_make_archive.py
Size : 243 bytes
Type : b'0'
work/check_archive_file.py
Size : 233 bytes
Type : b'0'

work/welcome.py
Size : 48 bytes
Type : b'0'

work/add_to_archive.py
Size : 491 bytes
```

```
Type : b'0'

work/shutil_unpack_archive.py
Size : 279 bytes
Type : b'0'
```

Now, we will extract the contents from an archive using the `extractall()` function. For that, create a script called `extract_contents.py` and write the following code in it:

```python
import tarfile
import os
os.mkdir('work')
with tarfile.open('work.tar', 'r') as t:
            t.extractall('work')
print(os.listdir('work'))
```

Run the script and you will get the following output:

```
student@ubuntu:~/work$ python3 extract_contents.py
```

Check your current working directory,and you will find the `work/` directory. Navigate to that directory and you can find your extracted files.

ZIP creation

In this section, we are going to work with ZIP files. We will learn about the `zipfile` module of `python`, how to create ZIP files, how to test whether an entered filename is a valid `zip` filename or not, reading the metadata, and so on.

First, we will learn how to create a `zip` file using the `make_archive()` function of the `shutil` module. Create a script called `make_zip_file.py` and write the following code in it:

```python
import shutil
shutil.make_archive('work', 'zip', 'work')
```

Run the script as follows:

```
student@ubuntu:~$ python3 make_zip_file.py
```

Now check your current working directory and you will see `work.zip`.

Now, we will test whether the entered filename is a `zip` file or not. For this purpose, the `zipfile` module has the `is_zipfile()` function.

Create a script called `check_zip_file.py` and write the following content in it:

```
import zipfile
for f_name in ['hello.py', 'work.zip', 'welcome.py', 'sample.txt',
'test.zip']:
        try:
                print('{:}                {}'.format(f_name,
zipfile.is_zipfile(f_name)))
        except IOError as err:
                print('{:}                {}'.format(f_name, err))
```

Run the script as follows:

```
student@ubuntu:~$ python3 check_zip_file.py
Output :
hello.py        False
work.zip        True
welcome.py    False
sample.txt      False
test.zip        True
```

In this example, we have used a `for` loop, where we are checking the filenames in a list. The `is_zipfile()` function will check, one by one, the filenames and will give Boolean values as a result.

Now, we will see how we can read the metadata from an archived ZIP file using the `zipfile` module of Python. Create a script called `read_metadata.py` and write the following content in it:

```
import zipfile

def meta_info(names):
        with zipfile.ZipFile(names) as zf:
                for info in zf.infolist():
                        print(info.filename)
                        if info.create_system == 0:
                                system = 'Windows'
                        elif info.create_system == 3:
                                system = 'Unix'
                        else:
                                system = 'UNKNOWN'
                        print("System        :", system)
                        print("Zip Version   :",
info.create_version)
                        print("Compressed    :",
info.compress_size, 'bytes')
                        print("Uncompressed  :",
```

```
                  info.file_size, 'bytes')
                                                    print()


if __name__ == '__main__':
    meta_info('work.zip')
```

Execute the script as follows:

```
student@ubuntu:~$ python3 read_metadata.py
Output:
sample.txt
System          : Unix
Zip Version     : 20
Compressed      : 2 bytes
Uncompressed    : 0 bytes

bye.py
System          : Unix
Zip Version     : 20
Compressed      : 32 bytes
Uncompressed    : 30 bytes

extract_contents.py
System          : Unix
Zip Version     : 20
Compressed      : 95 bytes
Uncompressed    : 132 bytes

shutil_make_archive.py
System          : Unix
Zip Version     : 20
Compressed      : 160 bytes
Uncompressed    : 243 bytes
```

To get the metadata information about the `zip` file, we used the `infolist()` method of the `ZipFile` class.

File encryption and decryption

In this section, we will learn about the `pyAesCrypt` module of Python. `pyAesCrypt` is a file encryption module that uses `AES256-CBC` to encrypt/decrypt files and binary streams.

Install `pyAesCrypt` as follows:

```
pip3 install pyAesCrypt
```

Create a script called `file_encrypt.py` and write the following code in it:

```
import pyAesCrypt

from os import stat, remove
# encryption/decryption buffer size - 64K
bufferSize = 64 * 1024
password = "#Training"
with open("sample.txt", "rb") as fIn:
 with open("sample.txt.aes", "wb") as fOut:
 pyAesCrypt.encryptStream(fIn, fOut, password, bufferSize)
# get encrypted file size
encFileSize = stat("sample.txt.aes").st_size
```

Run the script as follows:

```
student@ubuntu:~/work$ python3 file_encrypt.py
Output :
```

Please check your current working directory. You will find the `sample.txt.aes` encrypted file in it.

In this example, we've already mentioned the buffer size and password. Next, we mentioned our filename that will be encrypted. In `encryptStream`, we mentioned `fIn`, which is our file to encrypt, and `fOut`, which is our filename after encryption. We've stored our encrypted file as `sample.txt.aes`.

Now, we will decrypt the `sample.txt.aes` file to get the content of the file. Create a script called `file_decrypt.py` and write the following content in it:

```
import pyAesCrypt
from os import stat, remove
bufferSize = 64 * 1024
password = "#Training"
encFileSize = stat("sample.txt.aes").st_size
with open("sample.txt.aes", "rb") as fIn:
 with open("sampleout.txt", "wb") as fOut:
 try:
 pyAesCrypt.decryptStream(fIn, fOut, password, bufferSize, encFileSize)
 except ValueError:
 remove("sampleout.txt")
```

Run the script as follows:

```
student@ubuntu:~/work$ python3 file_decrypt.py
```

Now, check your current working directory. A file named `sampleout.txt` will be created. That's your decrypted file.

In this example, we mentioned the filename to decrypt, which is `sample.txt.aes`. Next, our decrypted file will be `sampleout.txt`. In `decryptStream()`, we mentioned `fIn`, which is our file to decrypt, and `fOut`, which is the name of the `decrypted` file.

Summary

In this chapter, we learned about creating and extracting archived files. Archiving plays an important role in managing files, directories, and data. It also stores the files and directories into a single file.

We learned in detail about the `tarfile` and `zipfile` Python modules that enable you to create, extract, and test archive files. You will be able to add a new file into the already archived file, read metadata, extract the files from an archive. You also learned about file encryption and decryption using the `pyAescrypt` module.

In the next chapter, you will learn about text processing and regular expressions in python. Python has a very powerful library called regular expressions that does tasks such as searching and extracting the data.

Questions

1. Can we compress the data using password protected? if yes how ?
2. What is context manager in python?
3. What is pickling and unpickling?
4. What are the different types of functions in python?

Further reading

- Data Compression and Archiving: `https://docs.python.org/3/library/archiving.html`
- `tempfile` documentation: `https://docs.python.org/2/library/tempfile.html`
- Cryptography Python documentation: `https://docs.python.org/3/library/crypto.html`
- `shutil` documentation: `https://docs.python.org/3/library/shutil.html`

7
Text Processing and Regular Expressions

In this chapter, we are going to learn about text processing and regular expressions. Text processing is a process of creating or modifying the text. Python has a very powerful library called regular expressions that does tasks such as searching and extracting the data. You will learn how to do it with files and also learn to read and write to files.

We are going to learn about the `re` Python module for regular expressions and processing text in Python. We are going to learn about the `match()`, `search()`, `findall()`, and `sub()` functions of `re` module. We are also going to learn about text wrapping in Python using the `textwrap` module. Finally, we will learn about unicode characters.

In this chapter, we will cover the following topics:

- Text wrapping
- Regular expressions
- Unicode strings

Text wrapping

In this section, we will learn about the `textwrap` Python module. This module provides the `TextWrapper` class that does all the work. The `textwrap` module is used for formatting and wrapping plain text. This module provides five main functions: `wrap()`, `fill()`, `dedent()`, `indent()`, and `shorten()`. We are going to learn these functions one by one now.

The wrap() function

The `wrap()` function is used to wrap an entire paragraph in to a single string. The output will be a list of output lines.

The syntax is `textwrap.wrap(text, width)`:

- `text`: Text to wrap.
- `width`: Maximum length allowed of a wrapped line. The default value is `70`.

Now, we will see an example of `wrap()`. Create a `wrap_example.py` script and write the following content in it:

```
import textwrap

sample_string = '''Python is an interpreted high-level programming language
for general-purpose programming. Created by Guido van Rossum and first
released in 1991, Python has a design philosophy that emphasizes code
readability, notably using significant whitespace.'''

w = textwrap.wrap(text=sample_string, width=30)
print(w)
```

Run the script and you will get the output as follows:

```
student@ubuntu:~/work$ python3 wrap_example.py
['Python is an interpreted high-', 'level programming language for',
'general-purpose programming.', 'Created by Guido van Rossum', 'and first
released in', '1991, Python has a design', 'philosophy that emphasizes',
'code readability,  notably', 'using significant whitespace.']
```

In the preceding example, we used the `textwrap` module of Python. First, we created a string named `sample_string`. Next, using the `TextWrapper` class we specified the width. Next, using the `wrap` function the string was wrapped to the width of `30`. And next, we printed the lines.

The fill() function

The `fill()` function works similarly to `textwrap.wrap`, except it returns the data joined into a single, newline-separated string. This function wraps the input in text and returns a single string containing the wrapped text.

The syntax for this function is:

```
textwrap.fill(text, width)
```

- `text`: Text to wrap.

- `width`: Maximum length allowed of a wrapped line. The default value is `70`.

Now, we will see an example of `fill()`. Create a `fill_example.py` script and write the following content in it:

```
import textwrap

sample_string = '''Python is an interpreted high-level programming
language.'''

w = textwrap.fill(text=sample_string, width=50)
print(w)
```

Run the script and you will get the output as follows:

```
student@ubuntu:~/work$ python3 fill_example.py
Python is an interpreted high-level programming
language.
```

In the preceding example, we used the `fill()` function. The procedure is the same as what we did in `wrap()`. First, we created a string variable. Next, we created the `textwrap` object. Then, we applied the `fill()` function. Finally, we printed the output.

The dedent() function

The `dedent()` is another function of the `textwrap` module. This function removes the common leading `whitespaces` from every line of your text.

The syntax for this function is as follows:

```
textwrap.dedent(text)
```

`text` is the text to `dedent`.

Now, we will see an example of `dedent()`. Create a `dedent_example.py` script and write the following content in it:

```
import textwrap

str1 = '''
            Hello Python World \tThis is Python 101
            Scripting language\n
            Python is an interpreted high-level programming language for
general-purpose programming.
            '''
print("Original: \n", str1)
print()

t = textwrap.dedent(str1)
print("Dedented: \n", t)
```

Run the script and you will get the output as follows:

```
student@ubuntu:~/work$ python3 dedent_example.py

Hello Python World    This is Python 101
Scripting language

Python is an interpreted high-level programming language for general-
purpose programming.
```

In the preceding example, we created a `str1` string variable. Then we used `textwrap.dedent()` to remove the common leading whitespaces. Tabs and spaces are considered whitespaces, but they are not equal. Therefore, the only common whitespace, which in our case is `tab`, is removed.

The indent() function

The `indent()` function is used to add the specified prefix to the beginning of the selected lines in your text.

The syntax for this function is:

```
textwrap.indent(text, prefix)
```

- `text`: The main string
- `prefix`: The prefix to add

Create a `indent_example.py` script and write the following content in it:

```
import textwrap

str1 = "Python is an interpreted high-level programming language for
general-purpose programming. Created by Guido van Rossum and first released
in 1991, \n\nPython has a design philosophy that emphasizes code
readability, notably using significant whitespace."

w = textwrap.fill(str1, width=30)
i = textwrap.indent(w, '*')
print(i)
```

Run the script and you will get the output as follows:

```
student@ubuntu:~/work$ python3 indent_example.py
*Python is an interpreted high-
*level programming language for
*general-purpose programming.
*Created by Guido van Rossum
*and first released in 1991,
*Python has a design philosophy
*that emphasizes code
*readability, notably using
*significant whitespace.
```

In the preceding example, we used the `fill()` and `indent()` functions of the `textwrap` module. First, we used the `fill` method to store the data into the `w` variable. Next, we used the `indent` method. Using `indent()`, each line in the output will have a * prefix. And next, we printed the output.

The shorten() function

This function of the `textwrap` module is used truncate the text to fit in the specified width. For example, if you want to create a summary or preview, use the `shorten()` function. Using `shorten()`, all the whitespaces in your text will get standardized into a single space.

The syntax for this function is:

```
textwrap.shorten(text, width)
```

Now we will see an example of `shorten()`. Create a `shorten_example.py` script and write the following content in it:

```
import textwrap

str1 = "Python is an interpreted high-level programming language for
general-purpose programming. Created by Guido van Rossum and first released
in 1991, \n\nPython has a design philosophy that emphasizes code
readability, notably using significant whitespace."

s = textwrap.shorten(str1, width=50)
print(s)
```

Run the script and you will get the output as follows:

```
student@ubuntu:~/work$ python3 shorten_example.py
Python is an interpreted high-level [...]
```

In the preceding example, we used the `shorten()` function to truncate our text and fit that text in a specified width. First, all the whitespaces truncated into the single space. If the result fited in the specified width, the result was displayed on the screen. If not, then the words of the specified width was displayed on the screen and the rest was placed in the placeholder.

Regular expressions

In this section, we are going to learn about regular expressions in Python. Regular expression is a specialized programming language, which is embedded in Python and is available to users through the `re` module. We can define the rules for the set of strings that we want to match. Using regular expressions, we can extract specific information from files, code, documents, spreadsheets, and so on.

In Python, a regular expression is denoted as `re` and can be imported through the `re` module. Regular expressions support four things:

- Identifiers
- Modifiers
- Whitespace characters
- Flags

The following table lists the identifiers, and there's a description for each one:

Identifier	Description
\w	Matches alphanumeric characters, including underscore (_)
\W	Matches non-alphanumeric characters, excluding underscore (_)
\d	Matches a digit
\D	Matches a non-digit
\s	Matches a space
\S	Matches anything but a space
.	Matches a period (.)
\b	Matches any character except a new line

The following table lists the modifiers, and there's a description for each one:

Modifier	Description
^	Matches start of the string
$	Matches end of the string
?	Matches 0 or 1
*	Matches 0 or more
+	Matches 1 or more
|	Matches either or x/y
[ ]	Matches range
{x}	Amount of preceding code

The following table lists the whitespace characters, and there's a description for each one:

Character	Description
\s	Space
\t	Tab
\n	New line
\e	Escape
\f	Form feed
\r	Return

The following table lists the flags, and there's a description for each one:

Flag	Description
re.IGNORECASE	Case-insensitive matching
re.DOTALL	Matches any character including new lines
re.MULTILINE	Multiline matching
Re.ASCII	Makes escape match only on ASCII characters

Now we are going to see some examples of regular expressions. We are going to learn about the match(), search(), findall(), and sub() functions.

 To use regular expressions in Python, you must import the re module in your scripts so that you will be able to use all the functions and methods for regular expressions.

Now we are going to learn about these functions one by one in the following sections.

The match() function

The match() function is a function of the re module. This function will match the specified re pattern with the string. If the match is found, a match object will be returned. A match object will contain the information about the match. If a match is not found, we will get the result as None. The match object has two methods:

- group(num): Returns an entire match
- groups(): Return all matching subgroups in tuple

The syntax for this function is as follows:

```
re.match(pattern, string)
```

Now, we are going see an example of re.match(). Create a re_match.py script and write the following content in it:

```
import re

str_line = "This is python tutorial. Do you enjoy learning python ?"
obj = re.match(r'(.*) enjoy (.*?) .*', str_line)
if obj:
        print(obj.groups())
```

Run the script and you will get the output as follows:

```
student@ubuntu:~/work$ python3 re_match.py
('This is python tutorial. Do you', 'learning')
```

In the preceding script, we imported the `re` module to use regular expressions in Python. Then we created a `str_line` string. Next, we created an `obj` match object and store the match pattern result in it. In this example, the `(.*) enjoy (.*?) .*` pattern will print everything before the `enjoy` keyword, and it will print only one word after the `enjoy` keyword. Next, we used the `groups()` method of `match` object. It will print all the matched substrings in a tuple. So, the output you will get will be, `('This is python tutorial. Do you', 'learning')`.

The search() function

The `search()` function of the `re` module will search through a string. It will look for any location for the specified `re` pattern. The `search()` will take a pattern and text and it will search through our specified string for a match. It will return a `match` object when a match is found. It will return `None` if no match found. The `match` object has two methods:

- `group(num)`: Returns an entire match
- `groups()`: Returns all matching subgroups in tuple

The syntax for this function is as follows:

```
re.search(pattern, string)
```

Create a `re_search.py` script and write following content in it:

```
import re

pattern = ['programming', 'hello']
str_line = 'Python programming is fun'
for p in pattern:
        print("Searching for %s in %s" % (p, str_line))
        if re.search(p, str_line):
                print("Match found")
        else:
                print("No match found")
```

Run the script and you will get the output as follows:

```
student@ubuntu:~/work$ python3 re_search.py
Searching for programming in Python programming is fun
```

```
Match found
Searching for hello in Python programming is fun
No match found
```

In the preceding example, we used the `search()` method of `match` object to find the `re` pattern. After importing the re module, we specified the pattern in a list. In that list, we wrote two strings: `programming` and `hello`. Next, we created a string: `Python programming is fun`. We wrote a for loop that will check for a specified pattern one by one. If a match is found, the `if` block will be executed. If no match is found, the `else` block will be executed.

The findall() function

This is one of the methods of the `match` object. The `findall()` method finds all the matches and then returns them as a list of strings. Each element of the list represents as a match. This method searches for the pattern without overlapping.

Create a `re_findall_example.py` script and write the following content in it:

```python
import re

pattern = 'Red'
colors = 'Red, Blue, Black, Red, Green'
p = re.findall(pattern, colors)
print(p)

str_line = 'Peter Piper picked a peck of pickled peppers. How many pickled
peppers did Peter Piper pick?'
pt = re.findall('pe\w+', str_line)
pt1 = re.findall('pic\w+', str_line)
print(pt)
print(pt1)

line = 'Hello hello HELLO bye'
p = re.findall('he\w+', line, re.IGNORECASE)
print(p)
```

Run the script and you will get the output as follows:

```
student@ubuntu:~/work$ python3 re_findall_example.py
['Red', 'Red']
['per', 'peck', 'peppers', 'peppers', 'per']
['picked', 'pickled', 'pickled', 'pick']
['Hello', 'hello', 'HELLO']
```

In the preceding script, we have written three examples of the `findall()` method. In the first example, we defined a pattern and a string. We found that pattern from the string using the `findall()` method and then printed it. In the second example, we created a string and we found the words whose first two letters are `pe` using `findall()` and then printing them. We will get the list of words whose first two letters are `pe`.

In addition, we found the words whose first three letters are `pic` and then print them. Here, also, we will get the list of strings. In the third example, we created a string in which we specified `hello` in uppercase and lowercase, and a word: `bye`. Using `findall()`, we find the words whose first two letters are `he`. Also in `findall()`, we used a `re.IGNORECASE` flag that will ignore the case of the word and printed them.

The sub() function

This is one of the most important functions of the re module. The `sub()` is used for replacing the `re` pattern with the specified replacement. It will replace all the occurrences of the `re` pattern with the replacement string. The syntax is as follows:

re.sub(pattern, repl_str, string, count=0)

- `pattern`: The `re` pattern.
- `repl_str`: The replacement string.
- `string`: The main string.
- `count`: The number of occurrences to be replaced. The default value is `0`, which means replacing all occurrences.

Now we are going to create a `re_sub.py` script and write the following content in it:

```
import re

str_line = 'Peter Piper picked a peck of pickled peppers. How many pickled peppers did Peter Piper pick?'

print("Original: ", str_line)
p = re.sub('Peter', 'Mary', str_line)
print("Replaced: ", p)

p = re.sub('Peter', 'Mary', str_line, count=1)
print("Replacing only one occurrence of Peter... ")
print("Replaced: ", p)
```

Run the script and you will get the output as follows:

```
student@ubuntu:~/work$ python3 re_sub.py
Original:  Peter Piper picked a peck of pickled peppers. How many pickled
peppers did Peter Piper pick?
Replaced:  Mary Piper picked a peck of pickled peppers. How many pickled
peppers did Mary Piper pick?
Replacing only one occurrence of Peter...
Replaced:  Mary Piper picked a peck of pickled peppers. How many pickled
peppers did Peter Piper pick?
```

In the preceding example, we used `sub()` to replace the `re` pattern with a specified replacement string. We replaced `Peter` with `Mary`. So, all the occurrences of Peter will be replaced by Mary. Next, we also included the `count` parameter. We mentioned `count=1`: it means only one occurrence of Peter will be replaced and other occurrences of Peter will remain the same.

Now, we will learn about the `subn()` function of the re module. The `subn()` function works the same as `sub()` with the additional functionality. The `subn()` function will return a tuple containing the new string and the number of replacements performed. Let's look at an the example of `subn()`. Create a `re_subn.py` script and write the following content in it:

```python
import re

print("str1:- ")
str1 = "Sky is blue. Sky is beautiful."

print("Original: ", str1)
p = re.subn('beautiful', 'stunning', str1)
print("Replaced: ", p)
print()

print("str_line:- ")
str_line = 'Peter Piper picked a peck of pickled peppers. How many pickled
peppers did Peter Piper pick?'

print("Original: ", str_line)
p = re.subn('Peter', 'Mary', str_line)
print("Replaced: ", p)
```

Run the script and you will get the output as follows:

```
student@ubuntu:~/work$ python3 re_subn.py
str1:-
Original:  Sky is blue. Sky is beautiful.
Replaced:  ('Sky is blue. Sky is stunning.', 1)
```

```
str_line:-
Original:  Peter Piper picked a peck of pickled peppers. How many pickled
peppers did Peter Piper pick?
Replaced:  ('Mary Piper picked a peck of pickled peppers. How many pickled
peppers did Mary Piper pick?', 2)
```

In the preceding example, we used the subn() function to replace the RE pattern. As a result, we got a tuple containing the replaced string and the number of replacements.

Unicode strings

In this section, we are going to learn about how to print Unicode strings in Python. Python handles Unicode strings in a very easy way. The string type actually holds Unicode strings, not a sequence of bytes.

Start the python3 console in your system and start writing the following:

```
student@ubuntu:~/work$ python3
Python 3.6.6 (default, Sep 12 2018, 18:26:19)
[GCC 8.0.1 20180414 (experimental) [trunk revision 259383]] on linux
Type "help", "copyright", "credits" or "license" for more information.
>>>
>>> print ('\u2713')
✓
>>> print ('\u2724')
✤
>>> print ('\u2750')
□
>>> print ('\u2780')
①
>>> chinese = '\u4e16\u754c\u60a8\u597d!'
>>> chinese
'你好，世界!'     ----- (Meaning "Hello world!")
>>>
>>> s = '\u092E\u0941\u0902\u092C\u0908'
>>> s
'मुंबई'                         ------(Unicode translated in Marathi)
>>>
>>> s = '\u10d2\u10d0\u10db\u10d0\u10e0\u10ef\u10dd\u10d1\u10d0'
>>> s
'გამარჯობა'            ------(Meaning "Hello" in Georgian)
>>>
>>> s = '\u03b3\u03b5\u03b9\u03b1\u03c3\u03b1\u03c2'
```

```
>>> s
'γειασας'                   ------(Meaning "Hello" in Greek)
>>>
```

Unicode code point

In this section, we are going to learn about the unicode code point. Python has a powerful built-in function named `ord()` to get a Unicode code point from a given character. So, let's see an example of getting a Unicode code point from a character, as shown in the following code:

```
>>> str1 = u'Office'
>>> for char in str1:
... print('U+%04x' % ord(char))
...
U+004f
U+0066
U+0066
U+0069
U+0063
U+0065
>>> str2 = '中文'
>>> for char in str2:
... print('U+%04x' % ord(char))
...
U+4e2d
U+6587
```

Encoding

The transformation from Unicode code point to byte string is known as encoding. So, let's see an example of how to encode Unicode code point, as shown in following code:

```
>>> str = u'Office'
>>> enc_str = type(str.encode('utf-8'))
>>> enc_str
<class 'bytes'>
```

Decoding

The transformation from a byte string to a Unicode code point is known as decoding. So, let's see an example of how to decode a byte string to get a Unicode code point as shown in following code:

```
>>> str = bytes('Office', encoding='utf-8')
>>> dec_str = str.decode('utf-8')
>>> dec_str
'Office'
```

Avoiding UnicodeDecodeError

UnicodeDecodeError occurs whenever byte strings cannot decode to Unicode code points. To avoid this exception, we can pass replace, backslashreplace, or ignore to the error argument in decode the as shown here:

```
>>> str = b"\xaf"
>>> str.decode('utf-8', 'strict')
    Traceback (most recent call last):
  File "<stdin>", line 1, in <module>
UnicodeDecodeError: 'utf-8' codec can't decode byte 0xaf in position 0:
invalid start byte

>>> str.decode('utf-8', "replace")
'\ufffd'
>>> str.decode('utf-8', "backslashreplace")
'\\xaf'
>>> str.decode('utf-8', "ignore")
' '
```

Summary

In this chapter, we learned about regular expressions, using which we can define the rules for a set of strings that we want to match. We learned about the four functions of the re module: match(), search(), findall(), and sub().

We learned about the textwrap module, which is used for formatting and wrapping plain text. We also learned about the wrap(), fill(), dedent(), indent(), and shorten() functions of the textwrap module. Finally, we learned about the Unicode characters and how to print the Unicode strings in Python.

In the next chapter, we are going to learn about standard documenting and reporting of information using Python.

Questions

1. What is a regular expression in Python?
2. Write a Python program to check that a string contains only a certain set of characters (in this case, a–z, A–Z, and 0–9).
3. Which module in Python supports regular expressions?
   a) `re`
   b) `regex`
   c) `pyregex`
   d) None of the above
4. What does the `re.match` function do?
   a) Matches a pattern at the start of the string
   b) Matches a pattern at any position in the string
   c) Such a function does not exist
   d) None of the above
5. What is the output of the following?
   Sentence: `"we are humans"`
   Matched: `re.match(r'(.*) (.*?) (.*)',sentence)`
   `print(matched.group())`

   a) `('we', 'are', 'humans')`
   b) `(we, are, humans)`
   c) `('we', 'humans')`
   d) `'we are humans'`

Further reading

- Regular expressions: `https://docs.python.org/3.2/library/re.html`
- Textwrap documentation: `https://docs.python.org/3/library/textwrap.html`
- Unicode documentation: `https://docs.python.org/3/howto/unicode.html`

Documentation and Reporting

In this chapter, you will learn how to document and report information using Python. You will also learn how to take input using Python scripts and how to print output. Writing scripts for receiving emails is easier in Python. You will learn how to format information.

In this chapter, you will learn about the following:

- Standard input and output
- Information formatting
- Sending emails

Standard input and output

In this section, we are going to learn about input and output in Python. We will learn about `stdin` and `stdout`, and the `input()` function.

`stdin` and `stdout` are file-like objects. These objects are provided by the operating system. Whenever a user runs a program in an interactive session, `stdin` acts as input and `stdout` will be the user's Terminal. As `stdin` is a file-like object, we have to read the data from `stdin` rather than reading data at runtime. `stdout` is used for the output. It is used as an output for expressions and `print()` function, as well as a prompt for the `input()` function.

Now, we will see an example of `stdin` and `stdout`. For that purpose, create a script, `stdin_stdout_example.py`, and write the following content in it:

```
import sys

print("Enter number1: ")
a = int(sys.stdin.readline())

print("Enter number2: ")
b = int(sys.stdin.readline())

c = a + b
sys.stdout.write("Result: %d " % c)
```

Run the script and you will get the output as follows:

```
student@ubuntu:~/work$ python3 stdin_stdout_example.py
Enter number1:
10
Enter number2:
20
Result: 30
```

In the preceding example, we have used `stdin` and `stdout` for taking input and displaying the output. The `sys.stdin.readline()` will read from `stdin`. The will write the data.

Now, we will learn about the `input()` and `print()` functions. The `input()` function is used for taking input from the user. The function has an optional parameter: prompt string.

Syntax:

```
input(prompt)
```

The `input()` function returns a string value. If you want a number value, simply write the 'int keyword before `input()`. You can do this as follows:

```
int(input(prompt))
```

Similarly, you can write `float` for float values. Now, we will look at an example. Create a `input_example.py` script and write the following code in it:

```
str1 = input("Enter a string: ")
print("Entered string is: ", str1)
print()

a = int(input("Enter the value of a: "))
```

```
b = int(input("Enter the value of b: "))
c = a + b
print("Value of c is: ", c)
print()

num1 = float(input("Enter num 1: "))
num2 = float(input("Enter num 2: "))
num3 = num1/num2
print("Value of num 3 is: ", num3)
```

Run the script and you will get the output as follows:

```
student@ubuntu:~/work$ python3 input_example.py
Output:
Enter a string: Hello
Entered string is:  Hello
Enter the value of a: 10
Enter the value of b: 20
Value of c is:   30
Enter num 1: 10.50
Enter num 2: 2.0
Value of num 3 is:   5.25
```

In the preceding example, we used input() function for three different values. Firstly for string, second for integer value, and third for float value. To use input() for integer and float, we have to use int() and float() type conversion functions to convert the received string into integer and float respectively.

Now, the print() function is used to output the data. We have to put in a comma-separated list of arguments. In input_example.py, to get the output, we used the print() function. Using the print() function, you can simply write the data on to your screen by enclosing them in the " " or ' '. To access just the value, just write the variable name in the print() function. If you want to write some text as well as accessing a value in the same print() function, then separate these two by putting a comma between them.

We will look at a simple example for the print() function. Create a print_example.py script and write the following content in it:

```
# printing a simple string on the screen.
print("Hello Python")

# Accessing only a value.
a = 80
print(a)
```

```
# printing a string on screen as well as accessing a value.
a = 50
b = 30
c = a/b
print("The value of c is: ", c)
```

Run the script and you will get the output as follows:

```
student@ubuntu:~/work$ python3 print_example.py
Hello Python
80
The value of c is:  1.6666666666666667
```

In the preceding example, first, we simply printed a string on the screen. Next, we just accessed the value of a and printed it on the screen. Lastly, we entered the values of a and b, then added them and stored the result in the variable c, and then we printed a statement and accessed a value from the same print() function.

Information formatting

In this section, we are going to learn about string formatting. We are going to learn how to format information in two ways: one by using the string format() method and the other by using the % operator.

First, we will learn string formatting using the string format() method. This method of the string class allows us to do value formatting. It also allows us to do variable substitutions. This will concatenate the elements through positional arguments.

Now, we are going to learn how to do this formatting using formatters. The string on which this method is called can contain literal text or replacement fields delimited by braces { }. Multiple pairs of { } can be used while formatting a string. This replacement field contains either an index of an argument, or the name of argument. As a result, you will get a copy of a string where each replacement field is replaced with the string value of an argument.

Now, we will look at an example of string formatting.

Create a format_example.py script and write the following content in it:

```
# Using single formatter
print("{}, My name is John".format("Hi"))
str1 = "This is John. I am learning {} scripting language."
print(str1.format("Python"))

print("Hi, My name is Sara and I am {} years old !!".format(26))
```

```
# Using multiple formatters
str2 = "This is Mary {}. I work at {} Resource department. I am {} years
old !!"
print(str2.format("Jacobs", "Human", 30))

print("Hello {}, Nice to meet you. I am {}.".format("Emily", "Jennifer"))
```

Run the script as follows:

```
student@ubuntu:~/work$ python3 format_example.py
Output:
Hi, My name is John
This is John. I am learning Python scripting language.
Hi, My name is Sara and I am 26 years old !!
This is Mary Jacobs. I work at Human Resource department. I am 30 years old
!!
Hello Emily, Nice to meet you. I am Jennifer.
```

In the preceding example, we did string formatting using the `format()` method of `string` class using single and multiple formatters.

Now, we are going to learn about string formatting using the `%` operator. There are format symbols used with the `%` operator. Here are some commonly used symbols:

- `%d`: Decimal integer
- `%s`: String
- `%f`: Floating point number
- `%c`: Character

Now, we will look at an example. Create a `string_formatting.py` script and write the following content in it:

```
# Basic formatting
a = 10
b = 30
print("The values of a and b are %d %d" % (a, b))
c = a + b
print("The value of c is %d" % c)

str1 = 'John'
print("My name is %s" % str1)

x = 10.5
y = 33.5
z = x * y
print("The value of z is %f" % z)
```

```
print()

# aligning
name = 'Mary'
print("Normal: Hello, I am %s !!" % name)

print("Right aligned: Hello, I am %10s !!" % name)

print("Left aligned: Hello, I am %-10s !!" % name)
print()

# truncating
print("The truncated string is %.4s" % ('Examination'))
print()

# formatting placeholders
students = {'Name' : 'John', 'Address' : 'New York'}
print("Student details: Name:%(Name)s Address:%(Address)s" % students)
```

Run the script and you will get the output as follows:

```
student@ubuntu:~/work$ python3 string_formatting.py
The values of a and b are 10 30
The value of c is 40
My name is John
The value of z is 351.750000
Normal: Hello, I am Mary !!
Right aligned: Hello, I am       Mary !!
Left aligned: Hello, I am Mary        !!
  The truncated string is Exam
  Student details: Name:John Address:New York
```

In the preceding example, we used the % operator to format strings: %d for numbers, %s for strings, and %f for float numbers. Then, we aligned the string to the left and right. We also learned how to truncate the string using the % operator. %.4s will display only the first four characters. Next, we created a dictionary named students and entered Name and Address key value pairs. Next, we placed our key names after the % operator to get the strings.

Sending email

In this section, we are going to learn about sending an email from Gmail through a Python script. To do this, Python has a module named smtplib. The smtplib module in Python provides SMTP client session object that is used to send an email to any internet machine with SMTP listener.

We are going to look at an example. In this example, we will send an email containing a simple text from Gmail to the recipients.

Create a `send_email.py` script and write the following content in it:

```
import smtplib
from email.mime.text import MIMEText
import getpass

host_name = 'smtp.gmail.com'
port = 465

u_name = 'username/emailid'
password = getpass.getpass()
sender = 'sender_name'
receivers = ['receiver1_email_address', 'receiver2_email_address']

text = MIMEText('Test mail')
text['Subject'] = 'Test'
text['From'] = sender
text['To'] = ', '.join(receivers)

s_obj = smtplib.SMTP_SSL(host_name, port)
s_obj.login(u_name, password)
s_obj.sendmail(sender, receivers, text.as_string())
s_obj.quit()
print("Mail sent successfully")
```

Run the script as follows:

```
student@ubuntu:~/work$ python3 send_text.py
```

Output:

```
Password:
Mail sent successfully
```

In the preceding example, we have sent an email from our Gmail ID to the receivers. The user name variable will store your email ID. In the password variable, either you can enter your password or else you can prompt for password using the `getpass` module. Here, we prompt for the password. Next, the sender variable will have your name. Now we are going to send this email to multiple receivers. Then, we included subject, from, and to for that email. Then in `login()`, we mentioned our username and password variables. Next, in `sendmail()`, we mentioned the sender, receivers, and text variables. So, using this process, we have sent the email successfully.

Now, we will look at one more example of sending an email with an attachment. In this example, we are going to send an image to the recipient. We are going to send this mail via Gmail. Create a `send_email_attachment.py` script and write the following content in it:

```python
import os
import smtplib
from email.mime.text import MIMEText
from email.mime.image import MIMEImage
from email.mime.multipart import MIMEMultipart
import getpass

host_name = 'smtp.gmail.com'
port = 465

u_name = 'username/emailid'
password = getpass.getpass()
sender = 'sender_name'
receivers = ['receiver1_email_address', 'receiver2_email_address']

text = MIMEMultipart()
text['Subject'] = 'Test Attachment'
text['From'] = sender
text['To'] = ', '.join(receivers)

txt = MIMEText('Sending a sample image.')
text.attach(txt)

f_path = '/home/student/Desktop/mountain.jpg'
with open(f_path, 'rb') as f:
    img = MIMEImage(f.read())

img.add_header('Content-Disposition',
               'attachment',
               filename=os.path.basename(f_path))

text.attach(img)

server = smtplib.SMTP_SSL(host_name, port)
server.login(u_name, password)
server.sendmail(sender, receivers, text.as_string())
print("Email with attachment sent successfully !!")
server.quit()
```

Run the script as follows:

```
student@ubuntu:~/work$ python3 send_email_attachment.py
```

Output:

```
Password:
Email with attachment sent successfully!!
```

In the preceding example, we sent an image as an attachment to the receivers. We mentioned the sender's and receivers' email IDs. Next, in the `f_path`, we mentioned the path of the image that we sent as an attachment. Next, we sent that image as an attachment to the receiver.

> In the previous two examples – `send_text.py` and `send_email_attachment.py` – we sent email via Gmail. You can send via any other email providers. To use any other email provider, just write that provider name in `host_name`. Don't forget to add `smtp` before it. In these example, we used `smtp.gmail.com`; for Yahoo! you can use `smtp.mail.yahoo.com`. So, you can change the hostname as well as the port, according to your email providers.

Summary

In this chapter, we learned about standard input and output. We learned how `stdin` and `stdout` act as keyboard input and user's Terminal respectively. We also learned about `input()` and `print()` functions. In addition to this, we learned about sending an email from Gmail to the receivers. We sent an email with simple text and also sent an attachment. Also, we learned about string formatting using the `format()` method and the `%` operator.

In the next chapter, you will learn about how to work with different files such as PDF, Excel, and `csv`.

Questions

1. What is the difference between `stdin` and input?
2. What is SMTP?
3. What would be the output of the following?

```
>>> name = "Eric"
>>> profession = "comedian"
>>> affiliation = "Monty Python"
>>> age = 25
>>> message = (
...     f"Hi {name}. "
...     f"You are a {profession}. "
...     f"You were in {affiliation}."
... )
>>> message
```

4. What would be the output of the following?

```
str1 = 'Hello'
str2 ='World!'
print('str1 + str2 = ', str1 + str2)
print('str1 * 3 =', str1 * 3)
```

Further reading

1. `string` documentation: https://docs.python.org/3.1/library/string.html
2. `smtplib` documentation: https://docs.python.org/3/library/smtplib.html

Working with Various Files

9

In this chapter, you will learn about working with various types of files, such as PDF files, Excel , CSV , and `txt` files. Python has modules for performing operations on these files. You will learn how to open, edit, and get data from these files using Python.

In this chapter, the following topics will be covered:

- Working with PDF files
- Working with Excel files
- Working with CSV files
- Working with `txt` files

Working with PDF files

In this section, we are going to learn about how to work with PDF files using Python modules. PDF is a widely used document format and PDF files have `.pdf` extensions. Python has a module named `PyPDF2`, that's useful to do various operations on `pdf` files. It is third-party module which is a Python library built as a PDF toolkit.

We must install this module first. To install `PyPDF2`, run the following command in your Terminal:

```
pip3 install PyPDF2
```

Now, we are going to look at some of the operations to work on PDF files, such as reading a PDF, getting the number of pages, extracting text, and rotating PDF pages.

Reading a PDF document and getting the number of pages

In this section, we are going read a PDF file using the `PyPDF2` module. Also, we are going to get the number of pages of that PDF. This module has a function called `PdfFileReader()` that helps in reading a PDF file. Make sure you have a PDF file in your system. Right now, I have the `test.pdf` file present in my system so I will use this file throughout this section. Enter your PDF filename in place of `test.pdf`. Create a script called `read_pdf.py` and write the following content in it:

```
import PyPDF2

with open('test.pdf', 'rb') as pdf:
    read_pdf= PyPDF2.PdfFileReader(pdf)
    print("Number of pages in pdf : ", read_pdf.numPages)
```

Run the script and you will get the following output:

```
student@ubuntu:~/work$ python3 read_pdf.py
```

Following is the output:

```
Number of pages in pdf :   20
```

In the preceding example, we used the `PyPDF2` module. Next, we created a `pdf` file object. `PdfFileReader()` will read the created object. After reading the PDF file, we are going to get the number of pages of that `pdf` file using the `numPages` property. In this case, it is `20` pages.

Extracting text

To extract the pages of the `pdf` file, the `PyPDF2` module has the `extractText()` method. Create a script called `extract_text.py` and write the following content in it:

```
import PyPDF2
with open('test.pdf', 'rb') as pdf:
    read_pdf = PyPDF2.PdfFileReader(pdf)
    pdf_page = read_pdf.getPage(1)
    pdf_content = pdf_page.extractText()
    print(pdf_content)
```

Run the script and you will get the following output:

```
student@ubuntu:~/work$ python3 extract_text.py
```

Following is the output:

```
3Pythoncommands
9
3.1Comments.......................................
.9
3.2Numbersandotherdatatypes.........................
......9
3.2.1The
type
function...............................9
3.2.2Strings.......................................
10
3.2.3Listsandtuples................................
..10
3.2.4The
range
function...............................11
3.2.5Booleanvalues.................................
.11
3.3Expressions.....................................
...11
3.4Operators.......................................
```

In the preceding example, we created a file reader object. The `pdf` reader object has a function called `getPage()`, which gets the page number (it starts from the `0th` index) as an argument and returns the page object. Next, we used the `extractText()` method, which will extract the text from the page number that we mentioned in `getPage()`. The page index starts from `0`.

Rotating PDF pages

In this section, we are going to see how to rotate PDF pages. For that, we will use the `rotate.Clockwise()` method of a `PDF` object. Create a script called `rotate_pdf.py` and write the following content in it:

```
import PyPDF2

with open('test.pdf', 'rb') as pdf:
    rd_pdf = PyPDF2.PdfFileReader(pdf)
    wr_pdf = PyPDF2.PdfFileWriter()
```

```
for pg_num in range(rd_pdf.numPages):
    pdf_page = rd_pdf.getPage(pg_num)
    pdf_page.rotateClockwise(90)
    wr_pdf.addPage(pdf_page)

with open('rotated.pdf', 'wb') as pdf_out:
    wr_pdf.write(pdf_out)

print("pdf successfully rotated")
```

Run the script and you will get the following output:

```
student@ubuntu:~/work$ python3 rotate_pdf.py
```

Following is the output:

```
pdf successfully rotated
```

In the preceding example, for the rotation of pdf, we first create a pdf file reader object of the original pdf file. Then the rotated pages will be written to a new pdf file . So, for writing to a new pdf, we use the PdfFileWriter() function of the PyPDF2 module. The new pdf file will be saved with the name rotated.pdf. Now, we will rotate the pages of the pdf file by using the rotateClockwise() method. Then, using the addPage() method, the pages to the rotated pdf. Now, we have to write those pdf pages to a new pdf file. So, first we have to open the new file object (pdf_out) and write pdf pages to it using the write() method of the pdf writer object. After all this, we're going to close the original (test.pdf) file object and the new (pdf_out) file object.

Working with Excel files

In this section, we are going to work with Excel files, which have the .xlsx extension. This file extension is for an open XML spreadsheet file format, which is used by Microsoft Excel.

Python has different modules: xlrd , pandas, and openpyxl to work with Excel files. In this section, we will learn how to handle Excel files using these three modules.

First, we will look at an example using the xlrd module. The xlrd module is used for reading, writing, and modifying Excel spreadsheets and doing a lot of work.

Using the xlrd module

First, we have to install the xlrd module. Run the following command in your Terminal to install the xlrd module:

```
pip3 install xlrd
```

 Note: Make sure you have an Excel file present in your system. I have sample.xlsx present in my system. So I'm going to use that file throughout this section.

We are going to look at how to read an Excel file and how to extract rows and columns from the Excel file.

Reading an Excel file

In this section, we will look at how to read an Excel file. We are going to use the xlrd module. Create a script called read_excel.py and write the following content in it:

```
import xlrd

excel_file = (r"/home/student/sample.xlsx")
book_obj = xlrd.open_workbook(excel_file)
excel_sheet = book_obj.sheet_by_index(0)
result = excel_sheet.cell_value(0, 1)
print(result)
```

Run the script and you will get the following output:

```
student@ubuntu:~$ python3 read_excel.py
```

Following is the output:

```
First Name
```

In the preceding example, we imported the xlrd module to read the Excel file. We also mentioned the location of the Excel file. Then, we created a file object, then we mentioned the index value, so that the reading will start from that index. Finally, we printed the results.

Extracting the names of columns

In this section, we are extracting column names from the Excel sheet. Create a script called `extract_column_names.py` and write the following content in it:

```
import xlrd

excel_file = ("/home/student/work/sample.xlsx")
book_obj = xlrd.open_workbook(excel_file)
excel_sheet = book_obj.sheet_by_index(0)
excel_sheet.cell_value(0, 0)
for i in range(excel_sheet.ncols):
            print(excel_sheet.cell_value(0, i))
```

Run the script and you will get the following output:

```
student@ubuntu:~/work$ python3 extract_column_names.py
```

Following is the output:

```
Id
First Name
Last Name
Gender
Age
Country
```

In the preceding example, we are extracting the column names from the Excel sheet. We fetched the column names using the `ncols` attribute.

Using pandas

Before proceeding to read Excel files using Pandas, first we have to install the `pandas` module. We can install `pandas` using the following command:

```
pip3 install pandas
```

 Note: Make sure you have an Excel file present in your system. I have `sample.xlsx` present in my system. So I am going to use that file throughout this section.

Now, we will look at some examples using `pandas`.

Reading an Excel file

In this section, we are going to read Excel files using the `pandas` module. Now, let's look at an example of reading an Excel file.

Create a script called `rd_excel_pandas.py` and write the following content in it:

```
import pandas as pd

excel_file = 'sample.xlsx'
df = pd.read_excel(excel_file)
print(df.head())
```

Run the preceding script and you will get the following output:

```
student@ubuntu:~/test$ python3 rd_excel_pandas.py
```

Following is the output:

```
    OrderDate    Region  ...   Unit Cost     Total
0   2014-01-09   Central  ...     125.00     250.00
1     6/17/15    Central  ...     125.00     625.00
2   2015-10-09   Central  ...       1.29       9.03
3    11/17/15    Central  ...       4.99      54.89
4    10/31/15    Central  ...       1.29      18.06
```

In the preceding example, we are reading an Excel file using the `pandas` module. First, we imported the `pandas` module. Then, we created a string called `excel_file` to hold the name of the file to be opened, which we want to manipulate using pandas. Later on, we created a `df data frame` object. In this example, we used the `read_excel` method of pandas to read data from the Excel file with default functions. The reading starts with index zero. Finally, we printed the `pandas` data frame.

Reading specific columns in an Excel file

When we use the pandas module to read an Excel file using the `read_excel` method, we can also read specific columns in that file. For reading specific columns, we need to use the `usecols` parameter in the `read_excel` method.

Now, let's look at an example to read specific columns in an Excel file. Create a script called `rd_excel_pandas1.py` and write the following content in it:

```python
import pandas as pd

excel_file = 'sample.xlsx'
cols = [1, 2, 3]
df = pd.read_excel(excel_file , sheet_names='sheet1', usecols=cols)

print(df.head())
```

Run the preceding script and you will get the following output:

```
student@ubuntu:~/test$ python3 rd_excel_pandas1.py
```

Following is the output:

```
     Region      Rep     Item
0   Central    Smith     Desk
1   Central   Kivell     Desk
2   Central     Gill   Pencil
3   Central  Jardine   Binder
4   Central  Andrews   Pencil
```

In the preceding example, first we imported the pandas module. Then, we created a string called `excel_file` to hold the filename. Then we defined the `cols` variable and put index values of the columns inside it. So, when we used the `read_excel` method, within that method, we also provided the `usecols` parameter to fetch a particular column through the index, which we defined previously in the `cols` variable. Therefore, after running the script, we are getting only specific columns from the Excel file.

We can also perform various operations on Excel files using the pandas module, such as reading an Excel file with missing data, skipping particular rows, and reading multiple Excel sheets.

Using openpyxl

`openpyxl` is a Python library that's used to read and write `xlsx`, `xlsm`, `xltx`, and `xltm` files. First, we have to install `openpyxl`. Run the following command:

```
pip3 install openpyxl
```

Now, we will look at some some examples of using `openpyxl`.

Creating a new Excel file

In this section, we will learn to create a new Excel file using `openpyxl`. Create a script called `create_excel.py` and write the following content in it:

```
from openpyxl import Workbook

book_obj = Workbook()
excel_sheet = book_obj.active
excel_sheet['A1'] = 'Name'
excel_sheet['A2'] = 'student'
excel_sheet['B1'] = 'age'
excel_sheet['B2'] = '24'

book_obj.save("test.xlsx")
print("Excel created successfully")
```

Run the script and you will get the following output:

```
student@ubuntu:~/work$ python3 create_excel.py
```

Following is the output:

```
Excel created successfully
```

Now, check your current working directory and you will find that `test.xlsx` has been created successfully. In the preceding example, we write data into four cells. Then, from the `openpyxl` module, we import the `Workbook` class. A workbook is the container for all other parts of the document. Next, we set the reference object to the active sheet and write values in the cells `A1`, `A2` and `B1`, `B2`. Finally, we've written the contents to the `test.xlsx` file with the `save()` method.

Appending values

In this section, we are going to append values in Excel. For that, we are going to use the `append()` method. We can add a group of values at the bottom of the current sheet in which we want to put the values. Create a script called `append_values.py` and write the following content in it:

```
from openpyxl import Workbook

book_obj = Workbook()
excel_sheet = book_obj.active
rows = (
    (11, 12, 13),
```

```
        (21, 22, 23),
        (31, 32, 33),
        (41, 42, 43)
    )
for values in rows:
    excel_sheet.append(values)
    print()

print("values are successfully appended")
book_obj.save('test.xlsx')wb.save('append_values.xlsx')
```

Run the script and you will get the following output:

```
student@ubuntu:~/work$ python3 append_values.py
```

Following is the output:

```
values are successfully appended
```

In the preceding example, we appended three columns of data in the
append_values.xlsx files sheet. The data we stored was in a tuple of tuples and to
append that data we went through the container row by row and inserted it using
the append() method.

Reading multiple cells

In this section, we are going to read multiple cells. We will use the openpyxl module.
Create a script called read_multiple.py and write the following content in it:

```
import openpyxl

book_obj = openpyxl.load_workbook('sample.xlsx')
excel_sheet = book_obj.active
cells = excel_sheet['A1': 'C6']
for c1, c2, c3 in cells:
            print("{0:6} {1:6} {2:6}".format(c1.value, c2.value, c3.value))
```

Run the script and you will get the following output:

```
student@ubuntu:~/work$ python3 read_multiple.py
```

Following is the output:

```
Id      First Name Last Name
   101 John    Smith
   102 Mary    Williams
   103 Rakesh Sharma
   104 Amit    Roy
   105 Sandra Ace
```

In the preceding example, we are reading the data of three columns by using the `range` operation. Then, we read the data from the cells `A1` - `C6`.

Similarly, we can perform lots of operations, such as merging and, splitting cells, on the Excel file using the `openpyxl` module.

Working with CSV files

The **CSV** format stands for **Comma Separated Values**. The commas are used to separate the fields in a record. These are commonly used for importing and exporting the format for spreadsheets and databases.

A CSV file is a plain text file that uses a specific type of structuring to arrange tabular data. Python has the built-in `csv` module that allows Python to parse these types of files. The `csv` module can be mostly used to work with data that is exported from spreadsheets, as well as databases in text file format, with fields and records.

The `csv` module has all of the required functions built-in, as follows:

- `csv.reader`: This function is used to return a `reader` object, which iterates over lines of a CSV file
- `csv.writer`: This function is used to return a `writer` object, which writes data into CSV file
- `csv.register_dialect`: This function is used to register a CSV dialect
- `csv.unregister_dialect`: This function is used to unregister a CSV dialect
- `csv.get_dialect`: This function is used to returns a dialect with a given name
- `csv.list_dialects`: This function is used to return all registered dialects
- `csv.field_size_limit`: This function is used to return the current maximum field size allowed by the parser

In this section, we are going to look at `csv.reader` and `csv.writer` only.

Reading a CSV file

Python has an in-built module, `csv`, which we are going to use here to work with CSV files. We will use the `csv.reader` module to read a CSV file. Create a script called `csv_read.py` and write the following content in it:

```python
import csv

csv_file = open('test.csv', 'r')
with csv_file:
    read_csv = csv.reader(csv_file)
    for row in read_csv:
        print(row)
```

Run the script and you will get the following output:

```
student@ubuntu:~$ python3 csv_read.py
```

Following is the output:

```
['Region', 'Country', 'Item Type', 'Sales Channel', 'Order Priority',
'Order Date', 'Order ID', 'Ship Date', 'Units Sold']
['Sub-Saharan Africa', 'Senegal', 'Cereal', 'Online', 'H', '4/18/2014',
'616607081', '5/30/2014', '6593']
['Asia', 'Kyrgyzstan', 'Vegetables', 'Online', 'H', '6/24/2011',
'814711606', '7/12/2011', '124']
['Sub-Saharan Africa', 'Cape Verde', 'Clothes', 'Offline', 'H', '8/2/2014',
'939825713', '8/19/2014', '4168']
['Asia', 'Bangladesh', 'Clothes', 'Online', 'L', '1/13/2017', '187310731',
'3/1/2017', '8263']
['Central America and the Caribbean', 'Honduras', 'Household', 'Offline',
'H', '2/8/2017', '522840487', '2/13/2017', '8974']
['Asia', 'Mongolia', 'Personal Care', 'Offline', 'C', '2/19/2014',
'832401311', '2/23/2014', '4901']
['Europe', 'Bulgaria', 'Clothes', 'Online', 'M', '4/23/2012', '972292029',
'6/3/2012', '1673']
['Asia', 'Sri Lanka', 'Cosmetics', 'Offline', 'M', '11/19/2016',
'419123971', '12/18/2016', '6952']
['Sub-Saharan Africa', 'Cameroon', 'Beverages', 'Offline', 'C', '4/1/2015',
'519820964', '4/18/2015', '5430']
['Asia', 'Turkmenistan', 'Household', 'Offline', 'L', '12/30/2010',
'441619336', '1/20/2011', '3830']
```

In the preceding program, we opened our `test.csv` file as `csv_file`. Then, we used the `csv.reader()` function to extract the data into the `reader` object, which we can iterate over to get each line of our data. Now, we are going to look at the second function, `csv.Writer()`

Writing into a CSV file

To write data in a `csv` file, we use the `csv.writer` module. In this section, we will store some data into the Python list and then put that data into the `csv` file. Create a script called `csv_write.py` and write the following content in it:

```
import csv

write_csv = [['Name', 'Sport'], ['Andres Iniesta', 'Football'], ['AB de
Villiers', 'Cricket'], ['Virat Kohli', 'Cricket'], ['Lionel Messi',
'Football']]

with open('csv_write.csv', 'w') as csvFile:
    writer = csv.writer(csvFile)
    writer.writerows(write_csv)
    print(write_csv)
```

Run the script and you will get the following output:

```
student@ubuntu:~$ python3 csv_write.py
```

Following is the output:

```
[['Name', 'Sport'], ['Andres Iniesta', 'Football'], ['AB de Villiers',
'Cricket'], ['Virat Kohli', 'Cricket'], ['Lionel Messi', 'Football']]
```

In the preceding program, we created a list named `write_csv` with a `Name` and its `Sport`. Then, after creating the list, we opened the newly created `csv_write.csv` file and inserted the `write_csv` list into it using the `csvWriter()` function.

Working with txt files

A plain text file is used to store data that represents only characters or strings and doesn't consider any structured metadata. In Python, there's no need to import any external library to read and write text files. Python provides an built-in function to create, open, close, and write and read text files. To do the operations, there are different access modes to govern the type of operation possible in an opened file.

The access modes in Python are as follows:

- **Read Only Mode ('r')**: This mode opens a text file for the purpose. If that file doesn't exist, it raises an I/O error. We can also call this mode the default mode in which the file will open.
- **Read and Write Mode ('r+')**: This mode opens a text file for reading as well as writing purposes and raises an I/O error if the file does not exist.
- **Write Only Mode ('w')**: This mode will open a text file for writing. It creates the file if the file does not exist and, for existing file, the data is overwritten.
- **Write and Read Mode ('w+')**: This mode will open a text file for reading and writing. For the existing file, the data is overwritten.
- **Append Only Mode ('a')**: This mode will open a text file for writing. It creates the file if the file does not exist and the data will be inserted at the end of existing data.
- **Append and Read Mode ('a+')**: This mode will open a text file for reading, as well as writing . It creates the file if the file does not exist and the data will be inserted at the end of the existing data.

The open() function

This function is used to open a file and does not require any external module to be imported.

The syntax is as follows:

```
Name_of_file_object = open("Name of file","Access_Mode")
```

For the preceding syntax, the file must be in the same directory that our Python program resides in. If the file is not in the same directory, then we also have to define the file path while opening the file. The syntax for such a condition is shown here:

```
Name_of_file_object = open("/home/....../Name of file","Access_Mode")
```

File opening

The open function to open the file is "test.txt" .

The file is in the same directory as the append mode:

```
text_file = open("test.txt","a")
```

If the file is not in the same directory, we have to define the path in the `append` mode:

```
text_file = open("/home/...../test.txt","a")
```

The close() function

This function is used to close the file, which frees the memory acquired by the file. This function is used when the file is not needed anymore or it is going to be opened in a different file mode.

The syntax is as follows:

```
Name_of_file_object.close()
```

The following code syntax can be use to simply open and close a file:

```
#Opening and closing a file test.txt:
text_file = open("test.txt","a")
text_file.close()
```

Writing a text file

By using Python, you can create a text file (`test.txt`). By using the code, writing to a text file is easy. To open a file for writing, we set the second parameter that is in access mode to `"w"`. To write the data into this `test.txt` file, we use the `write()` method of the `file handle` object. Create a script called `text_write.py` and write the following content in it:

```
text_file = open("test.txt", "w")
text_file.write("Monday\nTuesday\nWednesday\nThursday\nFriday\nSaturday\n")
text_file.close()
```

Run the preceding script and you will get the output as follows:

```
Desktop     Downloads          Music     Public        Templates  testing   Videos
Documents   examples.desktop   Pictures  __pycache__   test       test.txt  work
```

Now, check your current working directory. You'll find a `test.txt` file that we created. Now, check the contents of the file. You will find that the days that we have written in the `write()` function will be saved in `test.txt`.

In the preceding program, we've declared the `text_file` variable to open a file named `test.txt`. The `open` function takes two arguments: first, the file that we want to open, and second, the access mode that represents the permission or operation that we want to do or apply on the file. In our program, we used the `"w"` letter in our second argument, which indicates `write`. Then, we used `text_file.close()` to close the instance of the stored `test.txt` file.

Reading a text file

Reading a file is as easy as writing from a file. To open a file for reading, we set the second parameter that is the access mode to `"r"` instead of `"w"`. To read the data from this file, we use the `read()` method of the `file handle` object. Create a script called `text_read.py` and write the following content in it:

```
text_file = open("test.txt", "r")
data = text_file.read()
print(data)
text_file.close()
```

Following is the output:

```
student@ubuntu:~$ python3 text_read.py
Monday
Tuesday
Wednesday
Thursday
Friday
Saturday
```

In the preceding program, we've declared the `text_file` variable to open a file named `test.txt`. The `open` function takes two arguments: first, the file that we want to open, and second, the access mode that represents the permission or operation we want to do or apply on the file. In our program, we used the `"r"` letter in our second argument, which indicates a `read` operation. Then, we used `text_file.close()` to close the instance of the stored `test.txt` file. After running the Python program, we can easily see the content in our text file in our Terminal.

Summary

In this chapter, we learned about various files. We learned about PDF, Excel, CSV, and text files. We used Python modules to perform some operations on these types of files.

In the next chapter, we are going to learn about basic networking and internet modules in Python.

Questions

1. What is the difference between `readline()` and `readlines()` ?
2. What is the difference between `open()` and `with open()`?
3. What is the significance of `r c:\\Downloads` at starting?
4. What is the generators object?
5. What is the use of `pass`?
6. What is a lambda expression?

Further reading

- XLRD: `https://xlrd.readthedocs.io/en/latest/api.html`
- `openoyxl`: `http://www.python-excel.org/`
- Regarding generator concepts: `https://wiki.python.org/moin/Generators`

10
Basic Networking - Socket Programming

In this chapter, you will learn about sockets and three internet protocols: `http`, `ftplib`, and `urllib`. You will also learn about the `socket` module in Python, which is used for networking. `http` is a package that is used for working with the **Hypertext Transfer Protocol** (**HTTP**). The `ftplib` module is used for performing automated FTP-related work. `urllib` is a package that handles URL-related work.

In this chapter, you will learn about the following:

- Sockets
- The `http` package
- The `ftplib` module
- The `urllib` package

Sockets

In this section, we are going to learn about sockets. We are going to use Python's socket module. Sockets are endpoints for communication between machines, whether locally or across the internet. The socket module has a socket class, which is used to handle the data channel. It also has functions for network-related tasks. To use the functionality of the socket module, we first need to import the socket module.

Let's see how to create a socket. The socket class has a socket function, with two arguments: `address_family` and `socket type`.

The following is the syntax:

```
import socket
s = socket.socket(address_family, socket type)
```

`address_family` controls the OSI network layer protocol.

`socket type` controls the transport layer protocol.

Python supports three address families: `AF_INET`, `AF_INET6`, and `AF_UNIX`. The most commonly used is `AF_INET`, which is used for internet addressing. `AF_INET6` is used for IPv6 internet addressing. `AF_UNIX` is used for **Unix Domain Sockets** (**UDS**), which is an inter-process communication protocol.

There are two socket types: `SOCK_DGRAM` and `SOCK_STREAM`. The `SOCK_DGRAM` socket type is used for message-oriented datagram transport; these are associated with the UDP. Datagram sockets deliver individual messages. `SOCK_STREAM` is used for stream-oriented transport; these are associated with TCP. Stream sockets provide byte streams between the client and server.

Sockets can be configured as server and client sockets. When both TCP/IP sockets are connected, communication will be bi-directional. Now we are going explore an example of client-server communication. We will create two scripts: `server.py` and `client.py`.

The `server.py` script is as follows:

```python
import socket

host_name = socket.gethostname()
port = 5000
s_socket = socket.socket()
s_socket.bind((host_name, port))
s_socket.listen(2)

conn, address = s_socket.accept()
print("Connection from: " + str(address))

while True:
        recv_data = conn.recv(1024).decode()
        if not recv_data:
                break
        print("from connected user: " + str(recv_data))
        recv_data = input(' -> ')
        conn.send(recv_data.encode())

conn.close()
```

Now we will write a script for the client.

The `client.py` script is as follows:

```python
import socket

host_name = socket.gethostname()
port = 5000

c_socket = socket.socket()
c_socket.connect((host_name, port))
msg = input(" -> ")

while msg.lower().strip() != 'bye':
        c_socket.send(msg.encode())
        recv_data = c_socket.recv(1024).decode()
        print('Received from server: ' + recv_data)
        msg = input(" -> ")

c_socket.close()
```

Now we will run these two programs in two different Terminals. In the first Terminal, we'll run `server.py`, and in the second terminal, run `client.py`.

The output will be as follows:

Terminal 1: `python3 server.py`	**Terminal 2:** `python3 client.py`

`student@ubuntu:~/work$ python3 server.py`
`Connection from: ('127.0.0.1', 35120)`
`from connected user: Hello from client`
`-> Hello from server !`
	`student@ubuntu:~/work$ python3 client.py`
	`-> Hello from client`
	`Received from server: Hello from server !`
	`->`

The http package

In this section, we are going to learn about the `http` package. The `http` package has four modules:

- `http.client`: This is a low-level HTTP protocol client
- `http.server`: This contains basic HTTP server classes
- `http.cookies`: This is used for implementing state management with cookies
- `http.cookiejar`: This module provides cookie persistence

In this section, we are going to learn about the `http.client` and `http.server` modules.

The http.client module

We are going to see two `http` requests: `GET` and `POST`. We are also going to make an `http` connection.

First, we are going explore an example of making an `http` connection. For that, create a `make_connection.py` script and write the following content in it:

```
import http.client

con_obj = http.client.HTTPConnection('Enter_URL_name', 80, timeout=20)
print(con_obj)
```

Run the script and you will get the output as follows:

```
student@ubuntu:~/work$ python3 make_connection.py
<http.client.HTTPConnection object at 0x7f2c365dd898>
```

In the preceding example, we made a connection with the URL mentioned on port 80 for a specific timeout.

Now we will see the `http` `GET` request method; using this `GET` request method, we will see an example where we get a response code as well as a header list. Create a `get_example.py` script and write the following content in it:

```
import http.client

con_obj = http.client.HTTPSConnection("www.imdb.com")
con_obj.request("GET", "/")
response = con_obj.getresponse()

print("Status: {}".format(response.status))

headers_list = response.getheaders()
print("Headers: {}".format(headers_list))

con_obj.close()
```

Run the script as follows:

```
student@ubuntu:~/work$ python3 get_example.py
```

The output should be as follows:

```
Status: 200
Headers: [('Server', 'Server'), ('Date', 'Fri, 23 Nov 2018 09:49:12 GMT'),
('Content-Type', 'text/html;charset=UTF-8'), ('Transfer-Encoding',
'chunked'), ('Connection', 'keep-alive'), ('X-Frame-Options',
'SAMEORIGIN'), ('Content-Security-Policy', "frame-ancestors 'self' imdb.com
*.imdb.com *.media-imdb.com withoutabox.com *.withoutabox.com amazon.com
*.amazon.com amazon.co.uk *.amazon.co.uk amazon.de *.amazon.de
translate.google.com images.google.com www.google.com www.google.co.uk
search.aol.com bing.com www.bing.com"), ('Ad-Unit', 'imdb.home.homepage'),
('Entity-Id', ''), ('Section-Id', 'homepage'), ('Page-Id', 'homepage'),
('Content-Language', 'en-US'), ('Set-Cookie',
'uu=BCYsgIz6VTPefAjQB9YlJiZhwogwHmoU3sLx9YK-
A61kPgvXEKwHSJKU3XeaxIoL8DBQGhYLuFvR%0D%0AqPV6VVvx70AV6eL_sGzVaRQQAKf-
PUz2y0sTx9H4Yvib9iSYRPOzR5qHQkwuoHPKmpu2KsSbPaCb%0D%0AYbc-
R6nz9ObkbQf6RAYm5sTAdf5lSqM2ZzCEhfIt_H3tWQqnK5WlihYwfMZS2AJdtGXGRnRvEHlv%0D
%0AyA4Dcn9NyeX44-hAnS64zkDfDeGXoCUic_kH6ZnD5vv21HOiVodVKA%0D%0A;
Domain=.imdb.com; Expires=Wed, 11-Dec-2086 13:03:18 GMT; Path=/; Secure'),
('Set-Cookie', 'session-id=134-6809939-6044806; Domain=.imdb.com;
Expires=Wed, 11-Dec-2086 13:03:18 GMT; Path=/; Secure'), ('Set-Cookie',
'session-id-time=2173686551; Domain=.imdb.com; Expires=Wed, 11-Dec-2086
13:03:18 GMT; Path=/; Secure'), ('Vary', 'Accept-Encoding,X-Amzn-CDN-
Cache,User-Agent'), ('x-amz-rid', '7SWEYTYH4TX8YR2CF5JT')]
```

In the preceding example, we used HTTPSConnection, as the website is served over the HTTPS protocol. You can use HTTPSConnection or HTTPConnection, depending on the website you use. We provided a URL and checked the status with the connection object. After that, we got a header list. This header list contains information regarding the type of data sent back from the server. The getheaders() method will get list of headers.

Now we will see an example of a POST request. We can post data to the URL using HTTP POST. For that, create a post_example.py script and write following content in it:

```python
import http.client
import json

con_obj = http.client.HTTPSConnection('www.httpbin.org')
headers_list = {'Content-type': 'application/json'}
post_text = {'text': 'Hello World !!'}
json_data = json.dumps(post_text)
con_obj.request('POST', '/post', json_data, headers_list)
response = con_obj.getresponse()
print(response.read().decode())
```

Run the script as follows:

```
student@ubuntu:~/work$ python3 post_example.py
```

You should get the following output:

```
{
  "args": {},
  "data": "{\"text\": \"Hello World !!\"}",
  "files": {},
  "form": {},
  "headers": {
    "Accept-Encoding": "identity",
    "Connection": "close",
    "Content-Length": "26",
    "Content-Type": "application/json",
    "Host": "www.httpbin.org"
  },
  "json": {
    "text": "Hello World !!"
  },
  "origin": "1.186.106.115",
  "url": "https://www.httpbin.org/post"
}
```

In the preceding example, we first created an HTTPSConnection object. Next, we created a post_text object, which posts Hello World. After that, we wrote a POST request, to which we received a response.

The http.server module

In this section, we are going to learn about a module from the http package, the http.server module. This module defines the classes used for implementing HTTP servers. It has two methods: GET and HEAD. By using this module, we can share files over a network. You can run the http server on any port. Make sure the port number is greater than 1024. The default port number is 8000.

You can use http.server as follows.

First, navigate to your desired directory and run the following command:

```
student@ubuntu:~/Desktop$ python3 -m http.server 9000
```

Now open your browser and write `localhost:9000` in your address bar and press *Enter*. You will get the output following:

```
student@ubuntu:~/Desktop$ python3 -m http.server 9000
Serving HTTP on 0.0.0.0 port 9000 (http://0.0.0.0:9000/) ...
127.0.0.1 - - [23/Nov/2018 16:08:14] code 404, message File not found
127.0.0.1 - - [23/Nov/2018 16:08:14] "GET /Downloads/ HTTP/1.1" 404 -
127.0.0.1 - - [23/Nov/2018 16:08:14] code 404, message File not found
127.0.0.1 - - [23/Nov/2018 16:08:14] "GET /favicon.ico HTTP/1.1" 404 -
127.0.0.1 - - [23/Nov/2018 16:08:21] "GET / HTTP/1.1" 200 -
127.0.0.1 - - [23/Nov/2018 16:08:21] code 404, message File not found
127.0.0.1 - - [23/Nov/2018 16:08:21] "GET /favicon.ico HTTP/1.1" 404 -
127.0.0.1 - - [23/Nov/2018 16:08:26] "GET /hello/ HTTP/1.1" 200 -
127.0.0.1 - - [23/Nov/2018 16:08:26] code 404, message File not found
127.0.0.1 - - [23/Nov/2018 16:08:26] "GET /favicon.ico HTTP/1.1" 404 -
127.0.0.1 - - [23/Nov/2018 16:08:27] code 404, message File not found
127.0.0.1 - - [23/Nov/2018 16:08:27] "GET /favicon.ico HTTP/1.1" 404 -
```

The ftplib module

`ftplib` is a module in Python that provides all the functionality needed to perform various actions over the FTP protocol. `ftplib` contains the FTP client class, as well as some helper functions. Using this module, we can easily connect to an FTP server to retrieve multiple files and process them. By importing the `ftplib` module, we can use all the functionality it provides.

In this section, we are going to cover how to do FTP transfers by using the `ftplib` module. We are going see various FTP objects.

Downloading files

In this section, we are going to learn about downloading files from another machine using `ftplib`. For that, create a `get_ftp_files.py` script and write the following content in it:

```python
import os
from ftplib import FTP

ftp = FTP('your-ftp-domain-or-ip')
with ftp:
    ftp.login('your-username','your-password')
    ftp.cwd('/home/student/work/')
    files = ftp.nlst()
    print(files)
```

```
        # Print the files
        for file in files:
            if os.path.isfile(file):
                print("Downloading..." + file)
                ftp.retrbinary("RETR " + file ,open("/home/student/testing/" +
file, 'wb').write)

    ftp.close()
```

Run the script as follows:

```
student@ubuntu:~/work$ python3 get_ftp_files.py
```

You should get the following output:

```
Downloading...hello
Downloading...hello.c
Downloading...sample.txt
Downloading...strip_hello
Downloading...test.py
```

In the preceding example, we retrieved multiple files from the host by using the `ftplib` module. First, we mentioned the IP address, username, and password of the other machine. To get all the files from the host, we used the `ftp.nlst()` function, and to download those files to our computer, we used the `ftp.retrbinary()` function.

Getting a welcome message using getwelcome():

Once an initial connection is established, a server usually returns a welcome message. This message comes via the `getwelcome()` function, and sometimes includes disclaimers or helpful information that may be relevant to the user.

Now we will see an example of `getwelcome()`. Create a `get_welcome_msg.py` script and write the following content in it:

```
from ftplib import FTP

ftp = FTP('your-ftp-domain-or-ip')
ftp.login('your-username','your-password')

welcome_msg = ftp.getwelcome()
print(welcome_msg)

ftp.close()
```

Run the script as follows:

```
student@ubuntu:~/work$ python3 get_welcome_msg.py
220 (vsFTPd 3.0.3)
```

In the preceding code, we first mentioned the IP address, username, and password of the other machine. We used the `getwelcome()` function to get information after the initial connection was established.

Sending commands to the server using the sendcmd() function

In this section, we are going to learn about the `sendcmd()` function. We can use the `sendcmd()` function to send a simple `string` command to the server to get the String response. The client can send FTP commands such as `STAT`, `PWD`, `RETR`, and `STOR`. The `ftplib` module has multiple methods that can wrap these commands. The commands can be sent using the `sendcmd()` or `voidcmd()` methods. As an example, we are going to send a `STAT` command to check the status of a server.

Create a `send_command.py` script and write the following content in it:

```
from ftplib import FTP

ftp = FTP('your-ftp-domain-or-ip')
ftp.login('your-username','your-password')

ftp.cwd('/home/student/')
s_cmd_stat = ftp.sendcmd('STAT')
print(s_cmd_stat)
print()

s_cmd_pwd = ftp.sendcmd('PWD')
print(s_cmd_pwd)
print()

ftp.close()
```

Run the script as follows:

```
student@ubuntu:~/work$ python3 send_command.py
```

You will get the following output:

```
211-FTP server status:
    Connected to ::ffff:192.168.2.109
    Logged in as student
  TYPE: ASCII
    No session bandwidth limit
    Session timeout in seconds is 300
    Control connection is plain text
    Data connections will be plain text
    At session startup, client count was 1
    vsFTPd 3.0.3 - secure, fast, stable
211 End of status

257 "/home/student" is the current directory
```

In the preceding code, we first mentioned the IP address, username, and password of the other machine. Next, we used the `sendcmd()` method for the `STAT` command to the other machine. Then, we used `sendcmd()` for the `PWD` command.

The urllib package

Like `http`, `urllib` is also a package that has various modules for working with URLs. The `urllib` module allows you to access several websites via your script. We can also download data, parse data, modify headers, and more using this module.

`urllib` has a few different modules, which are listed here:

- `urllib.request`: This is used for opening and reading URLs.
- `urllib.error`: This contains exceptions raised by `urllib.request`.
- `urllib.parse`: This is used for parsing URLs.
- `urllib.robotparser`: This is used for parsing `robots.txt` files.

In this section, we are going to learn about opening a URL using `urllib` and how to read `html` files from the URL. We are going to see a simple example of the use of `urllib`. We will import `urllib.requests`. Then we assign the opening of the URL to a variable, then we will use a `.read()` command to read the data from the URL.

Create a `url_requests_example.py` script and write the following content in it:

```
import urllib.request

x = urllib.request.urlopen('https://www.imdb.com/')
print(x.read())
```

Run the script as follows:

```
student@ubuntu:~/work$ python3 url_requests_example.py
```

Here is the output:

```
b'\n\n<!DOCTYPE html>\n<html\n      xmlns:og="http://ogp.me/ns#"\n
xmlns:fb="http://www.facebook.com/2008/fbml">\n      <head>\n              \n
<meta charset="utf-8">\n           <meta http-equiv="X-UA-Compatible"
content="IE=edge">\n\n      \n     \n    \n\n     \n     \n    \n\n     <meta
name="apple-itunes-app" content="app-id=342792525, app-
argument=imdb:///?src=mdot">\n\n\n\n            <script
type="text/javascript">var IMDbTimer={starttime: new
Date().getTime(),pt:\'java\'};</script>\n\n<script>\n     if (typeof uet ==
\'function\') {\n      uet("bb", "LoadTitle", {wb: 1});\n      }\n</script>\n
<script>(function(t){ (t.events = t.events || {})["csm_head_pre_title"] =
new Date().getTime(); })(IMDbTimer);</script>\n            <title>IMDb -
Movies, TV and Celebrities - IMDb</title>\n  <script>(function(t){
(t.events = t.events || {})["csm_head_post_title"] = new Date().getTime();
})(IMDbTimer);</script>\n<script>\n     if (typeof uet == \'function\') {\n
uet("be", "LoadTitle", {wb: 1});\n      }\n</script>\n<script>\n      if
(typeof uex == \'function\') {\n       uex("ld", "LoadTitle", {wb: 1});\n
}\n</script>\n\n           <link rel="canonical" href="https://www.imdb.com/"
/>\n          <meta property="og:url" content="http://www.imdb.com/" />\n
<link rel="alternate" media="only screen and (max-width: 640px)"
href="https://m.imdb.com/">\n\n<script>\n      if (typeof uet ==
\'function\') {\n       uet("bb", "LoadIcons", {wb: 1});\n      }\n</script>\n
<script>(function(t){ (t.events = t.events || {})["csm_head_pre_icon"] =
new Date().getTime(); })(IMDbTimer);</script>\n            <link
href="https://m.media-amazon.com/images/G/01/imdb/images/safari-favicon-517
611381._CB483525257_.svg" mask rel="icon" sizes="any">\n           <link
rel="icon" type="image/ico"
href="https://m.media-amazon.com/images/G/01/imdb/images/favicon-2165806970
._CB470047330_.ico" />\n          <meta name="theme-color" content="#000000"
/>\n         <link rel="shortcut icon" type="image/x-icon"
href="https://m.media-amazon.com/images/G/01/imdb/images/desktop-favicon-21
65806970._CB484110913_.ico" />\n          <link
href="https://m.media-amazon.com/images/G/01/imdb/images/mobile/apple-touch
-icon-web-4151659188._CB483525313_.png" rel="apple-touch-icon"> \n
```

In the preceding example, we used the `read()` method, which returns the byte array. This prints the HTML data returned by the `Imdb` home page in a non-human-readable format, but we can use the HTML parser to extract some useful information from it.

Python urllib response headers

We can get response headers by calling the `info()` function on the response object. This returns a dictionary, so we can also extract specific header data from the response. Create a `url_response_header.py` script and write the following content in it:

```
import urllib.request

x = urllib.request.urlopen('https://www.imdb.com/')
print(x.info())
```

Run the script as follows:

```
student@ubuntu:~/work$ python3 url_response_header.py
```

Here is the output:

```
Server: Server
Date: Fri, 23 Nov 2018 11:22:48 GMT
Content-Type: text/html;charset=UTF-8
Transfer-Encoding: chunked
Connection: close
X-Frame-Options: SAMEORIGIN
Content-Security-Policy: frame-ancestors 'self' imdb.com *.imdb.com
*.media-imdb.com withoutabox.com *.withoutabox.com amazon.com *.amazon.com
amazon.co.uk *.amazon.co.uk amazon.de *.amazon.de translate.google.com
images.google.com www.google.com www.google.co.uk search.aol.com bing.com
www.bing.com
Content-Language: en-US
Set-Cookie: uu=BCYsJu-IKhmmXuZWHgogzgofKfB8CXXLkNXdfKrrvsCP-
RkcSn29epJviE8uRML4X14E7Iw9V09w%0D%0Anl3qKv1bEVJ-
hHWVeDFH6BF8j_MMf8pdVA2NWzguWQ2XbKvDXFa_rK1ymzWc-Q35RCk_Z6jTj-
Mk%0D%0AlEMrKkFyxbDYxLMe4hSjUo7NGrmV61LY3Aohaq7zE-
ZE8a6DhgdlcLfXsILNXTkv7L3hvbxmr4An%0D%0Af73atPNPOgyLTB2S615MnlZ3QpOeNH6E2fE
1DYXZnsIFEAb9FW2XfQ%0D%0A; Domain=.imdb.com; Expires=Wed, 11-Dec-2086
14:36:55 GMT; Path=/; Secure
Set-Cookie: session-id=000-0000000-0000000; Domain=.imdb.com; Expires=Wed,
11-Dec-2086 14:36:55 GMT; Path=/; Secure
Set-Cookie: session-id-time=2173692168; Domain=.imdb.com; Expires=Wed, 11-
Dec-2086 14:36:55 GMT; Path=/; Secure
Vary: Accept-Encoding,X-Amzn-CDN-Cache,User-Agent
x-amz-rid: GJDGQQTNA4MH7S3KJJKV
```

Summary

In this chapter, we learned about sockets, which are used for bi-directional client-server communication. We learned about three internet modules: `http`, `ftplib`, and `urllib`. The `http` package has modules for the client and server: `http.client` and `http.server` respectively. Using `ftplib`, we downloaded files from another machine. We also looked at welcome messages and sending `send` commands.

In the next chapter, we'll be covering building and sending emails. We will learn about message formats and adding multimedia content. Also, we are going to learn about SMTP, POP, and IMAP servers.

Questions

1. What is socket programming?
2. What is RPC?
3. What are the different ways to import to user-defined modules or files?
4. What is the difference between a list and a tuple ?
5. Can we have duplicate keys in a dictionary?
6. What are the differences between the `urllib`, `urllib2`, and `requests` modules?

Further reading

- `ftplib` documentation: `https://docs.python.org/3/library/ftplib.html`
- `xmlrpc` documentation: `https://docs.python.org/3/library/xmlrpc.html`

Handling Emails Using Python Scripting

11

In this chapter, you'll learn about how to use Python scripts to handle emails. You'll learn about the email message format. We're going to explore the `smtplib` module for sending and receiving emails. We're going to use the Python email package to send emails with attachments and HTML contents. You'll also learn about the different protocols used to handle emails.

In this chapter, you'll learn about the following:

- Email message format
- Adding HTML and multimedia content
- POP3 and IMAP servers

Email message format

In this section, we're going to learn about the email message format. Email messages consist of three primary components:

- The receiver's email address
- The sender's email address
- The message

There are other components also included in the message format, such as the subject line, email signatures, and attachments.

Now, we're going to see a simple example of sending a plain text email from your Gmail address, in which you'll learn about writing an email message and sending it. Now, create a script, `write_email_message.py`, and write the following content in it:

```
import smtplib
import getpass

host_name = "smtp.gmail.com"
port = 465

sender = 'sender_emil_id'
receiver = 'receiver_email_id'
password = getpass.getpass()

msg = """\
Subject: Test Mail
Hello from Sender !!"""

s = smtplib.SMTP_SSL(host_name, port)
s.login(sender, password)
s.sendmail(sender, receiver, msg)
s.quit()

print("Mail sent successfully")
```

Run the script and you'll get the following output:

```
student@ubuntu:~/work/Chapter_11$ python3 write_email_message.py
Output:
Password:
Mail sent successfully
```

In the preceding example, we used the `smtplib` Python module to send an email. Make sure you're sending an email from a Gmail ID to the receiver. The `sender` variable saves the sender's email address. In the `password` variable, you can either enter your password or you can prompt for a password using the `getpass` module. Here, we prompt for the password. Next, we created a variable named `msg`, which will be our actual email message. In that, we first mentioned a subject and then the message we want to send. Then, in `login()`, we mentioned the `sender` and `password` variables. Next, in `sendmail()`, we mentioned the `sender`, `receivers`, and `text` variables. So, using this process, we sent the email successfully.

Adding HTML and multimedia content

In this section, we're going to see how we can send multimedia content as an attachment and how we can add HTML content. To do this, we'll use the Python `email` package.

First, we'll see how we can add HTML content. For that, create a script, add_html_content.py, and write the following content in it:

```python
import os
import smtplib
from email.mime.text import MIMEText
from email.mime.multipart import MIMEMultipart
import getpass

host_name = 'smtp.gmail.com'
port = 465

sender = 'sender_emailid'
password = getpass.getpass()
receiver = 'receiver_emailid'

text = MIMEMultipart()
text['Subject'] = 'Test HTML Content'
text['From'] = sender
text['To'] = receiver

msg = """\
<html>
  <body>
    <p>Hello there, <br>
       Good day !!<br>
       <a href="http://www.imdb.com">Home</a>
    </p>
  </body>
</html>
"""

html_content = MIMEText(msg, "html")
text.attach(html_content)
s = smtplib.SMTP_SSL(host_name, port)
print("Mail sent successfully !!")

s.login(sender, password)
s.sendmail(sender, receiver, text.as_string())
s.quit()
```

Run the script and you'll get the following output:

```
student@ubuntu:~/work/Chapter_11$ python3 add_html_content.py
Output:
Password:
Mail sent successfully !!
```

In the preceding example, we used the email package to send HTML content as a message through a Python script. We created a `msg` variable in which we stored HTML content.

Now, we'll see how we can add an attachment and send it through a Python script. For that, create a script, `add_attachment.py`, and write the following content in it:

```
import os
import smtplib
from email.mime.text import MIMEText
from email.mime.image import MIMEImage
from email.mime.multipart import MIMEMultipart
import getpass

host_name = 'smtp.gmail.com'
port = 465

sender = 'sender_emailid'
password = getpass.getpass()
receiver = 'receiver_emailid'

text = MIMEMultipart()
text['Subject'] = 'Test Attachment'
text['From'] = sender
text['To'] = receiver

txt = MIMEText('Sending a sample image.')
text.attach(txt)
f_path = 'path_of_file'
with open(f_path, 'rb') as f:
    img = MIMEImage(f.read())
img.add_header('Content-Disposition',
               'attachment',
               filename=os.path.basename(f_path))

text.attach(img)
s = smtplib.SMTP_SSL(host_name, port)
print("Attachment sent successfully !!")
s.login(sender, password)
s.sendmail(sender, receiver, text.as_string())
s.quit()
```

Run the script and you'll get the output as follows:

```
student@ubuntu:~/work/Chapter_11$ python3 add_attachment.py
Output:
Password:
Attachment sent successfully !!
```

In the preceding example, we sent an image as an attachment to the receiver. We mentioned the sender's and receiver's email IDs. Next, in `f_path`, we mentioned the path of the image that we're sending as an attachment. Next, we send that image as an attachment to the receiver.

POP3 and IMAP servers

In this section, you'll learn about receiving emails via POP and IMAP servers. Python offers the `poplib` and `imaplib` libraries for receiving emails via Python scripts.

Receiving email using the poplib library

POP3 stands for **Post Office Protocol version 3**. This standard protocol helps you receive emails from a remote server to our local machine. The main advantage of POP3 is that it allows us to download emails on to our local machine and read the downloaded emails offline.

The POP3 protocol works on two ports:

- Port `110`: The default non-encrypted port
- Port `995`: The encrypted port

Now, we'll see some examples. First, we'll see an example where we get a number of emails. For that, create a script, `number_of_emails.py`, and write the following content in it:

```
import poplib
import getpass

pop3_server = 'pop.gmail.com'
username = 'Emaild_address'
password = getpass.getpass()

email_obj = poplib.POP3_SSL(pop3_server)
print(email_obj.getwelcome())
```

```
email_obj.user(username)
email_obj.pass_(password)
email_stat = email_obj.stat()
print("New arrived e-Mails are : %s (%s bytes)" % email_stat)
```

Run the script, as follows:

```
student@ubuntu:~$ python3 number_of_emails.py
```

As output, you'll get however many emails are present in your mailbox.

In the preceding example, first we're importing the poplib library, which is used in Python for the POP3 protocol to receive an email securely. Then, we state the specific email server and our email credentials—that is, our username and password. After that, we print the response message from the server and provide the username and password to the POP3 SSL server. After login, we get mailbox stats and print them to the Terminal in the form of a number of emails.

Now, we're going to write a script to get the latest email. For that, create a script, latest_email.py, and write the following content in it:

```
import poplib
import getpass

pop3_server = 'pop.gmail.com'
username = 'Emaild_address'
password = getpass.getpass()

email_obj = poplib.POP3_SSL(pop3_server)
print(email_obj.getwelcome())
email_obj.user(username)
email_obj.pass_(password)

print("\nLatest Mail\n")
latest_email = email_obj.retr(1)
print(latest_email[1])
```

Run the script, as follows:

```
student@ubuntu:~$ python3 latest_email.py
```

As output, you'll get the latest mail you received in your mailbox.

In the preceding example, we imported the `poplib` library used in Python to supply the POP3 protocol to receive an email securely. After stating the specific email server and the username and password, we printed the response message from the server and providing the username and password to the POP3 SSL server. Then, we're fetching the latest email from the mailbox.

Now, we're going to write a script to get all of the emails. For that, create a script, `all_emails.py`, and write the following content in it:

```python
import poplib
import getpass

pop3_server = 'pop.gmail.com'
username = 'Emaild_address'
password = getpass.getpass()

email_obj = poplib.POP3_SSL(pop3_server)
print(email_obj.getwelcome())
email_obj.user(username)
email_obj.pass_(password)

email_stat = email_obj.stat()
NumofMsgs = email_stat[0]
for i in range(NumofMsgs):
    for mail in email_obj.retr(i+1)[1]:
        print(mail)
```

Run the script, as follows:

```
student@ubuntu:~$ python3 latest_email.py
```

As output, you'll get all of the emails you've received in your mailbox.

Receiving email using the imaplib library

IMAP stands for Internet Message Access Protocol. It's used to access emails on a remote server through your local machine. IMAP allows simultaneous access by multiple clients to your email. IMAP is more suitable when you access your email via different locations.

The IMAP protocol works on two ports:

- Port 143: The default non-encrypted port
- Port 993: The encrypted port

Now, we're going to see an example using the imaplib library. Create a script, imap_email.py, and write the following content in it:

```
import imaplib
import pprint
import getpass

imap_server = 'imap.gmail.com'
username = 'Emaild_address'
password = getpass.getpass()

imap_obj = imaplib.IMAP4_SSL(imap_server)
imap_obj.login(username, password)
imap_obj.select('Inbox')
temp, data_obj = imap_obj.search(None, 'ALL')
for data in data_obj[0].split():
    temp, data_obj = imap_obj.fetch(data, '(RFC822)')
    print('Message: {0}\n'.format(data))
    pprint.pprint(data_obj[0][1])
    break

imap_obj.close()
```

Run the script, as follows:

```
student@ubuntu:~$ python3 imap_email.py
```

As output, you'll get all of the emails from the specified folder.

In the preceding example, first, we're importing the imaplib library, which is used in Python to receive an email securely via the IMAP protocol. Then, we state the specific email server and our user credentials—that is, our username and password. After that, we provide that username and password to the IMAP SSL server. We're using the 'select('Inbox')' function over imap_obj to display messages in the inbox. Then we use a for loop to display messages that have been fetched one by one. To display messages, we use "pretty print"—that is, the pprint.pprint() function-because it formats your object, writes it into the data stream, and passes it as an argument. Then, finally, the connection is closed.

Summary

In this chapter, we learned about how to write an email message in a Python script. We also learned about the Python smtplib module, which is used for sending and receiving emails via Python scripts. We also learned about how to receive emails through POP3 and IMAP protocols. Python supplies the poplib and imaplib libraries with which we can perform tasks.

In the next chapter, you'll learn about Telnet and SSH.

Questions

1. What are POP3 and IMAP?
2. What are break and continue used for? Give an appropriate example.
3. What is pprint?
4. What are negative indexes and why are they used?
5. What is the difference between the pyc and py file extensions?
6. Generate following pattern using looping's:

```
1010101
 10101
  101
   1
```

12
Remote Monitoring of Hosts Over Telnet and SSH

In this chapter, you will learn how to carry out basic configurations on a server with Telnet and SSH configured. We will begin by using the Telnet module, after which we will implement the same configurations using the preferred method: SSH using different modules in Python. You will also learn about how `telnetlib`, `subprocess`, `fabric`, `Netmiko`, and `paramiko` modules work. For this chapter, you must have a basic knowledge of networking.

In this chapter, we will cover the following topics:

- The `telnetlib()` module
- The `subprocess.Popen()` module
- SSH using fabric module
- SSH using Paramiko library
- SSH using Netmiko library

The telnetlib() module

In this section, we are going to learn about the Telnet protocol and then we will do Telnet operations using the `telnetlib` module over a remote server.

Telnet is a network protocol that allows a user to communicate with remote servers. It is mostly used by network administrators to remotely access and manage devices. To access the device, run the Telnet command with the IP address or hostname of a remote server in your Terminal.

Telnet uses TCP on the default port number 23. To use Telnet, make sure it is installed on your system. If not, run the following command to install it:

```
$ sudo apt-get install telnetd
```

To run Telnet using the simple Terminal, you just have to enter the following command:

```
$ telnet ip_address_of_your_remote_server
```

Python has the telnetlib module to perform Telnet functions through Python scripts. Before telnetting your remote device or router, make sure they are configured properly and, if not, you can do basic configuration by using the following command in the router's Terminal:

```
configure terminal
enable password 'set_Your_password_to_access_router'
username 'set_username' password 'set_password_for_remote_access'
line vty 0 4
login local
transport input all
interface f0/0
ip add 'set_ip_address_to_the_router' 'put_subnet_mask'
no shut
end
show ip interface brief
```

Now, let's see the example of Telnetting a remote device. For that, create a telnet_example.py script and write following content in it:

```
import telnetlib
import getpass
import sys

HOST_IP = "your host ip address"
host_user = input("Enter your telnet username: ")
password = getpass.getpass()

t = telnetlib.Telnet(HOST_IP)
t.read_until(b"Username:")
t.write(host_user.encode("ascii") + b"\n")
if password:
    t.read_until(b"Password:")
    t.write(password.encode("ascii") + b"\n")

t.write(b"enable\n")
t.write(b"enter_remote_device_password\n") #password of your remote device
t.write(b"conf t\n")
t.write(b"int loop 1\n")
```

```
t.write(b"ip add 10.1.1.1 255.255.255.255\n")
t.write(b"int loop 2\n")
t.write(b"ip add 20.2.2.2 255.255.255.255\n")
t.write(b"end\n")
t.write(b"exit\n")
print(t.read_all().decode("ascii") )
```

Run the script and you will get the output as follows:

```
student@ubuntu:~$ python3 telnet_example.py
Output:
Enter your telnet username: student
Password:


server>enable
Password:
server#conf t
Enter configuration commands, one per line.  End with CNTL/Z.
server(config)#int loop 1
server(config-if)#ip add 10.1.1.1 255.255.255.255
server(config-if)#int loop 23
server(config-if)#ip add 20.2.2.2 255.255.255.255
server(config-if)#end
server#exit
```

In the preceding example, we accessed and configured a Cisco router using the `telnetlib` module. In this script, first, we took the username and password from the user to initialize the Telnet connection with a remote device. When the connection was established, we did further configuration on the remote device. After telnetting, we will be able to access a remote server or device. But there is one very important disadvantage of this Telnet protocol, and that is all the data, including usernames and passwords is sent over a network in a text manner, which may cause a security risk. Because of that, nowadays Telnet is rarely used and has been replaced by a very secure protocol named Secure Shell, known as SSH.

SSH

SSH is a network protocol and is used to manage a device or servers through remote access. SSH uses public key encryption for security purposes. The important difference between Telnet and SSH is that SSH uses encryption, which means that all data transmitted over a network is protected from unauthorized real-time interception.

User who accesses a remote server or device must install an SSH client. Install SSH by running the following command in your Terminal:

```
$ sudo apt install ssh
```

Also, on a remote server where the user wants to communicate, an SSH server must be installed and running. SSH uses the TCP protocol and works on port number 22 by default.

You can run the ssh command through the Terminal as follows:

```
$ ssh host_name@host_ip_address
```

Now, you will learn to do SSH by using different modules in Python, such as subprocess, fabric, Netmiko, and Paramiko. Now, we will see those modules one by one.

The subprocess.Popen() module

The Popen class handles the process creation and management. By using this module, developers can handle less common cases. The child program execution will be done in a new process. To execute a child program on Unix/Linux, the class will use the os.execvp() function. To execute a child program in Windows, the class will use the CreateProcess() function.

Now, let's see some useful arguments of subprocess.Popen():

```
class subprocess.Popen(args, bufsize=0, executable=None, stdin=None,
stdout=None,
                                    stderr=None, preexec_fn=None,
close_fds=False, shell=False,
                                    cwd=None, env=None,
universal_newlines=False,
                startupinfo=None, creationflags=0)
```

Let's look at each argument:

- args: It can be a sequence of program arguments or a single string. If args is a sequence, the first item in args is executed. If args is a string, it recommends to pass args as a sequence.
- shell: The shell argument is by default set to False and it specifies whether to use shell for execution of the program. If shell is True, it recommends to pass args as a string. In Linux, if shell=True, the shell defaults to /bin/sh. If args is a string, the string specifies the command to execute through the shell.

- bufsize: If bufsize is 0 (by default, it is 0), it means unbuffered and if bufsize is 1, it means line buffered. If bufsize is any other positive value, use a buffer of the given size. If bufsize is any other negative value, it means fully buffered.
- executable: It specifies that the replacement program to be executed.
- stdin, stdout, and stderr: These arguments define the standard input, standard output, and standard error respectively.
- preexec_fn: This is set to a callable object and will be called just before the child is executed in the child process.
- close_fds: In Linux, if close_fds is true, all file descriptors except 0, 1, and 2 will be closed before the child process is executed. In Windows, if close_fds is true then the child process will inherit no handles.
- env: If the value is not None, then mapping will define environment variables for new process.
- universal_newlines: If the value is True then stdout and stderr will be opened as text files in newlines mode.

Now, we are going to see an example of subprocess.Popen(). For that, create a ssh_using_sub.py script and write the following content in it:

```
import subprocess
import sys

HOST="your host username@host ip"
COMMAND= "ls"

ssh_obj = subprocess.Popen(["ssh", "%s" % HOST, COMMAND],
 shell=False,
 stdout=subprocess.PIPE,
 stderr=subprocess.PIPE)

result = ssh_obj.stdout.readlines()
if result == []:
 err = ssh_obj.stderr.readlines()
 print(sys.stderr, "ERROR: %s" % err)
else:
 print(result)
```

Run the script and you will get the output as follows:

```
student@ubuntu:~$ python3 ssh_using_sub.py
Output :
student@192.168.0.106's password:
[b'Desktop\n', b'Documents\n', b'Downloads\n', b'examples.desktop\n',
b'Music\n', b'Pictures\n', b'Public\n', b'sample.py\n', b'spark\n',
```

```
b'spark-2.3.1-bin-hadoop2.7\n', b'spark-2.3.1-bin-hadoop2.7.tgz\n',
b'ssh\n', b'Templates\n', b'test_folder\n', b'test.txt\n',
b'Untitled1.ipynb\n', b'Untitled.ipynb\n', b'Videos\n', b'work\n']
```

In the preceding example, first, we imported the subprocess module, then we defined the host address where you want to establish the SSH connection. After that, we gave one simple command that executed over the remote device. After all this was set up, we put this information in the subprocess.Popen() function. This function executed the arguments defined inside that function to create a connection with the remote device. After the SSH connection was established, our defined command was executed and provided the result. Then we printed the result of SSH on the Terminal, as shown in the output.

SSH using fabric module

Fabric is a Python library as well as a command-line tool for the use of SSH. It is used for system administration and application deployment over the network. We can also execute shell commands over SSH.

To use fabric module, first you have to install it using the following command:

```
$ pip3 install fabric3
```

Now, we will see an example. Create a fabfile.py script and write the following content in it:

```
from fabric.api import *

env.hosts=["host_name@host_ip"]
env.password='your password'

def dir():
    run('mkdir fabric')
    print('Directory named fabric has been created on your host network')

def diskspace():
    run('df')
```

Run the script and you will get the output as follows:

```
student@ubuntu:~$ fab dir
Output:
[student@192.168.0.106] Executing task 'dir'
[student@192.168.0.106] run: mkdir fabric

Done.
Disconnecting from 192.168.0.106... done.
```

In the preceding example, first, we imported the `fabric.api` module, then we set the hostname and password to get connected with the host network. After that, we set different task to perform over SSH. Therefore, to execute our program instead of the Python3 `fabfile.py`, we used the `fab` utility (`fab dir`), and after that we stated that the required tasks should be performed from our `fabfile.py`. In our case, we performed the `dir` task, which creates a directory with the name `'fabric'` on your remote network. You can add your specific task in your Python file. It can be executed using the `fab` utility of the fabric module.

SSH using the Paramiko library

Paramiko is a library that implements the SSHv2 protocol for secure connections to remote devices. Paramiko is a pure Python interface around SSH.

Before using Paramiko, make sure you have installed it properly on your system. If it is not installed, you can install it by running the following command in your Terminal:

```
$ sudo pip3 install paramiko
```

Now, we will see an example of using `paramiko`. For this `paramiko` connection, we are using a Cisco device. Paramiko supports both password-based and key-pair based authentication for a secure connection with the server. In our script, we are using password-based authentication, which means we check for a password and, if available, authentication is attempted using plain username/password authentication. Before we are going to do SSH to your remote device or multi-layer router, make sure they are configured properly and, if not, you can do basic configuration by using the following command in a multi-layer router Terminal:

```
configure t
ip domain-name cciepython.com
crypto key generate rsa
How many bits in the modulus [512]: 1024
interface range f0/0 - 1
```

```
switchport mode access
switchport access vlan 1
no shut
int vlan 1
ip add 'set_ip_address_to_the_router' 'put_subnet_mask'
no shut
exit
enable password 'set_Your_password_to_access_router'
username 'set_username' password 'set_password_for_remote_access'
username 'username' privilege 15
line vty 0 4
login local
transport input all
end
```

Now, create a `pmiko.py` script and write the following content in it:

```
import paramiko
import time

ip_address = "host_ip_address"
usr = "host_username"
pwd = "host_password"

c = paramiko.SSHClient()
c.set_missing_host_key_policy(paramiko.AutoAddPolicy())
c.connect(hostname=ip_address,username=usr,password=pwd)

print("SSH connection is successfully established with ", ip_address)

rc = c.invoke_shell()
for n in range (2,6):
    print("Creating VLAN " + str(n))
    rc.send("vlan database\n")
    rc.send("vlan " + str(n) +  "\n")
    rc.send("exit\n")
    time.sleep(0.5)

time.sleep(1)
output = rc.recv(65535)
print(output)
c.close
```

Run the script and you will get the output as follows:

```
student@ubuntu:~$ python3 pmiko.py
Output:
SSH connection is successfuly established with  192.168.0.70
Creating VLAN 2
Creating VLAN 3
Creating VLAN 4
Creating VLAN 5
```

In the preceding example, first, we imported the `paramiko` module, then we defined the SSH credentials required to connect the remote device. After providing credentials, we created an instance `'c'` of `paramiko.SSHclient()`, which is the primary client used to establish connections with the remote device and execute commands or operations. The creation of an `SSHClient` object allows us to establish remote connections using the `.connect()` function. Then, we set the policy `paramiko` connection because, by default, `paramiko.SSHclient` sets the SSH policy in reject policy state. That causes the policy to reject any SSH connection without any validation. In our script, we are neglecting this possibility of SSH connection drop by using the `AutoAddPolicy()` function that automatically adds the server's host key without prompting it. We can use this policy for testing purposes only, but this is not a good option in a production environment because of security purpose.

When an SSH connection is established, you can do any configuration or operation that you want on your device. Here, we created a few virtual LANs on a remote device. After creating VLANs, we just closed the connection.

SSH using the Netmiko library

In this section, we will learn about Netmiko. The Netmiko library is an advanced version of Paramiko. It is a `multi_vendor` library that is based on Paramiko. Netmiko simplifies SSH connection to a network device and takes particular operation on the device. Before going doing SSH to your remote device or multi-layer router, make sure they are configured properly and, if not, you can do basic configuration by command mentioned in the Paramiko section.

Now, let's see an example. Create a `nmiko.py` script and write the following code in it:

```
from netmiko import ConnectHandler

remote_device={
    'device_type': 'cisco_ios',
    'ip':  'your remote_device ip address',
```

```python
        'username': 'username',
        'password': 'password',
}

remote_connection = ConnectHandler(**remote_device)
#net_connect.find_prompt()

for n in range (2,6):
    print("Creating VLAN " + str(n))
    commands = ['exit','vlan database','vlan ' + str(n), 'exit']
    output = remote_connection.send_config_set(commands)
    print(output)

command = remote_connection.send_command('show vlan-switch brief')
print(command)
```

Run the script and you will get the output as follows:

```
student@ubuntu:~$ python3 nmiko.py
Output:
Creating VLAN 2
config term
Enter configuration commands, one per line.  End with CNTL/Z.
server(config)#exit
server #vlan database
server (vlan)#vlan 2
VLAN 2 modified:
server (vlan)#exit
APPLY completed.
Exiting....
server #
 ..
 ..
 ..
 ..
switch#
Creating VLAN 5
config term
Enter configuration commands, one per line.  End with CNTL/Z.
server (config)#exit
server #vlan database
server (vlan)#vlan 5
VLAN 5 modified:
server (vlan)#exit
APPLY completed.
Exiting....
VLAN Name                                   Status    Ports
---- -------------------------------- --------- ----------------------------
```

```
----
1    default                         active    Fa0/0, Fa0/1, Fa0/2, Fa0/3,
Fa0/4, Fa0/5, Fa0/6, Fa0/7, Fa0/8, Fa0/9, Fa0/10, Fa0/11, Fa0/12, Fa0/13,
Fa0/14, Fa0/15
2    VLAN0002                        active
3    VLAN0003                        active
4    VLAN0004                        active
5    VLAN0005                        active
1002 fddi-default                    active
1003 token-ring-default         active
1004 fddinet-default             active
1005 trnet-default                   active
```

In the preceding example, we use Netmiko library to do SSH, instead of Paramiko. In this script, first, we imported `ConnectHandler` from the Netmiko library, which we used to establish an SSH connection to the remote network devices by passing in the device dictionary. In our case, that dictionary is `remote_device`. After the connection is established, we executed configuration commands to create a number of virtual LANs using the `send_config_set()` function.

When we use this type (`.send_config_set()`) of function to pass commands on a remote device, it automatically sets our device in configuration mode. After sending configuration commands, we also passed a simple command to get the information about the configured device.

Summary

In this chapter, you learned about Telnet and SSH. You also learned the different Python modules such as telnetlib, subprocess, fabric, Netmiko, and Paramiko, using which we perform Telnet and SSH. SSH uses the public key encryption for security purposes and is more secure than Telnet.

In the next chapter, we will use various Python libraries, with which you can make graphical user interfaces.

Questions

1. What is client-server architecture?
2. How do you run operating-specific commands in Python code?
3. What is the difference between LAN and VLAN?
4. What will the output of the following code be?

```
List = ['a', 'b', 'c', 'd', 'e']
Print(list [10:])
```

5. Write a Python program to display a calendar (hint: use the `calendar` module).
6. Write a Python program to count the number of lines in a text file.

Further reading

- Paramiko documentation: `https://github.com/paramiko/paramiko`
- Fabric documentation: `http://www.fabfile.org/`

13

Building Graphical User Interfaces

In this chapter, you will study **Graphical User Interface (GUI)** development. There are various Python libraries that you can use to make GUI. We are going to learn about the PyQt5 Python library for GUI creation.

In this chapter, you will learn the following topics:

- Introduction to GUI
- Using a library to create a GUI-based application
- Installing and using the Apache Log Viewer app

Introduction to GUI

In this section, we are going to learn about GUI. Python has various frameworks for GUI. In this section, we are going to look at PyQt5. PyQt5 has different graphics components, also known as object widgets, which can be displayed on screen and also interact with users. The components are listed here:

- **PyQt5 window**: The PyQt5 window will create a simple app window.
- **PyQt5 button**: The PyQt5 button is a button that causes an action whenever it is clicked.
- **PyQt5 textbox**: The PyQt5 textbox widget allows users to enter the text.
- **PyQt5 label**: The PyQt5 label widget displays a single-line text or an image.
- **PyQt5 combo box**: The PyQt5 combo box widget is a combined button and a popup list.
- **PyQt5 check box**: The PyQt5 check box widget is an option button that can be checked and unchecked.

- **PyQt5 radio button**: The PyQt5 radio button widget is an option button that can be checked or unchecked. In a group of radio buttons, only one of the buttons can be checked at a time.
- **PyQt5 message box**: The PyQt5 message box widget display a message.
- **PyQt5 menu**: The PyQt5 menu widget gives different choices that are displayed.
- **PyQt5 table**: The PyQt5 table widget provides standard table display functionality for applications, which can be constructed with a number of rows and columns.
- **PyQt5 signals/slots**: Signals will let you react to the event that has occurred and slot is simply a function that gets called whenever a signal occurs.
- **PyQt5 layouts**: The PyQt5 layouts consist of multiple widgets.

There are several PyQt5 classes available, which are divided into different modules. These modules are listed here:

- `QtGui`: `QtGui` contains classes for event handling, graphics, fonts, texts, and basic imaging.
- `QtWidgets`: `QtWidgets` contains classes to create desktop-style user interfaces.
- `QtCore`: `QtCore` contains core non-GUI functionality such as time, directories, files, streams, URLs, data types, threads, and processes.
- `QtBluetooth`: `QtBluetooth` contains classes for connecting with devices and interacting with them.
- `QtPositioning`: `QtPositioning` contains classes to determine the position.
- `QtMultimedia`: `QtMultimedia` contains classes for APIs and multimedia content.
- `QtNetwork`: `QtNetwork` contains classes for network programming.
- `QtWebKit`: `QtWebkit` contains classes for web browser implementation.
- `QtXml`: `QtXml` contains classes for XML files.
- `QtSql`: `QtSql` contains classes for databases.

The GUI is driven by the events. Now, what is an event? An event is a signal that indicates that something has happened in your program, for example, menu selection, mouse movement, or button clicks. The events are handled by functions and triggered when a user performs some actions on the objects. The listener will listen to the event and then it will invoke an event handler whenever an event occurs.

Using a library to create a GUI-based application

Now, we are actually going to use the PyQt5 library to create a simple GUI application. In this section, we are going to create a simple window. In that window, we will have one button and a label. After clicking on that button, some message will get printed in the label.

First, we will see how to create the button widget. The following line will create a button widget:

```
b = QPushButton('Click', self)
```

Now, we will see how to create a label. The following line will create a label:

```
l = QLabel(self)
```

Now, we will see how to create the button and label and how to perform an operation after clicking on that button. For that, create a `print_message.py` script and write following code in it:

```
import sys
from PyQt5.QtWidgets import QApplication, QLabel, QPushButton, QWidget
from PyQt5.QtCore import pyqtSlot
from PyQt5.QtGui import QIcon

class simple_app(QWidget):
        def __init__(self):
                    super().__init__()
                    self.title = 'Main app window'
                    self.left = 20
                    self.top = 20
                    self.height = 300
                    self.width = 400
                    self.app_initialize()

        def app_initialize(self):
                    self.setWindowTitle(self.title)
                    self.setGeometry(self.left, self.top, self.height,
self.width)

                    b = QPushButton('Click', self)
                    b.setToolTip('Click on the button !!')
                    b.move(100,70)
                    self.l = QLabel(self)
                    self.l.resize(100,50)
                    self.l.move(100,200)
                    b.clicked.connect(self.on_click)
```

```
                    self.show()

            @pyqtSlot()
            def on_click(self):
                        self.l.setText("Hello World")

    if __name__ == '__main__':
            appl = QApplication(sys.argv)
            ex = simple_app()
            sys.exit(appl.exec_())
```

Run the script and you will get the output as follows:

```
student@ubuntu:~/gui_example$ python3 print_message.py
```

In the preceding example, we imported the necessary PyQt5 modules. Then, we created the application. The QPushButton creates the widget and the first argument we entered is a text that will be printed on the button. Next, we have a QLabel widget on which we are printing a message, which will get printed when we will click on the button. Next, we created an on_click() function that will perform the printing operation after clicking on the button. The on_click() is the slot we created.

Now, we are going to see an example of the box layout. For that, create a `box_layout.py` script and write following code in it:

```
from PyQt5.QtWidgets import QApplication, QWidget, QPushButton, QVBoxLayout

appl = QApplication([])
make_window = QWidget()
layout = QVBoxLayout()

layout.addWidget(QPushButton('Button 1'))
layout.addWidget(QPushButton('Button 2'))

make_window.setLayout(l)
make_window.show()

appl.exec_()
```

Run the script and you will get the following output:

```
student@ubuntu:~/gui_example$ python3 box_layout.py
```

In the preceding example, we created a box layout. In that we have placed two buttons. This script is just for explaining the box layout. `l = QVBoxLayout()` will create a box layout.

Installing and using the Apache Log Viewer app

As we already have an Apache Log Viewer app, download the Apache Log Viewer app from the following link: `https://www.apacheviewer.com/download/`.

After downloading it, install the app on your computer. This app is useful for analyzing log files based on their connection status, IP addresses, and much more. Therefore, to analyze the log file we can simply browse access log file or error log file. After getting the file, we apply different operations on a log file such as applying a filter, for instance to sort the only files from `access.log` that have unsuccessful connections, or filtering by specific IP addresses.

The following screenshot shows Apache log viewer with the `access.log` file without applying a filter:

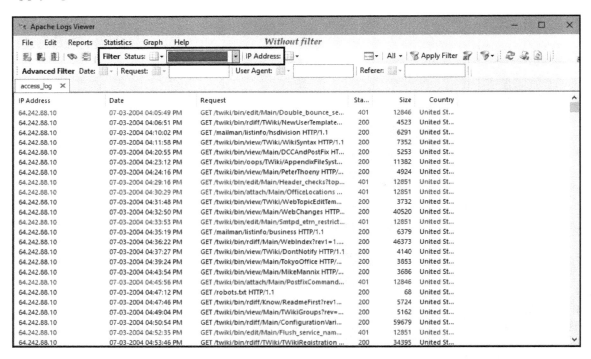

The following screenshot shows the Apache Log Viewer with the `access.log file` after applying a filter:

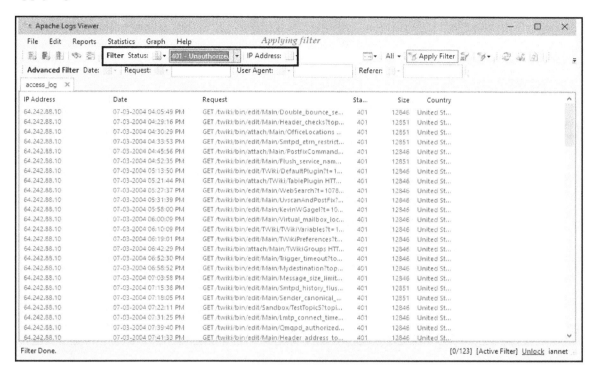

In the first case, we took the access log file and opened it in the Apache Logs Viewer. We can easily see that the access file that we opened in the Apache Logs Viewer contains all kinds of entries, such as authorized and unauthorized, with their status, IP address, request, and so on. However, in the second case we applied a filter on the access log file so that we can only see the log entries of unauthorized requests, as shown in the previous screenshot.

Summary

In this section, we learned about GUIs. We learned about the components used in GUI. We learned about the PyQt5 module in Python. Using the PyQt5 module, we created a simple application that will print a message in a label after clicking on a button.

In the next chapter, you will learn about working with Apache log files.

Questions

1. What is GUI ?
2. What are the constructors and destructors in Python?
3. What is the use of `self`?
4. Compare Tkinter, PyQt, and wxPython.
5. Create a Python program to copy the contents of one file into another
6. Create a Python program that reads a text file and counts the number of times a certain letter appears in the text file.

Further reading

- Tkinter library for GUI documentation: `https://docs.python.org/3/library/tk.html`
- PyQt library for GUI documentation: `https://wiki.python.org/moin/PyQt`

14
Working with Apache and Other Log Files

In this chapter, you are going to learn about log files. You will learn how to parse log files. You will also learn why you need to write exceptions in your programs. The different ways to parse different files are also important. You will also learn about `ErrorLog` and `AccessLog`. Finally, you will learn about how to parse other log files.

In this chapter, you will learn the following:

- Parsing complex log files
- The need for exceptions
- Tricks for parsing different files
- Error log
- Access log
- Parsing other log files

Parsing complex log files

First, we are going to examine the concept of parsing complex log files. Parsing log files is a challenging task because most log files are in plain text format, and that format does not follow any rules. Those files may be modified without showing any warning. The user can decide what kind of data they are going to store in a log file and in which format, as well as who is going to develop the application.

Before moving on to an example of log parsing or changing configurations in a log file, first we have to understand what we have got in a typical log file. According to that we have to decide, we will learn how to manipulate or get the information from it. We can also look for common terms in the log file so that we can use those common terms to fetch data.

Generally, you will see that most of the content generated in a log file is by the application containers and also either the entries of system access state (in other words, logging off and logging on) or the entries of a system accessed over a network. Therefore, when your system is accessed over a network remotely, the entry of such a remote connection will be saved into a log file. Let's take an example for such condition. We already have a file named `access.log` with some log information.

So, let's create a `read_apache_log.py` script and write the following content in it:

```
def read_apache_log(logfile):
        with open(logfile) as f:
                log_obj = f.read()
                print(log_obj)


if __name__ == '__main__':
        read_apache_log("access.log")
```

Run the script and you will get the output as follows:

```
student@ubuntu:~$ python3 read_apache_log.py
Output:
64.242.88.10 - - [07/Mar/2004:16:05:49 -0800] "GET
/twiki/bin/edit/Main/Double_bounce_sender?topicparent=Main.ConfigurationVar
iables HTTP/1.1" 401 12846
64.242.88.10 - - [07/Mar/2004:16:06:51 -0800] "GET
/twiki/bin/rdiff/TWiki/NewUserTemplate?rev1=1.3&rev2=1.2 HTTP/1.1" 200 4523
64.242.88.10 - - [07/Mar/2004:16:10:02 -0800] "GET
/mailman/listinfo/hsdivision HTTP/1.1" 200 6291
64.242.88.10 - - [07/Mar/2004:16:11:58 -0800] "GET
/twiki/bin/view/TWiki/WikiSyntax HTTP/1.1" 200 7352
64.242.88.10 - - [07/Mar/2004:16:20:55 -0800] "GET
/twiki/bin/view/Main/DCCAndPostFix HTTP/1.1" 200 5253
64.242.88.10 - - [07/Mar/2004:16:23:12 -0800] "GET
/twiki/bin/oops/TWiki/AppendixFileSystem?template=oopsmore&param1=1.12&para
m2=1.12 HTTP/1.1" 200 11382
64.242.88.10 - - [07/Mar/2004:16:24:16 -0800] "GET
/twiki/bin/view/Main/PeterThoeny HTTP/1.1" 200 4924
64.242.88.10 - - [07/Mar/2004:16:29:16 -0800] "GET
/twiki/bin/edit/Main/Header_checks?topicparent=Main.ConfigurationVariables
HTTP/1.1" 401 12851
64.242.88.10 - - [07/Mar/2004:16:30:29 -0800] "GET
/twiki/bin/attach/Main/OfficeLocations HTTP/1.1" 401 12851
64.242.88.10 - - [07/Mar/2004:16:31:48 -0800] "GET
/twiki/bin/view/TWiki/WebTopicEditTemplate HTTP/1.1" 200 3732
64.242.88.10 - - [07/Mar/2004:16:32:50 -0800] "GET
/twiki/bin/view/Main/WebChanges HTTP/1.1" 200 40520
64.242.88.10 - - [07/Mar/2004:16:33:53 -0800] "GET
```

```
/twiki/bin/edit/Main/Smtpd_etrn_restrictions?topicparent=Main.Configuration
Variables HTTP/1.1" 401 12851
64.242.88.10 - - [07/Mar/2004:16:35:19 -0800] "GET
/mailman/listinfo/business HTTP/1.1" 200 6379
.....
```

In the preceding example, we created one `read_apache_log` function to read Apache log files. Within that, we opened a log file and then printed the log entries in it. After defining the `read_apache_log()` function, we called it in the main function with the Apache log file's name. In our case, the Apache log file is named `access.log`.

After reading log entries in the `access.log` file, now we are going to parse the IP addresses from the log file. For that, create a `parse_ip_address.py` script and write the following content in it:

```
import re
from collections import Counter

r_e = r'\d{1,3}\.\d{1,3}\.\d{1,3}\.\d{1,3}'
with open("access.log") as f:
            print("Reading Apache log file")
            Apache_log = f.read()
            get_ip = re.findall(r_e,Apache_log)
            no_of_ip = Counter(get_ip)
            for k, v in no_of_ip.items():
                        print("Available IP Address in log file " + "=> " +
str(k) + " " + "Count " + "=> " + str(v))
```

Run the script and you will get the output as follows:

```
student@ubuntu:~/work/Chapter_15$ python3 parse_ip_address.py
Output:
Reading Apache log file
Available IP Address in log file => 64.242.88.1 Count => 452
Available IP Address in log file => 213.181.81.4 Count => 1
Available IP Address in log file => 213.54.168.1 Count => 12
Available IP Address in log file => 200.160.249.6 Count => 2
Available IP Address in log file => 128.227.88.7 Count => 14
Available IP Address in log file => 61.9.4.6 Count => 3
Available IP Address in log file => 212.92.37.6 Count => 14
Available IP Address in log file => 219.95.17.5 Count => 1
3Available IP Address in log file => 10.0.0.1 Count => 270
Available IP Address in log file => 66.213.206.2 Count => 1
Available IP Address in log file => 64.246.94.1 Count => 2
Available IP Address in log file => 195.246.13.1 Count => 12
Available IP Address in log file => 195.230.181.1 Count => 1
Available IP Address in log file => 207.195.59.1 Count => 20
```

```
Available IP Address in log file => 80.58.35.1 Count => 1
Available IP Address in log file => 200.222.33.3 Count => 1
Available IP Address in log file => 203.147.138.2 Count => 13
Available IP Address in log file => 212.21.228.2 Count => 1
Available IP Address in log file => 80.58.14.2 Count => 4
Available IP Address in log file => 142.27.64.3 Count => 7
......
```

In the preceding example, we created the Apache log parser to determine some specific IP addresses with their number of requests on your server. So, it is clear that we don't want entire log entries in the Apache log file, we just want to fetch IP addresses from the log file. To do that, we have to define a pattern to search IP addresses, and we can do that by using regular expressions. Because of that, we imported the `re` module. Then we imported the `Collection` module as the alternative to Python's built-in datatypes, `dict`, `list`, `set`, and `tuple`. This module has specialized container datatypes. After importing the required modules, we write a pattern using a regular expression to match specific conditions to map IP addresses from the log file.

In that matching pattern, `\d` can be any numeric digit between 0 to 9 and `\r` stands for raw string. Then, we opened the Apache log file named `access.log` and read it. After that, we applied a regular expression condition on the Apache log file, then uses the `counter` function of `collection` module to get a count of each IP address that we are fetching on the basis of the `re` conditions. Finally, we printed the result of the operation, as we can see in the output.

The need for exceptions

In this section, we are going to look at the need for exceptions in Python programming. The normal program flow consists of events and signals. The term exception revels that there is something wrong with your program. These exceptions can be of any type, such as zero division error, import error, attribute error, or assertion error. These exceptions will occur whenever the specified functions cannot perform their tasks properly. The moment the exception occurs the program execution stops and the interpreter will proceed with the exception handling process. The exception handling process consists of writing your code in a `try...except` block. The reason the exception handling is that something unexpected happened in your program.

Analyzing exceptions

In this section, we are going to understand analyzing exceptions. Every exception that occurs must be handled. Your log files should also contain few exceptions. If you are getting similar types of exceptions a number of times, then your program has some issue and you should make the necessary changes as soon as possible.

Consider the following example:

```
f = open('logfile', 'r')
print(f.read())
f.close()
```

After running the program, you get the output as follows:

```
Traceback (most recent call last):
  File "sample.py", line 1, in <module>
    f = open('logfile', 'r')
FileNotFoundError: [Errno 2] No such file or directory: 'logfile'
```

In this example, we are trying to read a file that is not present in our directory and as a result it shows an error. So, from the error we can analyze what kind of solution we have to provide. To handle such a case, we can use an exception handling technique. So, let's see an example of handling errors using an exception handling technique.

Consider the following example:

```
try:
    f = open('logfile', 'r')
    print(f.read())
    f.close()
except:
    print("file not found. Please check whether the file is present in your
directory or not.")
```

After running the program, you get the output as follows:

```
file not found. Please check whether the file is present in your directory
or not.
```

In this example, we are trying to read a file that is not present in our directory. But, as we used a file exception technique in this example, we put our code in `try:` and `except:` blocks. So, if any error or exception occurs in a `try:` block, it will skip that error and execute the code in an `except:` block. In our case, we just put a `print` statement in an `except:` block. Therefore, after running the script, when the exception occurs in the `try:` block, it skips that exception and executes the code in the `except:` block. So, the `print` statement in the `except` block gets executed, as we can see in the previous output.

Tricks for parsing different files

In this section, we are going to learn about the tricks to use to parse different files. Before we start with the actual parsing, we must read the data first. You need to understand where you will be getting all the data from. But, you must also remember all the log files come in different sizes. To make your task simpler, here is a list to follow:

- Remember the log files can be either plain text or compressed.
- All the Log files have a `.log` extension for a plain text file and `log.bz2` for a `bzip2` file.
- You should process the set of files based on their name.
- All the parsing of log files must be combined into a single report.
- The tool you are using must operate on all files, from a specified directory or from different directories. Log files from all sub-directories should also be included.

Error log

In this section, we are going to learn about the error log. The related directives for the error log are as follows:

- `ErrorLog`
- `LogLevel`

The location and the name of server log files are set by the `ErrorLog` directive. It is the most important log file. The Apache `httpd` sends the information in this and also records produced while processing. Whenever a problem occurs with the server, this will be the first place to look. It contains the details of the things that went wrong and the process of fixing it.

The error log is written into a file. On Unix systems, the errors can be sent to `syslog` by the server or you can pipe them to your program. The first thing in that log entry is the date and time of the message. The second entry records the severity of the error.

The `LogLevel` directive handles the errors sent to the error log by restricting the severity level. The third entry contains the information about the client who generated the error. That information will be the IP address. The next will be the message itself. It contains the information that the server has been configured to deny the client access. The server will then report the filesystem path of the requested document.

The various types of message can appear in the error log files. The error log file also contains the debugging output from CGI scripts. Whatever the information is written into the `stderr` will be directly copied to the error log.

The error log file is not customizable. The entries in the error log that deals with the requests will have corresponding entries in the access log. You should always monitor the error log for the problems during testing. On Unix systems, you can run the following command to accomplish this:

```
$ tail -f error_log
```

Access log

In this section, you are going to learn about the access log. The server access log will record all the requests processed by the server. The `CustomLog` directive controls the location and content of the access log. The `LogFormat` directive is used to select the contents of the logs.

Storing the information in the access log means starting log management. The next step will be analyzing the information that helps us get useful statistics. The Apache `httpd` has various versions, and these versions have used some other modules and directives to control access logging. You can configure the format of the access log. This format is specified using a format string.

Common log format

In this section, we are going to learn about common log format. The following syntax shows the configuration for the access log:

```
LogFormat "%h %l %u %t \"%r\" %>s %b" nick_name
CustomLog logs/access_log nick_name
```

This string will define a nickname and then it will associate that nickname with the log format string. The log format string is made of percent directives. Each percent directive tells the server to log specific information. This string may contain literal characters. Those characters will get copied directly in log output.

The CustomLog directive will set up a new log file with the help of a defined *nickname*. The filename for the access log is relative to the ServerRoot, unless it begins with a slash.

The configuration we stated previously will write the log entries in a **Common Log Format (CLF)**. This is a standard format and can be produced by many different web servers. Many log analysis programs read this log format.

Now, we will see what each percent directive means:

- %h: This shows us the IP address of the client who made the request to the web server. If HostnameLookups is on, then the server will determine the hostname and will log it in place of the IP address.
- %l: This term is used to indicate that the information is not available for a requested piece.
- %u: This is the user ID of the person who has requested the document. The same value is provided to CGI scripts in the REMOTE_USER environment variable.
- %t: This term is used to detect the time at which the processing request of server is finished. The format is as follows:

    [day/month/year:hour:minute:second zone]

For the day parameter, it takes two digits. For month, we have to define three letters. For year, as the year has four characters, we have to take four digits. Now after day, month, and year, we have to take two digits each for hour, minute, and seconds.

- \"%r\": This term is used as the request line, which is given in double quotes from the client. This request line has useful information. The request client uses the GET method and the protocol used is HTTP.
- %>s: This term defines the status code for the client. The status code is very important and useful, because it indicates whether the request sent by the client is successfully made to the server or not.
- %b: This term defines the total size of the object when it returns to the client. This total size does not include the size of the response header.

Parsing other log files

There are also different log files available within our system, including Apache log. In our Linux distribution, the log files are in the `/var/log/` folder within the root filesystem as shown here:

```
student@ubuntu:/var/log$ ls
alternatives.log        apport.log.1       btmp.1          dpkg.log.8.gz   lightdm             vmware                   wtmp
alternatives.log.1      apport.log.2.gz    cups            dpkg.log.9.gz   mcelog              vmware-network.1.log     wtmp.1
alternatives.log.10.gz  apport.log.3.gz    dist-upgrade    faillog         mysql               vmware-network.2.log     Xorg.0.log
alternatives.log.11.gz  apport.log.4.gz    dmesg           fontconfig.log  speech-dispatcher   vmware-network.3.log     Xorg.0.log.old
alternatives.log.12.gz  apport.log.5.gz    dpkg.log        fsck            syslog              vmware-network.4.log     Xorg.1.log
alternatives.log.2.gz   apport.log.6.gz    dpkg.log.1      gpu-manager.log syslog.1            vmware-network.5.log     Xorg.1.log.old
alternatives.log.3.gz   apport.log.7.gz    dpkg.log.10.gz  hp              syslog.2.gz         vmware-network.6.log     Xorg.2.log
alternatives.log.4.gz   apt                dpkg.log.11.gz  influxdb        syslog.3.gz         vmware-network.7.log     Xorg.2.log.old
alternatives.log.5.gz   auth.log           dpkg.log.12.gz  installer       syslog.4.gz         vmware-network.8.log     Xorg.failsafe.log
alternatives.log.6.gz   auth.log.1         dpkg.log.2.gz   kern.log        syslog.5.gz         vmware-network.9.log
alternatives.log.7.gz   auth.log.2.gz      dpkg.log.3.gz   kern.log.1      syslog.6.gz         vmware-network.log
alternatives.log.8.gz   auth.log.3.gz      dpkg.log.4.gz   kern.log.2.gz   syslog.7.gz         vmware-vmsvc.1.log
alternatives.log.9.gz   auth.log.4.gz      dpkg.log.5.gz   kern.log.3.gz   sysstat             vmware-vmsvc.2.log
apache2                 bootstrap.log      dpkg.log.6.gz   kern.log.4.gz   unattended-upgrades vmware-vmsvc.3.log
apport.log             btmp               dpkg.log.7.gz   lastlog         upstart             vmware-vmsvc.log
```

In the preceding screenshot, we can easily see the different types of log files (for instance, authentication log file `auth.log`, system log file `syslog`, and kernel log `kern.log`) available for different operations entries. As we perform operations on Apache log files, as shown previously, we can also perform the same kind of operations on local log files. Let's see an example for parsing one of the log files from before. Create a `simple_log.py` script and write the following content in it:

```python
f=open('/var/log/kern.log','r')

lines = f.readlines()
for line in lines:
        kern_log = line.split()
        print(kern_log)
f.close()
```

Run the script and you will get the output as follows:

```
student@ubuntu:~$ python3 simple_log.py
Output:
 ['Dec', '26', '14:39:38', 'ubuntu', 'NetworkManager[795]:', '<info>',
'[1545815378.2891]', 'device', '(ens33):', 'state', 'change:', 'prepare',
'->', 'config', '(reason', "'none')", '[40', '50', '0]']
 ['Dec', '26', '14:39:38', 'ubuntu', 'NetworkManager[795]:', '<info>',
'[1545815378.2953]', 'device', '(ens33):', 'state', 'change:', 'config',
'->', 'ip-config', '(reason', "'none')", '[50', '70', '0]']
 ['Dec', '26', '14:39:38', 'ubuntu', 'NetworkManager[795]:', '<info>',
'[1545815378.2997]', 'dhcp4', '(ens33):', 'activation:', 'beginning',
'transaction', '(timeout', 'in', '45', 'seconds)']
 ['Dec', '26', '14:39:38', 'ubuntu', 'NetworkManager[795]:', '<info>',
```

```
'[1545815378.3369]', 'dhcp4', '(ens33):', 'dhclient', 'started', 'with',
'pid', '5221']
['Dec', '26', '14:39:39', 'ubuntu', 'NetworkManager[795]:', '<info>',
'[1545815379.0008]', 'address', '192.168.0.108']
['Dec', '26', '14:39:39', 'ubuntu', 'NetworkManager[795]:', '<info>',
'[1545815379.0020]', 'plen', '24', '(255.255.255.0)']
['Dec', '26', '14:39:39', 'ubuntu', 'NetworkManager[795]:', '<info>',
'[1545815379.0028]', 'gateway', '192.168.0.1']
```

In the preceding example, first we created one simple file object, `f`, and opened the `kern.log` file in it with read mode. After that, we applied the `readlines()` function over `file` object to read the data in the file line-by-line in the `for` loop. Then we applied the `split()` function on each line of the kernel log file and then printed the whole file using the `print` function, as can be seen in the output.

Like reading the kernel log file, we can also perform various operations on it, just like we are going to perform some operations now. Now, we are going to access content in the kernel log file through indexing. It is possible because of the `split` function, as it splits all the information in the file as a different iteration. So, let's see an example of such a condition. Create a `simple_log1.py` script and put the following script in it:

```
f=open('/var/log/kern.log','r')

lines = f.readlines()
for line in lines:
            kern_log = line.split()[1:3]
            print(kern_log)
```

Run the script and you will get the following output:

```
student@ubuntu:~$ python3 simple_log1.py
Output:
['26', '14:37:20']
['26', '14:37:20']
['26', '14:37:32']
['26', '14:39:38']
['26', '14:39:38']
['26', '14:39:38']
['26', '14:39:38']
['26', '14:39:38']
['26', '14:39:38']
['26', '14:39:38']
['26', '14:39:38']
['26', '14:39:38']
```

In the preceding example, we just added `[1:3]` next to the `split` function, in other words, slicing. A sub-sequence of a sequence is known as a slice and the operation that extracts a sub-sequence is known as slicing. In our example, we use square brackets (`[ ]`) as the slice operator and have two integer values inside it, separated by a colon (`:`). The operator `[1:3]` returns the part of the sequence from the first element to the third element, including the first but excluding the last. When we slice any sequence, the sub-sequence we got always has the same type as the original sequence from which it was derived. However, the elements of a list (or tuple) can be of any type; no matter how we apply slicing over it, the derived slice of a list is a list. So, after applying slicing on log file, as a result of that we got the output shown previously.

Summary

In this chapter, you learned about how to work with different types of log files. You also learned about parsing complex log files and the need for exceptions while handling these files. The tricks for parsing log files will help in performing the parsing smoothly. You also learned about `ErrorLog` and `AccessLog`.

In the next chapter, you are going to learn about SOAP and REST communication.

Questions

1. What is the difference between runtime and compile time exceptions in Python?
2. What are regular expressions?
3. Explore the Linux commands `head`, `tail`, `cat`, and `awk`.
4. Write a Python program to append the contents of one file to another file.
5. Write a Python program to read the contents of a file in reverse order.
6. What would be the output of the following expressions?
    1. `re.search(r'C\Wke', 'C@ke').group()`
    2. `re.search(r'Co+kie', 'Cooookie').group()`
    3. `re.match(r'<.*?>', '<h1>TITLE</h1>').group()`

Further reading

- Python logging: `https://docs.python.org/3/library/logging.html`
- Regular expression: `https://docs.python.org/3/howto/regex.html`
- Exception handling: `https://www.pythonforbeginners.com/error-handling/python-try-and-except`

15
SOAP and REST API Communication

In this chapter, we will look at SOAP and REST API basics. We will also look at the Python libraries for SOAP and REST APIs. We are going to learn about the Zeep library for SOAP and requests for REST API. You will learn to work with the JSON data. We are going to see simple examples of working with JSON data, such as converting JSON strings into Python objects and converting Python objects into JSON strings.

In this chapter, you will learn the following:

- What is SOAP?
- Using libraries for SOAP
- What is a RESTful API?
- Using standard libraries for RESTful API
- Working with JSON data

What is SOAP?

SOAP is **Simple Object Access Protocol**. SOAP is the standard communication protocol system that permits processes to use different operating systems. These communicate via HTTP and XML. It is a web services technology. SOAP APIs are mainly designed for tasks such as creating, updating, deleting, and recovering data. SOAP API uses the Web Services Description language to describe the functionalities offered by web services. SOAP describes all the functions and the types of data. It builds an XML-based protocol.

Using libraries for SOAP

In this section, we are going to learn about Python libraries for SOAP. There are various libraries used for SOAP listed here:

- SOAPpy
- Zeep
- Ladon
- suds-jurko
- pysimplesoap

These are the SOAP API libraries for Python. In this section, we are going to learn about the Zeep library only.

To use the functionality of Zeep, you need to install it first. Run the following command in your Terminal to install Zeep:

```
$ pip3 install Zeep
```

The Zeep module is used for WSDL documents. It generates the code for the services and the documents and provides the programming interface to the SOAP server. The lxml library is used to parse the XML documents.

Now, we are going to see an example. Create a soap_example.py script and write the following code in it:

```
import zeep

w = 'http://www.soapclient.com/xml/soapresponder.wsdl'
c = zeep.Client(wsdl=w)
print(c.service.Method1('Hello', 'World'))
```

Run the script and you will get the following output:

```
student@ubuntu:~$ python3 soap_example.py
Output :
Your input parameters are Hello and World
```

In the preceding example, we first imported the zeep module. We first mentioned the website name. Then we created the zeep client object. The WSDL we used previously defines a simple Method1 function that is made available by zeep via client.service.Method1. It takes two arguments and returns a string.

What is a RESTful API?

REST stands for **Representational State Transfer**. RESTful API has an approach to communication used in the development of web services. It is a style of a web service that works as a channel of communication between different systems over the internet. It is an application interface and is used to GET, PUT, POST, and DELETE data using HTTP requests.

The advantage of REST is that it uses less bandwidth, which is suitable for internet usage. The REST API uses uniform interfaces. All the resources are handled by GET, POST, PUT, and DELETE operations. The REST API uses GET to retrieve a resource, uses PUT to update the resource or to change the state of resource, uses POST to create a resource, and uses DELETE to delete the resource. Systems using REST APIs deliver fast performance and reliability.

The REST API handles every request independently. The request from client to server must contain all the information that is necessary to understand that request.

Using standard libraries for RESTful APIs

In this section, we are going to learn how to use RESTful APIs. To do this, we are going to use the requests and JSON modules of Python. We will see an example now. First, we are going to use the requests module to get the information from an API. We will see GET and POST requests.

First, you must install the requests library as follows:

```
$ pip3 install requests
```

Now, we will see an example. Create a rest_get_example.py script and write the following content in it:

```
import requests

req_obj = requests.get('https://www.imdb.com/news/top?ref_=nv_tp_nw')
print(req_obj)
```

Run the script and you will get the output as follows:

```
student@ubuntu:~/work$ python3 rest_get_example.py
Output:
<Response [200]>
```

In the preceding example, we imported the `requests` module to get the request. Next, we created a request object, `req_obj`, and specified a link from where we want to get the request. And next, we printed it. The output we got is a status code `200`, which indicates success.

Now, we are going to see the `POST` request example. `POST` requests are used for sending data to a server. Create a `rest_post_example.py` script and write the following content in it:

```
import requests
import json

url_name = 'http://httpbin.org/post'
data = {"Name" : "John"}
data_json = json.dumps(data)
headers = {'Content-type': 'application/json'}
response = requests.post(url_name, data=data_json, headers=headers)
print(response)
```

Run the script and you will get the following output:

```
student@ubuntu:~/work$ python3 rest_post_example.py
Output:
<Response [200]>
```

In the preceding example, we learned about the `POST` request. First, we imported the necessary module requests and JSON. Next, we mentioned the URL. Also, we entered the data that we want to post in a dictionary format. Next, we mentioned headers. And then we posted, using a `POST` request. The output we got is status code `200`, which is a success code.

Working with JSON data

In this section, we are going to learn about JSON data. **JSON** stands for **JavaScript Object Notation**. JSON is a data interchange format. It encodes Python objects as JSON strings and decodes JSON strings into Python objects. Python has a JSON module that formats the JSON output. It has functions for serializing and deserializing JSON.

- `json.dump(obj, fileObj)`: This function will serialize an object as a JSON-formatted stream.
- `json.dumps(obj)`: This function will serialize an object as a JSON formatted string.

- `json.load(JSONfile)`: This function will deserialize a JSON file as a Python object.
- `json.loads(JSONfile)`: This function will deserializes a string-type JSON file to a Python object.

It also has two classes for encoding and decoding listed here:

- `JSONEncoder`: Used to convert Python objects into JSON format.
- `JSONDecoder`: Used to convert a JSON formatted file into a Python object.

Now, we are going to see some examples using a JSON module. First, we are going to see the conversion from JSON to Python. For that, create a script `json_to_python.py` and write the following code in it:

```
import json

j_obj = '{ "Name":"Harry", "Age":26, "Department":"HR"}'
p_obj = json.loads(j_obj)
print(p_obj["Name"])
print(p_obj["Department"])
```

Run the script and you will get the output as follows:

```
student@ubuntu:~/work$ python3 json_to_python.py
Output:
Harry
HR
```

In the preceding example, we have written a code that will covert a JSON string to a Python object. The `json.loads()` function is used to convert a JSON string to a Python object.

Now, we are going to see how to convert Python to JSON. For that, create a `python_to_json.py` script and write the following code in it:

```
import json

emp_dict1 = '{ "Name":"Harry", "Age":26, "Department":"HR"}'
json_obj = json.dumps(emp_dict1)
print(json_obj)
```

Run the script and you will get the following output:

```
student@ubuntu:~/work$ python3 python_to_json.py
Output:
"{ \"Name\":\"Harry\", \"Age\":26, \"Department\":\"HR\"}"
```

In the preceding example, we converted a Python object to a JSON string. The `json.dumps()` function is used for this conversion.

Now, we are going to see how to convert Python objects of various types into the JSON string. For that, create a `python_object_to_json.py` script and write the following content in it:

```python
import json

python_dict =  {"Name": "Harry", "Age": 26}
python_list =  ["Mumbai", "Pune"]
python_tuple =  ("Basketball", "Cricket")
python_str =  ("hello_world")
python_int =  (150)
python_float =  (59.66)
python_T =  (True)
python_F =  (False)
python_N =  (None)

json_obj = json.dumps(python_dict)
json_arr1 = json.dumps(python_list)
json_arr2 = json.dumps(python_tuple)
json_str = json.dumps(python_str)
json_num1 = json.dumps(python_int)
json_num2 = json.dumps(python_float)
json_t = json.dumps(python_T)
json_f = json.dumps(python_F)
json_n = json.dumps(python_N)

print("json object : ", json_obj)
print("json array1 : ", json_arr1)
print("json array2 : ", json_arr2)
print("json string : ", json_str)
print("json number1 : ", json_num1)
print("json number2 : ", json_num2)
print("json true", json_t)
print("json false", json_f)
print("json null", json_n)
```

Run the script and you will get the following output:

```
student@ubuntu:~/work$ python3 python_object_to_json.py
Output:
json object :   {"Name": "Harry", "Age": 26}
json array1 :   ["Mumbai", "Pune"]
json array2 :   ["Basketball", "Cricket"]
json string :   "hello_world"
json number1 :   150
```

```
json number2 :   59.66
json true true
json false false
json null null
```

In the preceding example, we converted various types of Python objects into JSON string using the `json.dumps()` function. After conversion, the Python list and tuples are converted into arrays. Integers and floats are treated as numbers in JSON. The following is the chart of conversion from Python to JSON:

Python	JSON
dict	Object
list	Array
tuple	Array
str	String
int	Number
float	Number
True	true
False	false
None	null

Summary

In this chapter, you learned about SOAP APIs and RESTful APIs. You learned about the `zeep` Python library for SOAP APIs and the requests library for REST APIs. You also learned to work with JSON data, for instance, converting JSON to Python and vice versa.

In the next chapter, you will learn about web scrapping and the Python library for performing this task.

Questions

1. What is the difference between SOAP and REST API?
2. What is the difference between `json.loads` and `json.load`?
3. Does JSON support all the platforms?

4. What is the output of the following code snippet?

```
boolean_value = False
print(json.dumps(boolean_value))
```

5. What is the output of the following code snippet?

```
>> weird_json = '{"x": 1, "x": 2, "x": 3}'
>>> json.loads(weird_json)
```

Further reading

- JSON documentation: https://docs.python.org/3/library/json.html
- REST API information: https://searchmicroservices.techtarget.com/definition/REST-representational-state-transfer

16
Web Scraping - Extracting Useful Data from Websites

In this chapter, you will learn about web scraping. You will also learn about the `beautifulsoup` library in Python, which is used for extracting information from websites.

In this chapter, we will cover the following topics:

- What is web scraping?
- Data extraction
- Extracting information from Wikipedia

What is web scraping?

Web scraping is the technique used to extract information from websites. This technique is used to transform unstructured data into structured data.

The use of web scraping is to extract the data from the websites. The extracted information is saved as a local file on your system, and you can store it to database in a table format as well. The web scraping software accesses the **World Wide Web** (**WWW**) directly using HTTP or a web browser. This is an automated process implemented using a web crawler or a bot.

Scraping a web page involves fetching the page and then extracting the data. A web crawler fetches a web page. A web crawler is a mandatory component in web scraping. After fetching, extraction takes place. You can search, parse, save the data into tables, and reformat the page.

Data extraction

In this section, we are going to see the actual data extraction process. Python has the beautifulsoup library to perform the data extraction task. We are also going to use the requests library of Python.

First, we must install these two libraries. Run the following commands to install the requests and beautifulsoup libraries:

```
$ pip3 install requests
$ pip3 install beautifulsoup4
```

The requests library

The use of the requests library is to use HTTP within our Python script in human-readable format. We can download the pages using the requests library in Python. The requests library has different types of requests. Here, we are going to learn about the GET request. The GET request is used to retrieve information from a web server. The GET request downloads the HTML content of a specified web page. Every request has a status code. The status codes return with every request we made to the server. These status codes give us the information about what happened with the request we made. The types of status code are listed here:

- 200: Indicates everything went OK and returns the result, if any
- 301: Indicates that the server is redirecting to a different endpoint if it has switched the domain name or the endpoint name must be changed
- 400: Indicates that you made a bad request
- 401: Indicates when we are not authenticated
- 403: Indicated that you are trying to access forbidden resources
- 404: Indicates that the resource you are trying to access is not available on the server

The beautifulsoup library

beautifulsoup is a library in Python, used for web scraping. It has simple methods for searching, navigating, and modifying. It is simply a toolkit used for extracting the data you needed from a web page.

Now, to use the `requests` and `beautifulsoup` functionality in your scripts you must import these two libraries using the `import` statement. Now, we are going to see an example of parsing a web page. Here, we are going to parse a web page, which is a top news page from the IMDb website. For that purpose, create a `parse_web_page.py` script and write the following content in it:

```
import requests
from bs4 import BeautifulSoup

page_result = requests.get('https://www.imdb.com/news/top?ref_=nv_nw_tp')
parse_obj = BeautifulSoup(page_result.content, 'html.parser')

print(parse_obj)
```

Run the script and you will get the output as follows:

```
student@ubuntu:~/work$ python3 parse_web_page.py
Output:
<!DOCTYPE html>

<html xmlns:fb="http://www.facebook.com/2008/fbml"
xmlns:og="http://ogp.me/ns#">
<head>
<meta charset="utf-8"/>
<meta content="IE=edge" http-equiv="X-UA-Compatible"/>
<meta content="app-id=342792525, app-argument=imdb:///?src=mdot"
name="apple-itunes-app"/>
<script type="text/javascript">var IMDbTimer={starttime: new
Date().getTime(),pt:'java'};</script>
<script>
    if (typeof uet == 'function') {
      uet("bb", "LoadTitle", {wb: 1});
    }
</script>
<script>(function(t){ (t.events = t.events || {})["csm_head_pre_title"] =
new Date().getTime(); })(IMDbTimer);</script>
<title>Top News - IMDb</title>
<script>(function(t){ (t.events = t.events || {})["csm_head_post_title"] =
new Date().getTime(); })(IMDbTimer);</script>
<script>
    if (typeof uet == 'function') {
      uet("be", "LoadTitle", {wb: 1});
    }
</script>
<script>
    if (typeof uex == 'function') {
      uex("ld", "LoadTitle", {wb: 1});
```

```
        }
</script>
<link href="https://www.imdb.com/news/top" rel="canonical"/>
<meta content="http://www.imdb.com/news/top" property="og:url">
<script>
    if (typeof uet == 'function') {
      uet("bb", "LoadIcons", {wb: 1});
    }
```

In the preceding example, we collected a page and parsed it using beautifulsoup. First, we imported the requests and beautifulsoup modules. Then, we collected the URL using the GET request and assigned that URL to the page_result variable. Next, we created a beautifulsoup object parse_obj. This object will take page_result.content as its argument from requests and then the page parsed using html.parser.

Now, we are going to extract the content from a class and a tag. To perform this operation, go to your web browser and right-click on the content, that you want to extract and scroll down so you can see the **Inspect** option. Click on that and you will get the class name. Mention it in your program and run your script. For that, create a extract_from_class.py script and write the following content in it:

```
import requests
from bs4 import BeautifulSoup

page_result = requests.get('https://www.imdb.com/news/top?ref_=nv_nw_tp')
parse_obj = BeautifulSoup(page_result.content, 'html.parser')

top_news = parse_obj.find(class_='news-article__content')
print(top_news)
```

Run the script and you will get the following output:

```
student@ubuntu:~/work$ python3 extract_from_class.py
Output :
<div class="news-article__content">
<a href="/name/nm4793987/">Issa Rae</a> and <a
href="/name/nm0000368/">Laura Dern</a> are teaming up to star in a limited
series called "The Dolls" currently in development at <a
href="/company/co0700043/">HBO</a>.<br/><br/>Inspired by true events, the
series recounts the aftermath of Christmas Eve riots in two small Arkansas
towns in 1983, riots which erupted over Cabbage Patch Dolls. The series
explores class, race, privilege and what it takes to be a "good
mother."<br/><br/>Rae will serve as a writer and executive producer on the
series in addition to starring, with Dern also executive producing. <a
href="/name/nm3308450/">Laura Kittrell</a> and <a
href="/name/nm4276354/">Amy Aniobi</a> will also serve as writers and co-
executive producers. <a href="/name/nm0501536/">Jayme Lemons</a> of Dern's
```

```
<a href="/company/co0641481/">Jaywalker Pictures</a> and <a
href="/name/nm3973260/">Deniese Davis</a> of <a
href="/company/co0363033/">Issa Rae Productions</a> will also executive
produce.<br/><br/>Both Rae and Dern currently star in HBO shows, with Dern
appearing in the acclaimed drama "<a href="/title/tt3920596/">Big Little
Lies</a>" and Rae starring in and having created the hit comedy "<a
href="/title/tt5024912/">Insecure</a>." Dern also recently starred in the
film "<a href="/title/tt4015500/">The Tale</a>,
            </div>
```

In the preceding example, we first imported the requests and beautifulsoup modules. Then, we created a request object and assigned an URL to it. Next, we created a beautifulsoup object parse_obj. This object takes page_result.content as its argument from requests and then the page was parsed using html.parser. Next, we used beautifulsoup's find() method to get the content from the 'news-article__content' class.

Now, we are going to see an example of extracting content from a particular tag. In this example, we are going to extract the content from the <a> tag. Create an extract_from_tag.py script and write the following content in it:

```
import requests
from bs4 import BeautifulSoup

page_result = requests.get('https://www.imdb.com/news/top?ref_=nv_nw_tp')
parse_obj = BeautifulSoup(page_result.content, 'html.parser')

top_news = parse_obj.find(class_='news-article__content')
top_news_a_content = top_news.find_all('a')
print(top_news_a_content)
```

Run the script and you will get the output as follows:

```
student@ubuntu:~/work$ python3 extract_from_tag.py
Output:
[<a href="/name/nm4793987/">Issa Rae</a>, <a href="/name/nm0000368/">Laura
Dern</a>, <a href="/company/co0700043/">HBO</a>, <a
href="/name/nm3308450/">Laura Kittrell</a>, <a href="/name/nm4276354/">Amy
Aniobi</a>, <a href="/name/nm0501536/">Jayme Lemons</a>, <a
href="/company/co0641481/">Jaywalker Pictures</a>, <a
href="/name/nm3973260/">Deniese Davis</a>, <a
href="/company/co0363033/">Issa Rae Productions</a>, <a
href="/title/tt3920596/">Big Little Lies</a>, <a
href="/title/tt5024912/">Insecure</a>, <a href="/title/tt4015500/">The
Tale</a>]
```

In the preceding example, we are extracting contents from the <a> tag. We used the find_all() method to extract all <a> tag contents from the 'news-article__content' class.

Extracting information from Wikipedia

In this section, we are going to see an example of a list of dance forms from Wikipedia. We are going to list all classical Indian dances. For that, create a extract_from_wikipedia.py script and write the following content in it:

```
import requests
from bs4 import BeautifulSoup

page_result = requests.get('https://en.wikipedia.org/wiki/Portal:History')
parse_obj = BeautifulSoup(page_result.content, 'html.parser')

h_obj = parse_obj.find(class_='hlist noprint')
h_obj_a_content = h_obj.find_all('a')

print(h_obj)
print(h_obj_a_content)
```

Run the script and you will get the following output:

```
student@ubuntu:~/work$ python3 extract_from_wikipedia.py
Output:
<div class="hlist noprint" id="portals-browsebar" style="text-align:
center;">
<dl><dt><a href="/wiki/Portal:Contents/Portals"
title="Portal:Contents/Portals">Portal topics</a></dt>
<dd><a href="/wiki/Portal:Contents/Portals#Human_activities"
title="Portal:Contents/Portals">Activities</a></dd>
<dd><a href="/wiki/Portal:Contents/Portals#Culture_and_the_arts"
title="Portal:Contents/Portals">Culture</a></dd>
<dd><a href="/wiki/Portal:Contents/Portals#Geography_and_places"
title="Portal:Contents/Portals">Geography</a></dd>
<dd><a href="/wiki/Portal:Contents/Portals#Health_and_fitness"
title="Portal:Contents/Portals">Health</a></dd>
<dd><a href="/wiki/Portal:Contents/Portals#History_and_events"
title="Portal:Contents/Portals">History</a></dd>
<dd><a href="/wiki/Portal:Contents/Portals#Mathematics_and_logic"
title="Portal:Contents/Portals">Mathematics</a></dd>
<dd><a href="/wiki/Portal:Contents/Portals#Natural_and_physical_sciences"
title="Portal:Contents/Portals">Nature</a></dd>
<dd><a href="/wiki/Portal:Contents/Portals#People_and_self"
```

```
title="Portal:Contents/Portals">People</a></dd>
In the preceding example, we extracted the content from Wikipedia. In this
example also, we extracted the content from class as well as tag.
....
```

Summary

In this chapter, you learned about what web scraping is. We learned about two libraries that are used in extracting the data from a web page. We also extracted information from Wikipedia.

In the next chapter, you will learn about statistics gathering and reporting. You will learn about the NumPy module, data visualization, and displaying data using plots, graphs, and charts.

Questions

1. What is web scrapping?
2. What are the web crawlers?
3. Can you scrape data behind a login page?
4. Can you crawl Twitter?
5. Is it possible to scrap the Java script pages? If yes, how?

Further reading

- Urllib documentation: https://docs.python.org/3/library/urllib.html
- Mechanize: https://mechanize.readthedocs.io/en/latest/
- Scrapemark: https://pypi.org/project/scrape/
- Scrapy: https://doc.scrapy.org/en/latest/index.html

17
Statistics Gathering and Reporting

In this chapter, you will learn about the advanced Python libraries used in statistics for scientific calculations. You are going to learn about the NumPY, Pandas, Matplotlib, and Plotly modules of Python. You will learn about the data visualization techniques and also how to plot the gathered data.

In this chapter, we will cover the following topics:

- NumPY module
- Pandas module
- Data visualization

NumPY module

NumPY is a Python module that provides efficient operations on arrays. NumPY is the fundamental package for scientific computing with Python. This package is commonly used for Python data analysis. A NumPY array is a grid of multiple values.

Install NumPY by running the following command in your Terminal:

```
$ pip3 install numpy
```

We are going to use this numpy library to do operations on a numpy array. Now we are going to see how to create numpy arrays. For that, create a script called simple_array.py and write following code in it:

```
import numpy as np

my_list1 = [1,2,3,4]
my_array1 = np.array(my_list1)
print(my_list11, type(my_list1))
print(my_array1, type(my_array1))
```

Run the script and you will get the following output:

```
student@ubuntu:~$ python3 simple_array.py
```

The output is as follows:

```
[1, 2, 3, 4] <class 'list'>
[1 2 3 4] <class 'numpy.ndarray'>
```

In the preceding example, we have imported the numpy library as np to use numpy functionality. Then we created a simple list, which we converted into an array and for that we used the np.array() function. Finally, we printed the numpy array with type to easily understand a normal array and a numpy array.

The previous example was of a single dimensional array. Now we are going to look at an example of a multi-dimensional array. For that, we that we have to create another list. Let's look at another example. Create a script called mult_dim_array.py and write the following content in it:

```
import numpy as np

my_list1 = [1,2,3,4]
my_list2 = [11,22,33,44]

my_lists = [my_list1, my_list2]
my_array = np.array(my_lists)
print(my_lists, type(my_lists))
print(my_array, type(my_array))
```

Run the script and you will get the following output:

```
student@ubuntu:~$ python3 mult_dim_array.py
```

The output is as follows:

```
[[1, 2, 3, 4], [11, 22, 33, 44]] <class 'list'>
[[ 1  2  3  4]
 [11 22 33 44]] <class 'numpy.ndarray'>
```

In the preceding example, we imported the numpy module. After that, we created two lists: my_list1 and my_list2. Then we made another list of lists (my_list1 and my_list2) and applied the np.array() function on the list (my_lists) and stored it in an object called my_array. Finally, we printed the numpy array.

Now, we are going to look at more operations that can be done with an array. We are going to study how to know the size as well as the data type of our created array; that is, my_array. For that, we just have to apply the shape() function and we will get the size of the array and dtype() function to know the data type of the array on our created array. Let's look at an example of this. Create a script called size_and_dtype.py and write the following in it:

```python
import numpy as np

my_list1 = [1,2,3,4]
my_list2 = [11,22,33,44]

my_lists = [my_list1,my_list2]
my_array = np.array(my_lists)
print(my_array)

size = my_array.shape
print(size)

data_type = my_array.dtype
print(data_type)
```

Run the script and you will get the following output:

```
student@ubuntu:~$ python3 size_and_dtype.py
```

The output is as follows:

```
[[ 1  2  3  4]
 [11 22 33 44]]
(2, 4)
int64
```

In the preceding example, we applied the shape function as `my_array.shape` to get the size of our array. The output was `(2, 4)`. Then we applied the `dtype` function as `my_array.dtype` on the array and the output was `int64`.

Now, we are going to look at some examples of special case arrays.

First, we will make an array with all zeros using the `np.zeros()` function, as shown here:

```
student@ubuntu:~$ python3
Python 3.6.7 (default, Oct 22 2018, 11:32:17)
[GCC 8.2.0] on linux
Type "help", "copyright", "credits" or "license" for more information.
>>> import numpy as np
>>> np.zeros(5)
array([0., 0., 0., 0., 0.])
>>>
```

After making the array with all zeros, we are going to make the array with all 1's using the `np.ones()` function of `numpy`, as shown here:

```
>>> np.ones((5,5))
array([[1., 1., 1., 1., 1.],
       [1., 1., 1., 1., 1.],
       [1., 1., 1., 1., 1.],
       [1., 1., 1., 1., 1.],
       [1., 1., 1., 1., 1.]])
>>>
```

`np.ones((5,5))` creates an array of 5*5 with all values being 1.

Now, we are going to make an empty array using the `np.empty()` function of `numpy`, as shown here:

```
>>> np.empty([2,2])
array([[6.86506982e-317, 0.00000000e+000],
       [6.89930557e-310, 2.49398949e-306]])
>>>
```

`np.empty()` does not set the array values to zero, like the `np.zeros()` function does. Therefore, it may be faster. Besides, it requires the user to enter all the values manually in the array and should therefore be used with caution.

Now, let's see how to make an identity array using the `np.eye()` function, which results in the array with its diagonal value `1`, as shown here:

```
>>> np.eye(5)
array([[1., 0., 0., 0., 0.],
       [0., 1., 0., 0., 0.],
       [0., 0., 1., 0., 0.],
       [0., 0., 0., 1., 0.],
       [0., 0., 0., 0., 1.]])
>>>
```

Now, we are going to see the `range` function, which is used to create an array using the `np.arange()` function of `numpy`, as shown here:

```
>>> np.arange(10)
array([0, 1, 2, 3, 4, 5, 6, 7, 8, 9])
>>>
```

The `np.arange(10)` function creates the array of range `0-9`. We defined the range value `10`, and because of that, the array index value starts with `0`.

Using arrays and scalars

In this section, we are going to look at various arithmetic operations on arrays using `numpy`. For that, first we will create a multidimensional array, as follows:

```
student@ubuntu:~$ python3
Python 3.6.7 (default, Oct 22 2018, 11:32:17)
[GCC 8.2.0] on linux
Type "help", "copyright", "credits" or "license" for more information.
>>> import numpy as np
>>> from __future__ import division
>>> arr = np.array([[4,5,6],[7,8,9]])
>>> arr
array([[4, 5, 6],
       [7, 8, 9]])
>>>
```

Here, we imported the `numpy` module to use the `numpy` functionality, and then we imported the `__future__` module that will take care of floats. After that, we created a two dimensional array, `arr`, to perform various operations on it.

Now, let's look at some arithmetic operations on arrays. First, we will study the multiplication of arrays, as shown here:

```
>>> arr*arr
array([[16, 25, 36],
       [49, 64, 81]])
>>>
```

In the preceding multiplication operation, we multiplied the `arr` array twice to get a multiplied array. You can also multiply two different arrays.

Now, we are going to look at a subtraction operation on an array, as shown here:

```
>>> arr-arr
array([[0, 0, 0],
       [0, 0, 0]])
>>>
```

As shown in the preceding example, we just use the – operator to do the subtraction of two arrays. After the subtraction of the arrays, we got the resultant array, as shown in the preceding code.

Now we are going to look at arithmetic operations on arrays with scalars. Let's look at some operations:

```
>>> 1 / arr
array([[0.25       ,  0.2       ,   0.16666667],
       [0.14285714 ,  0.125     ,   0.11111111]])
>>>
```

In the preceding example, we divided 1 by our array and got the output. Remember, we imported the __future__ module, which is actually useful for such operations, to take care of float values in the array.

Now we will look at the exponential operation on the numpy array, as shown here:

```
>>> arr ** 3
array([[ 64, 125, 216],
       [343, 512, 729]])
>>>
```

In the preceding example, we took a cube of our array and it gave the output as the cube of each value in the array.

Array indexing

The indexing of arrays is done using an array as an index. With an index array, a copy of the original array is returned. numpy arrays can be indexed using any other sequence or by using any other array, excluding tuples. The last element in the array can be indexed by -1 and the second last element can be indexed by -2, and so on.

So, to perform indexing operations on the array, first we create a new numpy array and for that we are going to use the range() function to create the array, as shown here:

```
student@ubuntu:~$ python3
Python 3.6.7 (default, Oct 22 2018, 11:32:17)
[GCC 8.2.0] on linux
Type "help", "copyright", "credits" or "license" for more information.
>>> import numpy as np
>>> arr = np.arange(0,16)
>>> arr
array([ 0,  1,  2,  3,  4,  5,  6,  7,  8,  9, 10, 11, 12, 13, 14, 15])
>>>
```

In the preceding example, we created the array arr with the range 16; that is, 0-15.

Now, we are going to perform a different indexing operation on array arr. First, let's get the value in the array at a particular index:

```
>>> arr[7]
7
>>>
```

In the preceding example, we accessed the array by its index value and after passing the index number to the array arr, the array returned the value 7, which is the particular indexed number that we pass.

After getting the value at a particular index, we are going to get values in a range. Let's look at the following example:

```
>>> arr[2:10]
array([2, 3, 4, 5, 6, 7, 8, 9])
>>> arr[2:10:2]
array([2, 4, 6, 8])
>>>
```

In the preceding example, first we accessed the array and got values in a range of (2-10). As a result, it shows the output as `array([2, 3, 4, 5, 6, 7, 8, 9])`. In the second term, `arr[2:10:2]`, it actually states that access array in the range of 2-10 in the interval of two step. The syntax of this kind of indexing is `arr[_start_value_:_stop_value_:_steps_]`. So, as the output of second term, we get `array([2, 4, 6, 8])`.

We can also get values in the array from the index until the end, as show in the following example:

```
>>> arr[5:]
array([ 5,  6,  7,  8,  9, 10, 11, 12, 13, 14, 15])
>>>
```

As we seen in the preceding example, we accessed the values in the array from the 5th index value until the end. As a result, we got the output as `array([ 5, 6, 7, 8, 9, 10, 11, 12, 13, 14, 15])`.

Now we are going to look at slicing of the numpy array. In slicing, we actually take some part of our original array and store it in a specified array name. Let's look at an example:

```
>>> arr_slice = arr[0:8]
>>> arr_slice
array([0, 1, 2, 3, 4, 5, 6, 7])
>>>
```

In the preceding example, we take slice of the original array. As a result, we got a slice of the array with values 0, 1, 2, ..., 7. We can also give updated values to the slice of the array. Let's look at an an example:

```
>>> arr_slice[:] = 29
>>> arr_slice
array([29, 29, 29, 29, 29, 29, 29, 29])
>>>
```

In the the preceding example, we set all values in the array slice to 29, . But the important thing while assigning values to the array slice is that the value assigned to the slice will also get assigned to the original set of the array.

Let's see the result after giving values to the slice of the array and the effect on our original array:

```
>>> arr
array([29, 29, 29, 29, 29, 29, 29, 29,  8,  9, 10, 11, 12, 13, 14, 15])
>>>
```

Now, we are going to look at another operation; that is, copying the array. The difference between slicing and copying of arrays is that when we do the slicing of the array, the changes made are going to be applied on the original array. When we get a copy of the array, it gives an explicit copy of the original array. Therefore, the changes applied onto the copy of the array do not affect the original array. So let's look at an example of copying an array:

```
>>> cpying_arr = arr.copy()
>>> cpying_arr
array([29, 29, 29, 29, 29, 29, 29, 29,  8,  9, 10, 11, 12, 13, 14, 15])
>>>
```

In the preceding example, we just take a copy of the original array. For that, we use the `array_name.copy()` function and the output is the copy the original array.

Indexing a 2D array

A 2D array is an array of arrays. In this, the position of the data element normally refers to two indices instead of one and it represents the table with rows and columns of data. Now we are going to do indexing of such a type of arrays.

So, let's look at an example of a 2D array:

```
>>> td_array = np.array(([5,6,7],[8,9,10],[11,12,13]))
>>> td_array
array([[ 5,  6,   7],
       [ 8,  9,  10],
       [11, 12,  13]])
>>>
```

In the preceding example, we created a 2D array named `td_array`. After creating an array, we printed `td_array`. Now we are also going to fetch the values in `td_array` through indexing. Let's look at an example to access values through indexing:

```
>>> td_array[1]
array([ 8,  9, 10])
>>>
```

In the preceding example, we accessed the first index value of the array and we got the output. In such a type of indexing, when we access the value, we get the whole array. Instead of getting the whole array, we can also get access to particular value. Let's look at an example:

```
>>> td_array[1,0]
8
>>>
```

In the preceding example, we accessed td_array by passing two values for the row and column. As seen in the output, we got the value 8.

We can also set up the two-dimensional array in a different way. First, set our 2D array with increased length. Let's set the length to 10. So, for that, we create a sample array with all zeros in it and, after that, we are going to put values in it. Let's look at an example:

```
>>> td_array = np.zeros((10,10))
>>> td_array
array([[0., 0., 0., 0., 0., 0., 0., 0., 0., 0.],
       [0., 0., 0., 0., 0., 0., 0., 0., 0., 0.],
       [0., 0., 0., 0., 0., 0., 0., 0., 0., 0.],
       [0., 0., 0., 0., 0., 0., 0., 0., 0., 0.],
       [0., 0., 0., 0., 0., 0., 0., 0., 0., 0.],
       [0., 0., 0., 0., 0., 0., 0., 0., 0., 0.],
       [0., 0., 0., 0., 0., 0., 0., 0., 0., 0.],
       [0., 0., 0., 0., 0., 0., 0., 0., 0., 0.],
       [0., 0., 0., 0., 0., 0., 0., 0., 0., 0.],
       [0., 0., 0., 0., 0., 0., 0., 0., 0., 0.]])
>>> for i in range(10):
...     td_array[i] = i
...
>>> td_array
array([[0., 0., 0., 0., 0., 0., 0., 0., 0., 0.],
       [1., 1., 1., 1., 1., 1., 1., 1., 1., 1.],
       [2., 2., 2., 2., 2., 2., 2., 2., 2., 2.],
       [3., 3., 3., 3., 3., 3., 3., 3., 3., 3.],
       [4., 4., 4., 4., 4., 4., 4., 4., 4., 4.],
       [5., 5., 5., 5., 5., 5., 5., 5., 5., 5.],
       [6., 6., 6., 6., 6., 6., 6., 6., 6., 6.],
       [7., 7., 7., 7., 7., 7., 7., 7., 7., 7.],
       [8., 8., 8., 8., 8., 8., 8., 8., 8., 8.],
       [9., 9., 9., 9., 9., 9., 9., 9., 9., 9.]])
>>>
```

In the preceding example, we created one two-dimensional array with the length 10 by 10.

Now let's do some fancy indexing on it, as shown in the following example:

```
>>> td_array[[1,3,5,7]]
array([[1., 1., 1., 1., 1., 1., 1., 1., 1., 1.],
       [3., 3., 3., 3., 3., 3., 3., 3., 3., 3.],
       [5., 5., 5., 5., 5., 5., 5., 5., 5., 5.],
       [7., 7., 7., 7., 7., 7., 7., 7., 7., 7.]])
>>>
```

In the preceding example, we fetch particular index values. So, in the result, we got the output.

Universal array functions

Universal functions perform the operations on all the elements in a numpy array. Now, we are going to look at an example to perform multiple universal functions on an array. First, we are going to take the square root of the array. Create a script called sqrt_array.py and write the following content in it:

```
import numpy as np

array = np.arange(16)
print("The Array is : ",array)
Square_root = np.sqrt(array)
print("Square root of given array is : ", Square_root)
```

Run the script and you will get the following output:

```
student@ubuntu:~/work$ python3 sqrt_array.py
```

The output is as follows:

```
The Array is : [ 0 1 2 3 4 5 6 7 8 9 10 11 12 13 14 15]
Square root of given array is : [0. 1. 1.41421356 1.73205081 2. 2.23606798
 2.44948974 2.64575131 2.82842712 3. 3.16227766 3.31662479
 3.46410162 3.60555128 3.74165739 3.87298335]
```

In the preceding example, we created one simple array using range as a function of numpy. Then we applied the sqrt() function on the generated array to get the square root of the array. After taking the square root of the array, we are going to apply another universal function on the array, which is the exponential exp() function. Let's look at an example. Create a script called expo_array.py and write the following content in it:

```python
import numpy as np

array = np.arange(16)
print("The Array is : ",array)
exp = np.exp(array)
print("exponential of given array is : ", exp)
```

Run the script and you will get the following output:

```
student@ubuntu:~/work$ python3 expo_array.py
```

The output is as follows:

```
The Array is :   [ 0  1  2  3  4  5  6  7  8  9 10 11 12 13 14 15]
exponential of given array is :   [1.00000000e+00 2.71828183e+00
7.38905610e+00 2.00855369e+01
 5.45981500e+01 1.48413159e+02 4.03428793e+02 1.09663316e+03
 2.98095799e+03 8.10308393e+03 2.20264658e+04 5.98741417e+04
 1.62754791e+05 4.42413392e+05 1.20260428e+06 3.26901737e+06]
```

In the preceding example, we created one simple array using the range function of numpy. Then we applied the exp() function on the generated array to get the exponential of the array.

Pandas module

In this section, we are going to learn about the pandas module. The pandas module provides fast and flexible data structures that are designed for working with structured and time series data. The pandas module is used for data analysis. The pandas module is built on packages such as NumPY and Matplotlib and gives us a place to do most of our analysis and visualization work in. To use the functionality of this module, you must import it first.

First, install the following packages that we need in our examples by running the following commands:

```
$ pip3 install pandas
$ pip3 install matplotlib
```

Here, we are going to look at some examples of using the pandas module. We will learn about two data structures: Series and DataFrames. We are also going to see how we can read the data from a `csv` file using pandas.

Series

The pandas series is a one-dimensional array. It can hold any data type. The labels are referred to as the index. Now, we are going to look at an example of series without declaring an index and series with declaring an index. First, we will look at an example of series without declaring an index. For that, create a script called `series_without_index.py` and write the following content in it:

```
import pandas as pd
import numpy as np

s_data = pd.Series([10, 20, 30, 40], name = 'numbers')
print(s_data)
```

Run the script and you will get the following output:

```
student@ubuntu:~/work$ python3 series_without_index.py
```

The output is as follows :

```
0  10
1  20
2  30
3  40
Name: numbers, dtype: int64
```

In the preceding example, we learned about series without declaring an index. First, we imported two modules: pandas and `numpy`. Next, we created the `s_data` object that will store the series data. In that series, we created a list and instead of declaring an index, we provided the name attribute, which will give a name to the list, and then we printed the data. In the output, the left column is your index for the data. Even if we never provide the index, pandas will give it implicitly. The index will always start from 0. Underneath the columns is the name of our series and the data type of the values.

Now, we are going to look at an example of a series when declaring an index. Here we are also going to perform indexing and slicing operations. For that, create a script called `series_with_index.py` and write the following content in it:

```
import pandas as pd
import numpy as np

s_data = pd.Series([10, 20, 30, 40], index = ['a', 'b', 'c', 'd'], name =
'numbers')
print(s_data)
print()
print("The data at index 2 is: ", s_data[2])
print("The data from range 1 to 3 are:\n", s_data[1:3])
```

Run the script and you will get the following output:

```
student@ubuntu:~/work$ python3 series_with_index.py
a    10
b    20
c    30
d    40
Name: numbers, dtype: int64


The data at index 2 is:  30
The data from range 1 to 3 are:
 b    20
c    30
Name: numbers, dtype: int64
```

In the preceding example, we provided an index value for our data in the `index` attribute. In the output, the left column is the index values that we provided.

DataFrames

In this section, we are going to learn about pandas DataFrames. DataFrames are two-dimensional labeled data structures that have columns and may be of different data types. DataFrames are similar to SQL tables or a spreadsheet. They are the most common object when working with pandas.

Now, we are going to look at an example of reading data from a `csv` file into a DataFrame. For that, you must have a `csv` file present in your system. If you don't have a `csv` file in your system, create a file named `employee.csv`, as follows:

```
Id, Name, Department, Country
101, John, Finance, US
102, Mary, HR, Australia
103, Geeta, IT, India
104, Rahul, Marketing, India
105, Tom, Sales, Russia
```

Now, we are going to read this `csv` file into a DataFrame. For that, create a script called `read_csv_dataframe.py` and write the following content in it:

```python
import pandas as pd

file_name = 'employee.csv'
df = pd.read_csv(file_name)
print(df)
print()
print(df.head(3))
print()
print(df.tail(1))
```

Run the script and you will get the following output:

```
student@ubuntu:~/work$ python3 read_csv_dataframe.py
Output:
    Id     Name  Department    Country
0  101     John     Finance         US
1  102     Mary          HR  Australia
2  103    Geeta          IT      India
3  104    Rahul   Marketing      India
4  105      Tom       Sales     Russia


    Id     Name  Department    Country
0  101     John     Finance         US
1  102     Mary          HR  Australia
2  103    Geeta          IT      India

    Id  Name  Department  Country
4  105   Tom       Sales   Russia
```

In the preceding example, we first created a `csv` file called `employee.csv`. We are using the pandas module to create data frames. The goal is to read that `csv` file into the DataFrame. Next, we created a `df` object and we are reading the contents of a `csv` file into it. Next we are printing a DataFrame. Here, we used the `head()` and `tail()` methods to get the particular number of lines of data. We specified `head(3)`, which means we are printing the first three lines of data. We also specified `tail(1)`, which means we are printing the last line of data.

Data visualization

Data visualization is the term that describes the efforts in understanding the significance of data, placing it in a visual manner. In this section, we are going to look at the following data visualization techniques:

- Matplotlib
- Plotly

Matplotlib

Matplotlib is the data visualization library in Python and it allows us to generate plots, histograms, power spectra, bar charts, error charts, scatter plots, and so on, using a few lines of code. Matplotlib usually make things easier and the hardest things possible.

To use `matplotlib` in your Python program, first we have to install `matplotlib`. Run the following command in your Terminal to install `matplotlib`:

```
$ pip3 install matplotlib
```

Now, you have to install one more package, `tkinter`, for graphical representations. Install it using the following command:

```
$ sudo apt install python3-tk
```

Now that `matplotlib` is installed in your system, we will look at some examples. While plotting, there are two important components: figures and axes. The figure is the container that acts as the window on which everything is drawn. It can have various types of independent figures. The axis is the area where you can plot your data and any labels associated with it. Axes consist of an x axis and a y axis.

Now, we are going to look at some examples of `matplotlib`. Let's start with a simple example. Create a script called `simple_plot.py` and write the following content in it:

```
import matplotlib.pyplot as plt
import numpy as np

x = np.linspace(0, 5, 10)
y = x**2
plt.plot(x,y)
plt.title("sample plot")
plt.xlabel("x axis")
plt.ylabel("y axis")
plt.show()
```

Run the script and you will get the following output:

```
student@ubuntu:~/work$ python3 simple_plot.py
```

The output is as follows:

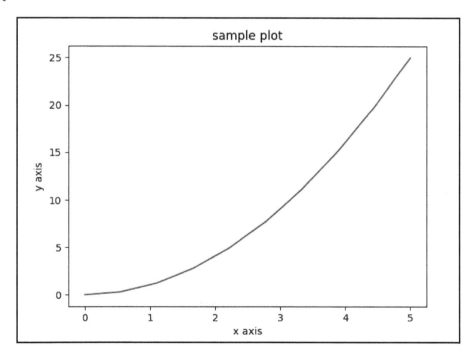

In the preceding example, we imported two modules, matplotlib and numpy, to visualize the data as well as to create the arrays *x* and *y*, respectively. After this, we plotted two arrays as plt.plot(x,y). Then we added a title and labels to the plot using the xlabel(), ylabel(), and title() functions, and to display this plotting, we used the plt.show() function. Because we are using Matplotlib within a Python script, don't forget to add plt.show() at the end line to display your plot.

Now we are going to create two arrays to display two lines of curves in the plot and we are going to apply style to both the curves. In the following example, we will use the ggplot style to plot the graph. ggplot is a system used for creating graphics declaratively, and is based on the grammar of graphics. To plot ghraph, we just provide the data and then tell ggplot how to map variables and what graphical primitives to use, and it takes care of the details. In most cases, we start with the ggplot() style.

Now, create a script called simple_plot2.py and write the following content in it:

```python
import matplotlib.pyplot as plt
from matplotlib import style

style.use('ggplot')

x1 = [0,5,10]
y1 = [12,16,6]
x2 = [6,9,11]
y2 = [6,16,8]

plt.subplot(2,1,1)
plt.plot(x1, y1, linewidth=3)
plt.title("sample plot")
plt.xlabel("x axis")
plt.ylabel("y axis")
plt.subplot(2,1,2)
plt.plot(x2, y2, color = 'r', linewidth=3)
plt.xlabel("x2 axis")
plt.ylabel("y2 axis")

plt.show()
```

Run the script and you will get the following output:

```
student@ubuntu:~/work$ python3 simple_plot2.py
```

The output is as follows:

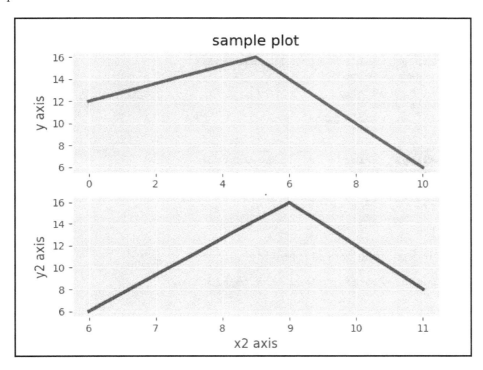

In the preceding example, first we imported the required module, and then we used the ggplot style to plot the graph. We created two sets of array; that is, x1, y1 and x2, y2. Then we used the subplot function, plt.subplot(), because it allows us to plot different things within the same canvas. You can also use the plt.figure() function instead of plt.subplot(), if you want to display these two plots on a different canvas.

Now, we are going to see how to plot the arrays using the plt.figure() function and save our generated figure using Matplotlib. You can save them in different formats, such as png, jpg, pdf, and so on, by using the savefig() method. We'll save the preceding figure in a file named my_sample_plot.jpg. Now, we will look at an example. For that, create a script called simple_plot3.py and write the following content in it:

```
import matplotlib.pyplot as plt
from matplotlib import style

style.use('ggplot')

x1 = [0,5,10]
```

```
y1 = [12,16,6]
x2 = [6,9,11]
y2 = [6,16,8]

plt.figure(1)
plt.plot(x1, y1, color = 'g', linewidth=3)
plt.title("sample plot")
plt.xlabel("x axis")
plt.ylabel("y axis")
plt.savefig('my_sample_plot1.jpg')
plt.figure(2)

plt.plot(x2, y2, color = 'r', linewidth=3)
plt.xlabel("x2 axis")
plt.ylabel("y2 axis")
plt.savefig('my_sample_plot2.jpg')

plt.show()
```

Run the script and you will get the following output:

```
student@ubuntu:~/work$ python3 simple_plot3.py
```

The output is as follows:

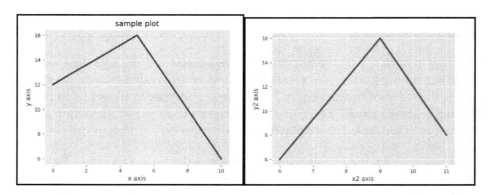

In the preceding example, we used the `plt.figure()` function to plot the things on a different canvas. After that, we used the `plt.plot()` function. This function has different arguments, which are useful to plot the graph. In the preceding example, we used some of arguments; that is `x1`, `x2`, `y1`, and `y2`. These are the respective axis points used to plot.

Then we used the `color` argument to provide a particular color to the graph line and, in the third argument, we used `linewidth`, which decides the width of the graph line. After that, we also used the `savefig()` method to save our figure in a particular image format. You can check them in your current directory (if you did not mention the path) where you run your Python script.

You can open those images by directly accessing that directory or you can also use following method to open those generated images using `matplotlib`. Now, we will look at an example to open saved figures. For that, create a script called `open_image.py` and write the following content in it:

```
import matplotlib.pyplot as plt
import matplotlib.image as mpimg

plt.imshow(mpimg.imread('my_sample_plot1.jpg'))
plt.show()
```

Run the script and you will get the following output:

```
student@ubuntu:~/work$ python3 open_image.py
```

The output is as follows:

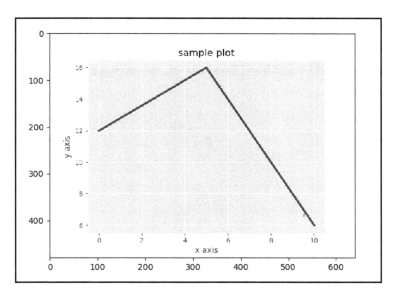

In the preceding example, we used the imshow() function of Matplotlib to open the saved image of the figure.

Now, we will look at different types of plots. Matplotlib allows us to create different types of plots to deal with data in arrays, such as histograms, scatter plots, bar charts, and so on. The use of different kinds of plots depends on the purpose of the data visualization. Let's look at some of these plots.

Histograms

This type of plot helps us to examine the distribution of numerical data in such a way that you are unable to make do with mean or median alone. We are going to use the hist() method to create a simple histogram. Let's look at an example to create a simple histogram. For that, create a script called histogram_example.py and write the following content in it:

```
import matplotlib.pyplot as plt
import numpy as np

x = np.random.randn(500)
plt.hist(x)
plt.show()
```

Run the script and you will get the following output:

```
student@ubuntu:~/work$ python3 histogram_example.py
```

The output is as follows:

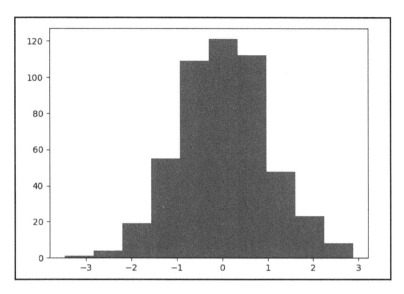

In the preceding example, we created an array of random numbers using numpy. Then we plotted that numerical data using the plt.hist() method.

Scatter plots

This type of plot shows us the data as a collection of points. It offers a convenient way to visualize how numeric values are related. It also helps us to understand the relationships between multiple variables. We are going to use the scatter() method to plot the data in a scatter plot. In a scatter plot, the position of points depends on its x and y axis values; that is, two-dimensional values, so each value in a dataset is a position in either the horizontal or the vertical dimension. Let's look at an example of a scatter plot. Create a script called scatterplot_example.py and write the following content in it:

```
import matplotlib.pyplot as plt
import numpy as np

x = np.linspace(-2, 2, 100)
y = np.random.randn(100)
colors = np.random.rand(100)
plt.scatter(x, y, c=colors)
plt.show()
```

Run the script and you will get the following output:

```
student@ubuntu:~/work$ python3 scatterplot_example.py
```

The output is as follows:

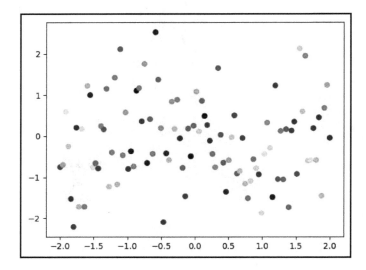

In the preceding example, we got values of x and y. Then we plotted those values using the plt.scatter() method to get a scatter plot for the x and y values.

Bar charts

A bar chart is a chart that represents your data in rectangular bars. You can plot them vertically or horizontally. Create a script called bar_chart.py and write the following content in it:

```
import matplotlib.pyplot as plt
from matplotlib import style

style.use('ggplot')

x1 = [4,8,12]
y1 = [12,16,6]
x2 = [5,9,11]
y2 = [6,16,8]

plt.bar(x1,y1,color = 'g',linewidth=3)
plt.bar(x2,y2,color = 'r',linewidth=3)
```

```
plt.title("Bar plot")

plt.xlabel("x axis")
plt.ylabel("y axis")

plt.show()
```

Run the script and you will get the following output:

```
student@ubuntu:~/work$ python3 bar_chart.py
```

The output is as follows:

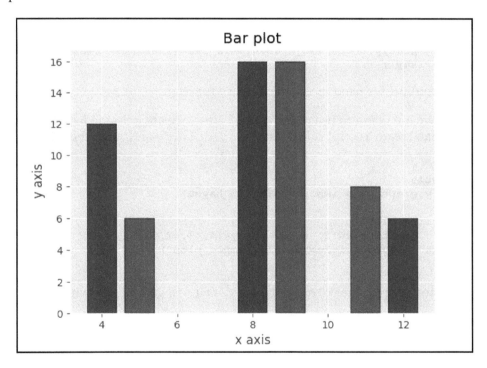

In the preceding example, we have two sets of values: x1, y1 and x2, y2. After getting the numerical data, we used the plt.bar() method to plot the bar chart for the present data.

There are multiple techniques available to plot the data. Among them, there are a few techniques or methods of data visualization using matplotlib, which we have seen. We can also perform such operations using another tool of data visualization: plotly.

Plotly

Plotly is an interactive, open source graphing library in Python. It is a charting library that provides over 30 chart types, such as scientific charts, 3D graphs, statistical charts, financial charts, and more.

To use `plotly` in Python, first we have to install it in our system. To install `plotly`, run the following command in your Terminal:

```
$ pip3 install plotly
```

We can use `plotly` online as well as offline. For online usage, you need to have a `plotly` account and after that you need to set up your credentials in Python:

```
plotly.tools.set_credentials_file(username='Username',
api_key='APIkey')
```

To use `plotly` offline, we need to use the `plotly` function: `plotly.offline.plot()`

In this section, we are going to use plotly offline. Now, we are going to look at a simple example. For that, create a script called `sample_plotly.py` and write the following content in it:

```python
import plotly
from plotly.graph_objs import Scatter, Layout

plotly.offline.plot({
    "data": [Scatter(x=[1, 4, 3, 4], y=[4, 3, 2, 1])],
    "layout": Layout(title="plotly_sample_plot")
})
```

Run the preceding script as `sample_plotly.py`. You will get the following output:

```
student@ubuntu:~/work$ python3 sample_plotly.py
```

The output is as follows:

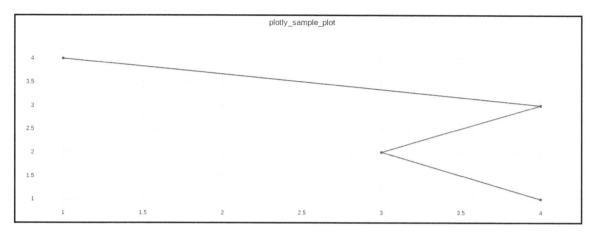

In the preceding example, we imported the `plotly` module and then we set `plotly` for offline use. We put arguments in it, which are useful to plot a graph. In the example, we used some of arguments: `data` and `layout`. In the `data` argument, we define the scatter function with x and y arrays, which have values to plot over the x and y axes, respectively. Then we use the `layout` argument, in which we define the layout function to provide the title for the graph. The output of the preceding program is saved as an HTML file and gets opened in your default browser. This HTML file is in the same directory as your script.

Now let's look at some different types of charts for visualizing the data. So, first, we are going to start with the scatter plot.

Scatter plots

Create a script called `scatter_plot_plotly.py` and write the following content in it:

```
import plotly
import plotly.graph_objs as go
import numpy as np

x_axis = np.random.randn(100)
y_axis = np.random.randn(100)

trace = go.Scatter(x=x_axis, y=y_axis, mode = 'markers')
data_set = [trace]
plotly.offline.plot(data_set, filename='scatter_plot.html')
```

Run the script and you will get the following output:

```
student@ubuntu:~/work$ python3 scatter_plot_plotly.py
```

The output is as follows:

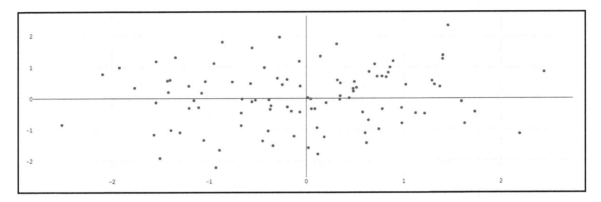

In the preceding example, we imported `plotly` and then created random data by using `numpy` and, for that, import the `numpy` module in your script. After generating the dataset, we created one object named `trace` and inserted our numerical data in it to be scattered. Then, finally, we place the data in the `trace` object into the `plotly.offline.plot()` function to get the scatter plot of data. Like our first sample graph, the output of this example is also saved in HTML format and displayed in your default web browser.

Line scatter plots

We can also create some more informative plots, such as a line scatter plot. Let's look at an example. Create a script called `line_scatter_plot.py` and write the following content in it:

```python
import plotly
import plotly.graph_objs as go
import numpy as np

x_axis = np.linspace(0, 1, 50)
y0_axis = np.random.randn(50)+5
y1_axis = np.random.randn(50)
y2_axis = np.random.randn(50)-5

trace0 = go.Scatter(x = x_axis,y = y0_axis,mode = 'markers',name =
'markers')
trace1 = go.Scatter(x = x_axis,y = y1_axis,mode = 'lines+markers',name =
```

```
'lines+markers')
trace2 = go.Scatter(x = x_axis,y = y2_axis,mode = 'lines',name = 'lines')

data_sets = [trace0, trace1, trace2]
plotly.offline.plot(data_sets, filename='line_scatter_plot.html')
```

Run the script and you will get the following output:

```
student@ubuntu:~/work$ python3 line_scatter_plot.py
```

The output is as follows:

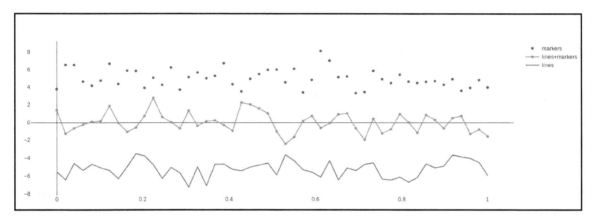

In the preceding example, we imported `plotly`, as well as the `numpy` module. Then we generated some random values for the x-axis and also for three different y-axes. After that, we put that data in the created `trace` object and, finally, put that dataset in plotly's offline function. Then we get the output in the format of scatter as well as line. The output file of this example is saved with the name `line_scatter_plot.html` in your current directory.

Box plots

The box plot is usually informative and also helpful, especially when you have too much to show with very less data. Let's look at an example. Create a script called `plotly_box_plot.py` and write the following content in it:

```
import random
import plotly
from numpy import *

N = 50.
c = ['hsl('+str(h)+','50%'+',50%)' for h in linspace(0, 360, N)]
```

```
data_set = [{
    'y': 3.5*sin(pi * i/N) + i/N+(1.5+0.5*cos(pi*i/N))*random.rand(20),
    'type':'box',
    'marker':{'color': c[i]}
    } for i in range(int(N))]

layout = {'xaxis': {'showgrid':False,'zeroline':False,
'tickangle':45,'showticklabels':False},
          'yaxis': {'zeroline':False,'gridcolor':'white'},
          'paper_bgcolor': 'rgb(233,233,233)',
          'plot_bgcolor': 'rgb(233,233,233)',
          }

plotly.offline.plot(data_set)
```

Run the script and you will get the following output:

```
student@ubuntu:~/work$ python3 plotly_box_plot.py
```

The output is as follows:

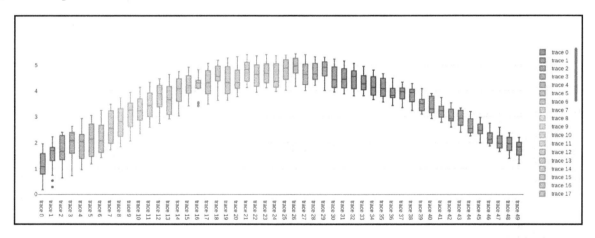

In the preceding example, we imported `plotly`, as well as the `numpy` module. Then we declared N as the total number boxes in the box plot and generated an array of rainbow colors by fixing the saturation and lightness of the HSL representation of color and marching around the hue. Each box is represented by a dictionary that contains the data, the type, and the color. We use list comprehension to describe N boxes, each with a different color and with different randomly generated data. After that, we format the layout of the output and plot the data through the offline `plotly` function.

Contour plots

The contour plot is most commonly used as a scientific plot and used a lot while showing heat map data. Let's look at an example of a contour plot. Create a script called `contour_plotly.py` and write the following content in it:

```
from plotly import tools
import plotly
import plotly.graph_objs as go

trace0 = go.Contour(
    z=[[1, 2, 3, 4, 5, 6, 7, 8],
       [2, 4, 7, 12, 13, 14, 15, 16],
       [3, 1, 6, 11, 12, 13, 16, 17],
       [4, 2, 7, 7, 11, 14, 17, 18],
       [5, 3, 8, 8, 13, 15, 18, 19],
       [7, 4, 10, 9, 16, 18, 20, 19],
       [9, 10, 5, 27, 23, 21, 21, 21]],
    line=dict(smoothing=0),
)
trace1 = go.Contour(
    z=[[1, 2, 3, 4, 5, 6, 7, 8],
       [2, 4, 7, 12, 13, 14, 15, 16],
       [3, 1, 6, 11, 12, 13, 16, 17],
       [4, 2, 7, 7, 11, 14, 17, 18],
       [5, 3, 8, 8, 13, 15, 18, 19],
       [7, 4, 10, 9, 16, 18, 20, 19],
       [9, 10, 5, 27, 23, 21, 21, 21]],
    line=dict(smoothing=0.95),
)
data = tools.make_subplots(rows=1, cols=2,
                           subplot_titles=('Smoothing_not_applied',
'smoothing_applied'))
data.append_trace(trace0, 1, 1)
data.append_trace(trace1, 1, 2)

plotly.offline.plot(data)
```

Run the script and you will get the following output:

```
student@ubuntu:~/work$ python3 contour_plotly.py
This is the format of your plot grid:
[ (1,1) x1,y1 ]   [ (1,2) x2,y2 ]
```

The output is as follows:

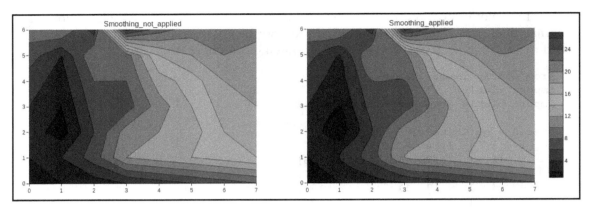

In the preceding example, we took a dataset and applied the `contour()` function on it. Then we appended that contour data in `data_set` and, finally, applied the `plotly` function on the data to get the output. These are some techniques from plotly to plot data in a visual manner.

Summary

In this chapter, we learned about the NumPY and Pandas modules, as well as data visualization techniques. In the NumPY module section, we learned about indexing and slicing the array and the universal array function. In the pandas module section, we learned about Series and DataFrames. We also learned how to read a `csv` file into a DataFrame. In data visualization, we learned about the libraries in Python, which are used for data visualization: `matplotlib` and `plotly`.

In the next chapter, you will learn about MySQL and SQLite database administrations.

Questions

1. What is a NumPy array?
2. What is the output of the following code snippet?

```
import numpy as np
# input array
in_arr1 = np.array([[ 1, 2, 3], [ -1, -2, -3]] )
print ("1st Input array : \n", in_arr1)
in_arr2 = np.array([[ 4, 5, 6], [ -4, -5, -6]] )
print ("2nd Input array : \n", in_arr2)
# Stacking the two arrays horizontally
out_arr = np.hstack((in_arr1, in_arr2))
print ("Output stacked array :\n ", out_arr)
```

3. How do you sum a small array faster than np.sum?
4. How do you delete indices, rows, or columns from a Pandas DataFrame?
5. How do you write a Pandas DataFrame to a file?
6. What is NaN in pandas ?
7. How do you remove duplicates from a pandas DataFrame ?
8. How do you change the size of figures drawn with Matplotlib?
9. What are the alternatives available for plotting graphs using Python ?

Further reading

- 10 minutes to pandas documentation: https://pandas.pydata.org/pandas-docs/stable/
- NumPy tutorial: https://docs.scipy.org/doc/numpy/user/quickstart.html
- Graph plotting using plotly: https://plot.ly/d3-js-for-python-and-pandas-charts/

18
MySQL and SQLite Database Administrations

In this chapter, you will learn about MySQL and SQLite database administration. You will learn to install MySQL and SQLite. You will also learn how to create users, grant privileges, create databases, create tables, insert data into a table, and view all records from the table specific records, and update and delete the data.

In this chapter, you will learn the following:

- MySQL database administration
- SQLite database administration

MySQL database administration

This section will cover MySQL database administration using Python. You already know Python has various modules for `mysql` database administration. So, we will learn about the MySQLdb module here. The `mysqldb` module is an interface for MySQL database server and is used to provide Python database API.

Let's learn how to install MySQL and a Python `mysqldb` package. For this, run the following command in your Terminal:

```
$ sudo apt install mysql-server
```

This command installs the MySQL server and various other packages. While installing the package, we are prompted to enter a password for the MySQL root account:

- The following code is used for checking for the `mysqldb` package to install:

  ```
  $ apt-cache search MySQLdb
  ```

- And the following is for installing the Python interface for MySQL:

  ```
  $ sudo apt-get install python3-mysqldb
  ```

- Now, we will check if `mysql` is installed properly or not. For this, run the following command in Terminal:

  ```
  student@ubuntu:~$ sudo mysql -u root -p
  ```

Once the command runs, you will get the following output:

```
Enter password:
Welcome to the MySQL monitor.  Commands end with ; or \g.
Your MySQL connection id is 10
Server version: 5.7.24-0ubuntu0.18.04.1 (Ubuntu)


Copyright (c) 2000, 2018, Oracle and/or its affiliates. All rights
reserved.

Oracle is a registered trademark of Oracle Corporation and/or its
affiliates. Other names may be trademarks of their respective
owners.


Type 'help;' or '\h' for help. Type '\c' to clear the current input
statement.

mysql>
```

By running `sudo mysql -u root -p`, you will get the `mysql` console. There are some commands used for listing databases and tables, and using the database to store our work. We will see them one by one:

- This is for listing all the databases:

  ```
  show databases;
  ```

- And this is for using the database:

```
use database_name;
```

Whenever we come out of the MySQL console and log in again after some time, we must use the `use database_name;` statement. The purpose of using this command is that our work will be saved in our database. We can understand this in detail with the following examples:

- The following code is used for listing all the tables:

```
show tables;
```

These are the commands we use for listing databases, using the database, and listing the tables.

Now, we will create a database using a create database statement in the `mysql` console. Now, open the `mysql` console using `mysql -u root -p`, then enter your password, which you entered while installing, and press *Enter*. Next, create your database. In this section, we are going to create a database named `test` and we will use this database throughout this section:

```
student@ubuntu:~/work/mysql_testing$ sudo mysql -u root -p

Output:
Enter password:
Welcome to the MySQL monitor.  Commands end with ; or \g.
Your MySQL connection id is 16
Server version: 5.7.24-0ubuntu0.18.04.1 (Ubuntu)

Copyright (c) 2000, 2018, Oracle and/or its affiliates. All rights
reserved.

Oracle is a registered trademark of Oracle Corporation and/or its
affiliates. Other names may be trademarks of their respective
owners.


Type 'help;' or '\h' for help. Type '\c' to clear the current input
statement.


mysql>
mysql> show databases;
+--------------------+
| Database           |
+--------------------+
```

```
| information_schema |
| mysql              |
| performance_schema |
| sys                |
+--------------------+
4 rows in set (0.10 sec)

mysql> create database test;
Query OK, 1 row affected (0.00 sec)

mysql> show databases;
+--------------------+
| Database           |
+--------------------+
| information_schema |
| mysql              |
| performance_schema |
| sys                |
| test               |
+--------------------+
5 rows in set (0.00 sec)

mysql> use test;
Database changed
mysql>
```

First, we listed all the databases using show databases. Next, we created our database test using the create `database` statement. Again, we executed show databases to find whether our database is created or not. Our database is now created. Next, we used that database to store the work we are doing.

Now, we are going to create a user and grant the privileges to that user. Run the following commands:

```
mysql> create user 'test_user'@'localhost' identified by 'test123';
Query OK, 0 rows affected (0.06 sec)

mysql> grant all on test.* to 'test_user'@'localhost';
Query OK, 0 rows affected (0.02 sec)

mysql>
```

We created a `test_user` user; the password for that user is `test123`. Next, we grant all the privileges to our `test_user` user. Now, come out of the `mysql` console by running a `quit;` or `exit;` command.

Now, we are going to see some examples for getting a database version, creating a table, inserting some data into the table, updating the data, and deleting the data.

Getting a database version

First, we will see an example of getting the database version. For that, we will create a `get_database_version.py` script and write the following content in it:

```
import MySQLdb as mdb
import sys

con_obj = mdb.connect('localhost', 'test_user', 'test123', 'test')
cur_obj = con_obj.cursor()
cur_obj.execute("SELECT VERSION()")
version = cur_obj.fetchone()
print ("Database version: %s " % version)

con_obj.close()
```

It is very important to follow the previous steps before running this script; they should not be skipped.

Run the script and you will get the following output:

```
student@ubuntu:~/work/mysql_testing$ python3 get_database_version.py
Output:
Database version: 5.7.24-0ubuntu0.18.04.1
```

In the preceding example, we got the database version. For that, first we imported the MySQLdb module. Then we wrote the connection string. In the connection string, we mentioned our username, password, and database name. Next, we created a cursor object that is used for executing a SQL query. In `execute()`, we passed an SQL query. `fetchone()` retrieves the next row of query result. Next, we printed the result. The `close()` method closes the database connection.

Creating a table and inserting data

Now, we are going to create a table and we will insert some data into it. For that, create a `create_insert_data.py` script and write the following content in it:

```python
import MySQLdb as mdb

con_obj = mdb.connect('localhost', 'test_user', 'test123', 'test')
with con_obj:
        cur_obj = con_obj.cursor()
        cur_obj.execute("DROP TABLE IF EXISTS books")
        cur_obj.execute("CREATE TABLE books(Id INT PRIMARY KEY
AUTO_INCREMENT, Name VARCHAR(100))")
        cur_obj.execute("INSERT INTO books(Name) VALUES('Harry
Potter')")
        cur_obj.execute("INSERT INTO books(Name) VALUES('Lord of the
rings')")
        cur_obj.execute("INSERT INTO books(Name) VALUES('Murder on the
Orient Express')")
        cur_obj.execute("INSERT INTO books(Name) VALUES('The adventures
of Sherlock Holmes')")
        cur_obj.execute("INSERT INTO books(Name) VALUES('Death on the
Nile')")

print("Table Created !!")
print("Data inserted Successfully !!")
```

Run the script and you will get the following output:

```
student@ubuntu:~/work/mysql_testing$ python3 create_insert_data.py

Output:
Table Created !!
Data inserted Successfully !!
```

To check whether your table is created successfully or not, open your `mysql` console and run the following commands:

```
student@ubuntu:~/work/mysql_testing$ sudo mysql -u root -p

Enter password:
Welcome to the MySQL monitor.  Commands end with ; or \g.
Your MySQL connection id is 6
Server version: 5.7.24-0ubuntu0.18.04.1 (Ubuntu)

Copyright (c) 2000, 2018, Oracle and/or its affiliates. All rights
reserved.
```

```
Oracle is a registered trademark of Oracle Corporation and/or its
affiliates. Other names may be trademarks of their respective
owners.

Type 'help;' or '\h' for help. Type '\c' to clear the current input
statement.


mysql>
mysql>
mysql> use test;
Reading table information for completion of table and column names
You can turn off this feature to get a quicker startup with -A


Database changed
mysql> show tables;
+----------------+
| Tables_in_test |
+----------------+
| books          |
+----------------+
1 row in set (0.00 sec)
```

You can see that your table books is created.

Retrieving the data

To retrieve the data from the table, we use the `select` statement. Now, we are going to retrieve the data from our books table. For that, create a `retrieve_data.py` script and write the following content in it:

```
import MySQLdb as mdb

con_obj = mdb.connect('localhost', 'test_user', 'test123', 'test')
with con_obj:
            cur_obj = con_obj.cursor()
            cur_obj.execute("SELECT * FROM books")
            records = cur_obj.fetchall()
            for r in records:
                        print(r)
```

Run the script and you will get the output as follows:

```
student@ubuntu:~/work/mysql_testing$ python3 retrieve_data.py
```

```
Output:
(1, 'Harry Potter')
(2, 'Lord of the rings')
(3, 'Murder on the Orient Express')
(4, 'The adventures of Sherlock Holmes')
(5, 'Death on the Nile')
```

In the preceding example, we retrieved data from tables. We used the MySQLdb module. We wrote a connection string and created a cursor object to execute the SQL query. In execute(), we wrote an SQL select statement. And last, we printed the records.

Updating the data

Now, if we want to make some changes in the records, we can use an SQL update statement. We are going to see an example of an update statement. For that, create a update_data.py script and write following content in it:

```python
import MySQLdb as mdb

con_obj = mdb.connect('localhost', 'test_user', 'test123', 'test')
cur_obj = con_obj.cursor()
cur_obj.execute("UPDATE books SET Name = 'Fantastic Beasts' WHERE Id = 1")
try:
    con_obj.commit()
except:
    con_obj.rollback()
```

Run the script as follows:

```
student@ubuntu:~/work/mysql_testing$ python3 update_data.py
```

Now, to check if your record is updated or not, run retrieve_data.py as follows:

```
student@ubuntu:~/work/mysql_testing$ python3 retrieve_data.py
```

```
Output:
(1, 'Fantastic Beasts')
(2, 'Lord of the rings')
(3, 'Murder on the Orient Express')
(4, 'The adventures of Sherlock Holmes')
(5, 'Death on the Nile')
```

You can see your data for ID 1 is updated. In the preceding example, in execute(), we have written an update statement that will update the data for ID 1.

Deleting the data

To delete a particular record from your table, use a delete statement. We are going to see an example of deleting data. Create a delete_data.py script and write the following content in it:

```
import MySQLdb as mdb

con_obj = mdb.connect('localhost', 'test_user', 'test123', 'test')
cur_obj = con_obj.cursor()
cur_obj.execute("DELETE FROM books WHERE Id = 5");
try:
        con_obj.commit()
except:
        con_obj.rollback()
```

Run the script as follows:

```
student@ubuntu:~/work/mysql_testing$ python3 delete_data.py
```

Now, to check whether your record is deleted or not, run the retrieve_data.py script as follows:

```
student@ubuntu:~/work/mysql_testing$ python3 retrieve_data.py

Output:
(1, 'Fantastic Beasts')
(2, 'Lord of the rings')
(3, 'Murder on the Orient Express')
(4, 'The adventures of Sherlock Holmes')
```

You can see your record, whose ID is 5, is deleted. In the preceding example, we used the delete statement to delete a particular record. Here, we deleted the record whose ID is 5. You can also delete the record according to any field name of your choice.

SQLite database administration

In this section, we are going to learn how to install and use SQLite. Python has the `sqlite3` module to do SQLite database tasks. SQLite is a serverless, zero configuration, transactional SQL database engine. SQLite is very fast and lightweight. The entire database is stored in a single disk file.

Now, we will install SQLite first. Run the following command in your Terminal:

```
$ sudo apt install sqlite3
```

In this section, we are going to learn following the operations: creating database, creating tables, inserting data into table, retrieving the data, and updating and deleting the data from table. We will see each operation one by one.

Now, first, we will see how to create a database in SQLite. To create a database, you simply have to write the command in your Terminal as follows:

```
$ sqlite3 test.db
```

After running this command, you will get the `sqlite` console opened in your Terminal as follows:

```
student@ubuntu:~$ sqlite3 test.db
SQLite version 3.22.0 2018-01-22 18:45:57
Enter ".help" for usage hints.
sqlite>
```

There you go, your database has been created by simply running `sqlite3 test.db`.

Connecting to the database

Now, we will see how to connect to the database. For that, we are going to create a script. Python already has a `sqlite3` module included in the standard library. We just have to import it whenever we are going to work with SQLite. Create a `connect_database.py` script and write the following content in it:

```python
import sqlite3

con_obj = sqlite3.connect('test.db')
print ("Database connected successfully !!")
```

Run the script and you will get the following output:

```
student@ubuntu:~/work $ python3 connect_database.py

Output:
Database connected successfully !!
```

In the preceding example, we imported the `sqlite3` module to perform the functionality. Now, check your directory and you will find the `test.db` file created in your directory.

Creating a table

Now, we are going to create a table in our database. For that, we will create a `create_table.py` script and write the following content in it:

```
import sqlite3

con_obj = sqlite3.connect("test.db")
with con_obj:
            cur_obj = con_obj.cursor()
            cur_obj.execute("""CREATE TABLE books(title text, author
text)""")

print ("Table created")
```

Run the script and you will get the output as follows:

```
student@ubuntu:~/work $ python3 create_table.py

Output:
Table created
```

In the preceding example, we created a table books using a CREATE TABLE statement. First, we established a connection with our database using `test.db`. Next, we created a cursor object that we used to execute the SQL query on our database.

Inserting the data

Now, we will insert the data into our table. For that, we will create a `insert_data.py` script and write the following content in it:

```
import sqlite3

con_obj = sqlite3.connect("test.db")
```

```
with con_obj:
        cur_obj = con_obj.cursor()
        cur_obj.execute("INSERT INTO books VALUES ('Pride and
Prejudice', 'Jane Austen')")
        cur_obj.execute("INSERT INTO books VALUES ('Harry Potter', 'J.K
Rowling')")
        cur_obj.execute("INSERT INTO books VALUES ('The Lord of the
Rings', 'J. R. R. Tolkien')")
        cur_obj.execute("INSERT INTO books VALUES ('Murder on the
Orient Express', 'Agatha Christie')")
        cur_obj.execute("INSERT INTO books VALUES ('A Study in
Scarlet', 'Arthur Conan Doyle')")
        con_obj.commit()

print("Data inserted Successfully !!")
```

Run the script and you will get the following output:

```
student@ubuntu:~/work$ python3 insert_data.py

Output:
Data inserted Successfully !!
```

In the preceding example, we inserted some data into our table. For that, we used `insert` in the SQL statement. By using `commit()`, we are telling the database to save all the current transactions.

Retrieving the data

Now, we are going to retrieve the data from the table. For that, create a `retrieve_data.py` script and write the following content in it:

```
import sqlite3

con_obj = sqlite3.connect('test.db')
cur_obj = con_obj.execute("SELECT title, author from books")
for row in cur_obj:
        print ("Title = ", row[0])
        print ("Author = ", row[1], "\n")

con_obj.close()
```

Run the script and you will get the output as follows:

```
student@ubuntu:~/work$ python3 retrieve_data.py

Output:
Title =  Pride and Prejudice
Author =  Jane Austen

Title =  Harry Potter
Author =  J.K Rowling

Title =  The Lord of the Rings
Author =  J. R. R. Tolkien

Title =  Murder on the Orient Express
Author =  Agatha Christie

Title =  A Study in Scarlet
Author =  Arthur Conan Doyle
```

In the preceding example, we imported the sqlite3 module. Next, we connected with our test.db database . To retrieve the data, we used the select statement. And, last, we printed the retrieved data.

You can also retrieve the data in the sqlite3 console. For that, start the SQLite console first and then retrieve the data as follows:

```
student@ubuntu:~/work/sqlite3_testing$ sqlite3 test.db

Output:
SQLite version 3.22.0 2018-01-22 18:45:57
Enter ".help" for usage hints.
sqlite>
sqlite> select * from books;
Pride and Prejudice|Jane Austen
Harry Potter|J.K Rowling
The Lord of the Rings|J. R. R. Tolkien
Murder on the Orient Express|Agatha Christie
A Study in Scarlet|Arthur Conan Doyle
sqlite>
```

Updating the data

We can update the data from our table using the update statement. Now, we are going to see an example of updating data. For that, create a update_data.py script and write the following content in it:

```
import sqlite3

con_obj = sqlite3.connect("test.db")
with con_obj:
        cur_obj = con_obj.cursor()
        sql = """
                UPDATE books
                SET author = 'John Smith'
                WHERE author = 'J.K Rowling'
                """
        cur_obj.execute(sql)

print("Data updated Successfully !!")
```

Run the script and you will get the following output:

```
student@ubuntu:~/work $ python3 update_data.py

Output:
Data updated Successfully !!
```

Now, to check that the data is actually updated or not, you can run retrieve_data.py, or else you can go to the SQLite console and run select * from books;. You will get the updated output as follows:

```
By running retrieve_data.py:

Output:
student@ubuntu:~/work$ python3 retrieve_data.py
Title =  Pride and Prejudice
Author =  Jane Austen

Title =  Harry Potter
Author =  John Smith

Title =  The Lord of the Rings
Author =  J. R. R. Tolkien

Title =  Murder on the Orient Express
Author =  Agatha Christie
```

```
Title =  A Study in Scarlet
Author =  Arthur Conan Doyle
```

Checking on SQLite console:

```
Output:
student@ubuntu:~/work$ sqlite3 test.db
SQLite version 3.22.0 2018-01-22 18:45:57
Enter ".help" for usage hints.
sqlite>
sqlite> select * from books;
Pride and Prejudice|Jane Austen
Harry Potter|John Smith
The Lord of the Rings|J. R. R. Tolkien
Murder on the Orient Express|Agatha Christie
A Study in Scarlet|Arthur Conan Doyle
sqlite>
```

Deleting the data

Now, we will see an example of deleting data from a table. We are going to do this using the delete statement. Create a delete_data.py script and write the following content in it:

```python
import sqlite3

con_obj = sqlite3.connect("test.db")
with con_obj:
        cur_obj = con_obj.cursor()
        sql = """
                DELETE FROM books
                WHERE author = 'John Smith'
                """
        cur_obj.execute(sql)

print("Data deleted successfully !!")
```

Run the script and you will get the following output:

```
student@ubuntu:~/work $ python3 delete_data.py

Output:
Data deleted successfully !!
```

In the preceding example, we deleted a record from a table. We used the `delete` SQL statement. Now, to check whether the data is deleted successfully or not, run `retrieve_data.py` or start the SQLite console, as follows:

```
By running retrieve_data.py

Output:
student@ubuntu:~/work$ python3 retrieve_data.py
Title =  Pride and Prejudice
Author =  Jane Austen

Title =  The Lord of the Rings
Author =  J. R. R. Tolkien

Title =  Murder on the Orient Express
Author =  Agatha Christie

Title =  A Study in Scarlet
Author =  Arthur Conan Doyle
```

You can see the record whose author was `john smith` is deleted:

```
Checking on SQLite console:

Output:
student@ubuntu:~/work$ sqlite3 test.db
SQLite version 3.22.0 2018-01-22 18:45:57
Enter ".help" for usage hints.
sqlite>
sqlite> select * from books;
Pride and Prejudice|Jane Austen
The Lord of the Rings|J. R. R. Tolkien
Murder on the Orient Express|Agatha Christie
A Study in Scarlet|Arthur Conan Doyle
sqlite>
```

Summary

In this chapter, we learned about MySQL as well as SQLite database administration. We created databases and tables. We then inserted a few records in tables. Using the `select` statement, we retrieved the records. We also learned about updating and deleting the data.

Questions

1. What is database used for?
2. What is CRUD in a database?
3. Can we connect a remote database? If yes, explain with an example.
4. Can we write triggers and procedures inside Python code?
5. What are DML and DDL statements?

Further reading

- Using PyMySQL library: `http://zetcode.com/python/pymysql/`
- MySQLdb, a Python connection guide: `https://mysqlclient.readthedocs.io/`
- The DB-API 2.0 interface for SQLite databases: `https://docs.python.org/3/library/sqlite3.html`

Assessments

Chapter 1, Python Scripting Overview

1. An iterator is an object that can be iterated upon. It is an object that will return data, one element at a time. A generator is a function that returns an object that we can iterate over.
2. Lists are mutable.
3. Data structures in Python are structures that can hold some data together. In other words, they are used to store a collection of related data.
4. We can access the values from a list by using index values.
5. Modules are just files that contain Python statements and definitions.

Chapter 2, Debugging and Profiling Python Scripts

1. To debug the program, the `pdb` module is used.

2. a) Before running `ipython3`, install using `sudo apt-get install ipython3`.
   b) `%lsmagic`.
3. A global interpreter lock is a mechanism used in computer language interpreters to synchronize the execution of threads so that only one native thread can execute at a time
4. Following are the answers:

   a) `PYTHONPATH`: It has a role similar to PATH. This variable tells the Python interpreter where to locate the module files imported into a program. It should include the Python source library directory and the directories containing Python source code. `PYTHONPATH` is sometimes preset by the Python installer.

b) PYTHONSTARTUP: It contains the path of an initialization file containing Python source code. It is executed every time you start the interpreter. It is named as .pythonrc.py in Unix and it contains commands that load utilities or modify PYTHONPATH.

c) PYTHONCASEOK: It is used in Windows to instruct Python to find the first case-insensitive match in an import statement. Set this variable to any value to activate it.

d) PYTHONHOME: It is an alternative module search path. It is usually embedded in the PYTHONSTARTUP or PYTHONPATH directories to make switching module libraries easy.

5. Answer: [0].
   A new list object is created in the function and the reference is lost. This can be checked by comparing the ID of k before and after k = [1].

6. Answer: b. Variable names should not start with a number.

Chapter 3, Unit Testing – Introduction to the Unit Testing Framework

1. Unit testing is a level of software testing where individual units/components of the software are tested. The purpose is to validate that each unit of the software performs as designed.
   Automation testing is an automatic technique where the tester writes scripts on their own and uses suitable software to test the software. It is basically an automation process of a manual process.
   Manual testing is a process of finding out the defects or bugs in a software program. In this method, the tester plays an important role of end user and verifies that all the features of the application are working correctly.

2. Unittest, mock, nose, pytest.

3. A test case is a set of actions executed to verify a particular feature or functionality of your software application. This tutorial describes test case designing and the importance of its various components.

4. PEP 8 is Python's style guide. It's a set of rules for how to format your Python code to maximize its readability. Writing code to a specification helps to make large code bases, with lots of writers. It is more uniform and predictable, too.

Chapter 4, Automating Regular Administrative Activities

1. The `readline()` method reads one entire line from the file. A trailing newline character is kept in the string. If the size argument is present and non-negative, it is a maximum byte count including the trailing newline, and an incomplete line may be returned.

2. Reading: `cat`.
   Creating the new file : `touch`.
   Deletion of the file : `rm`.
   List the file in current directory: `ls`.

3. Following is the answer:

   ```
   os.system("shell_command")
   subprocess.getstatusoutput("shell_command")
   ```

4. Following is the answer:

   ```
   import configparser as config
   config.set(section, option, value)
   ```

5. Following is the answer:

   ```
   psutil, fabric, salt, asnible, buildbot, shinken
   ```

6. Following is the answer:

   ```
   input()
   sys.stdin.readline()
   ```

7. Use `list.sort()` when you want to mutate the list, `sorted()` when you want a new sorted object back. Use `sorted()` when you want to sort something that is an iterable, which is not a list yet. For lists, `list.sort()` is faster than `sorted()` because it doesn't have to create a copy.

Chapter 5, Handling Files, Directories, and Data

1. By using the `pathlib` library.

2. Following is the answer:

   ```
   print(*objects, sep=' ', end='\n', file=sys.stdout, flush=False)
   ```

3. If called without an argument, return the names in the current scope. Otherwise, return an alphabetized list of names comprising (some of) the attributes of the given object, and the attributes reachable from it.

4. A DataFrame is a two-dimensional size, mutable, and potentially heterogeneous tabular data structure with labeled axes.
   Series is the data structure for a single column of a DataFrame, not only conceptually, but literally; that is, the data in a DataFrame is actually stored in memory as a collection of series.

5. List comprehensions provide a concise way to create new lists.

6. Yes:

   ```
   Set comprehension {s**2 for s in range(10)}
   Dict comprehension {n: n**2 for n in range(5)}
   ```

7. Following is the answer:

   ```
   df.head(number of lines) default blank
   df.tail(number of lines) default blank
   ```

8. Following is the answer:

   ```
   [i for i in range(10) if i%2]
   ```

9. Answer: b. It is a list of elements.

Chapter 6, File Archiving, Encrypting, and Decrypting

1. Yes, using the `pyminizip` library of Python.

2. Context managers are a way of allocating and releasing some sort of the resource exactly where you need it. The simplest example is file access:

```
with open ("foo", 'w+') as foo:
foo.write("Hello!")
is similar to
foo = open ("foo", 'w+'):
 foo.write("Hello!")
foo.close()
```

3. Pickling in Python refers to the process of serializing objects into binary streams, while unpickling is the inverse of that.

4. Function with no argument and no return value
   Function with no argument and with return value
   Function with argument and no return value
   Function with argument and return value

Chapter 7, Text Processing and Regular Expressions

1. A regular expression is a method used in programming for pattern matching. Regular expressions provide a flexible and concise means to match strings of text.

2. Following is the answer:

```
import redef is_allowed_specific_char(string):
    charRe = re.compile(r'[^a-zA-Z0-9.]')
    string = charRe.search(string)
    return not bool(string)
 print(is_allowed_specific_char("ABCDEFabcdef123450"))
 print(is_allowed_specific_char("*&%@#!}{"))
```

3. Answer: a.
   `re` is a part of the standard library and can be imported using `import re`.

4. Answer: a.
   It will look for the pattern at the beginning and return None if it isn't found.
5. Answer: d.
   This function returns the entire match.

Chapter 8, Documentation and Reporting

1. The main difference is that when you use the input and print function, all the output formatting job is done behind the scenes. stdin is used for all interactive input, including calls to input(); stdout is used for the output of print() and expression statements and for the prompts of input().

2. **Simple Mail Transfer Protocol (SMTP)** is an internet standard for email transmission. First defined by RFC 821 in 1982, it was updated in 2008 with extended SMTP additions by RFC 5321, which is the protocol in widespread use today.

3. Following is the answer:

   ```
   Hi Eric. You are a comedian. You were in Monty Python.
   ```

4. Following is the answer:

   ```
   str1 + str2 = HelloWorld!
   str1 * 3 = HelloHelloHello
   ```

Chapter 9, Working with Various Files

1. f.readline() reads a single line from the file; a newline character, (\n), is left at the end of the string, and is only omitted on the last line of the file if the file doesn't end in a newline. If you want to read all the lines of a file in a list, you can also use list(f) or f.readlines().

2. Basically, using with open() just ensures that you don't forget to close() the file, making it safer/preventing memory issues.

3. r means the string will be treated as raw string.

4. Generators simplify the creation of iterators. A generator is a function that produces a sequence of results instead of a single value.

5. The pass statement in Python is used when a statement is required syntactically but you do not want any command or code to execute. The pass statement is a null operation; nothing happens when it executes.

6. In Python, an anonymous function is a function that is defined without a name. While normal functions are defined using the `def` keyword, in Python anonymous functions are defined using the `lambda` keyword. Hence, anonymous functions are also called lambda functions.

Chapter 10, Basic Networking – Socket Programming

1. Socket programming involves writing computer programs that enable processes to communicate with each other across a computer network.

2. In distributed computing, a remote procedure call is when a computer program causes a procedure to execute in a different address space, which is coded as if it were a normal procedure call, without the programmer explicitly coding the details for the remote interaction.

3. Following is the answer:

```
import filename (import file)
from filename import function1 (import specific function)
from filename import function1, function2(import multiple
functions)
from filename import * (import all the functions)
```

4. The main difference between lists and a tuples is the fact that lists are mutable whereas tuples are immutable. A mutable data type means that a Python object of this type can be modified. Immutable means that a Python object of this type cannot be modified.

5. You can't have a dict with duplicate keys, because in the backend it uses an hashing mechanism.

6. `urllib` and `urllib2` are both Python modules that perform URL request related stuff but offer different functionalities.
`urllib2` can accept a request object to set the headers for a URL request, `urllib` accepts only a URL. Python requests encode the parameters automatically so you just pass them as simple arguments.

Chapter 11, Handling Emails Using Python Scripting

1. In computing, the Post Office Protocol is an application-layer internet standard protocol used by email clients to retrieve email from a mail server. POP version 3 is the version in common use. The **Internet Message Access Protocol (IMAP)** is an internet standard protocol used by email clients to retrieve email messages from a mail server over a TCP/IP connection. IMAP is defined by RFC 3501.

2. The break statement terminates the loop containing it. Control of the program flows to the statement immediately after the body of the loop. If a break statement is inside a nested loop (a loop inside another loop), the break will terminate the innermost loop. Here's an example:

```
for val in "string":
 if val == "i":
 break
 print(val)
print("The end")
```

3. The continue statement is used to skip the rest of the code inside a loop for the current iteration only. The loop does not terminate but continues on with the next iteration:

```
for val in "string":
 if val == "i":
 continue
 print(val)
print("The end")
```

4. The `pprint` module provides a capability to pretty-print arbitrary Python data structures in a form that can be used as input to the interpreter. If the formatted structures include objects that are not fundamental Python types, the representation may not be loadable. This may be the case if objects such as files, sockets, classes, or instances are included, as well as many other built-in objects that are not representable as Python constants.

5. A negative index is used in Python to index starting from the last element of the list, tuple, or any other container class that supports indexing. −1 refers to the *last index*, −2 refers to the *second last index*, and so on.

6. Python compiles the `.py` files and saves them as `.pyc` files , so it can reference them in subsequent invocations. `.pyc` contains the compiled bytecode of Python source files. `.pyc` contains the compiled bytecode of Python source files, which is what the Python interpreter compiles the source to. This code is then executed by Python's virtual machine . There's no harm in deleting them `.pyc`, but they will save compilation time if you're doing lots of processing.

7. Following is the answer:

```
num = 7
for index in range(num,0,-1):
if index % 2 != 0:
for row in range(0,num-index):
print(end=" ")
for row in range(0,index):
if row % 2== 0:
print("1",end=" ")
else:
print("0",end=" ")
print()
```

Chapter 12, Remote Monitoring of Hosts Over Telnet and SSH

1. A client-server model is a distributed application structure that partitions tasks or workloads between the providers of a resource or service, called servers, and service requesters, called clients.

2. By using the following:

```
os.commands(command_name)
subprocess.getstatusoutput(command_name)
```

3. A virtual LAN is any broadcast domain that is partitioned and isolated in a computer network at the data link layer. LAN is the abbreviation for local area network and in this context virtual refers to a physical object recreated and altered by additional logic.

4. Answer: []．
   It prints a blank list because the size of list is less than 10.

5. Following is the answer:

```
import calender
calendar.month(1,1)
```

6. Following is the answer:

```
def file_lengthy(fname):
 with open(fname) as f:
 for i, l in enumerate(f):
 pass
 return i + 1
print("Number of lines in the file: ",file_lengthy("test.txt"))
```

Chapter 13, Building Graphical User Interfaces

1. Graphical User Interface, which allows a user to interact with electronic devices.
2. A constructor is a special type of method (function) that is used to initialize the instance members of the class. Implementation of the__init__ method. A destructor is a special method called automatically during the destruction of an object. Implementation of the__del__ method.
3. Self is an object reference to the object itself; therefore, they are the same.
4. Tkinter is a Python binding to the Tk GUI toolkit. It is the standard Python interface to the Tk GUI toolkit, and is Python's de facto standard GUI. Tkinter is included with standard Linux, Microsoft Windows, and macOS X installs of Python. The name Tkinter comes from the Tk interface. PyQt is a Python binding of the cross-platform GUI toolkit Qt, implemented as a Python plugin. PyQt is free software developed by the British firm Riverbank Computing. wxPython is a wrapper for the cross-platform GUI API wxWidgets for the Python programming language. It is one of the alternatives to Tkinter, which is bundled with Python. It is implemented as a Python extension module. Other popular alternatives are PyGTK, its successor PyGObject, and PyQt.
5. Following is the answer:

```
def copy(source, destination):
    with open(source, "w") as fw, open(destination,"r") as fr:
        fw.writelines(fr)
copy(source_file_name1, file_name2)
```

6. Following is the answer:

```
fname = input("Enter file name: ")
l=input("Enter letter to be searched:")
k = 0
with open(fname, 'r') as f:
    for line in f:
        words = line.split()
        for i in words:
            for letter in i:
                if(letter==l):
                    k=k+1
print("Occurrences of the letter:")
print(k)
```

Chapter 14, Working with Apache and Other Log Files

1. Runtime exceptions occur during execution of the program and they exit abruptly in between. Compile time exceptions are those that are found before program executions start.

2. A regular expression, regex, or regexp is a sequence of characters that define a search pattern. Usually this pattern is used by string searching algorithms for find or find and replace operations on strings, or for input validation.

3. Here's a description of the Linux commands:
   - `head`: used to see the first N number of lines of plain files.
   - `tail`: used to see the last N number of lines of plain files.
   - `cat`: used to see the content of plain files.
   - `awk`: AWK is a programming language designed for text processing and typically used as a data extraction and reporting tool. It is a standard feature of most Unix-like operating systems.

4. Following is the answer:

```
def append(source, destination):
    with open(source, "a") as fw, open(destination,"r") as fr:
        fw.writelines(fr)
append(source_file_name1, file_name2)
```

5. Following is the answer:

```
filename=input("Enter file name: ")
for line in reversed(list(open(filename))):
    print(line.rstrip())
```

6. The output for the expressions are as follows:
    1. C@ke
    2. Cooookie
    3. <h1>

Chapter 15, SOAP and REST API Communication

1. REST is basically an architectural style of the web services that work as a channel of communication between different computers or systems on the internet. SOAP is a standard communication protocol system that permits processes using different operating systems, such as Linux and Windows, to communicate via HTTP and its XML. SOAP-based APIs are designed to create, recover, update, and delete records, such as accounts, passwords, leads, and custom objects.
2. json.load can deserialize a file itself; that is, it accepts file objects.
3. Yes. JSON is platform independent.
4. Answer: false.
5. Answer: {'x': 3}.

Chapter 16, Web Scraping – Extracting Useful Data from Websites

1. Web scraping, web harvesting, or web data extraction is data scraping used for extracting data from websites. Web scraping software may access the World Wide Web directly using the Hypertext Transfer Protocol, or through a web browser.
2. A web crawler (also known as a web spider or web robot) is a program or automated script that browses the World Wide Web in a methodical, automated manner. This process is called web crawling or spidering.

3. Yes.

4. Yes, using Tweepy.

5. Yes, by using the Selenium-Python web driver. Other libraries are also available, such as PhantomJS and dryscrape.

Chapter 17, Statistics Gathering and Reporting

1. NumPy's main object is the homogeneous multidimensional array. It is a table of elements (usually numbers), all of the same type, indexed by a tuple of positive integers. In NumPy, dimensions are called axes.

2. Following is the output:

```
1st Input array :
 [[ 1  2  3]
 [-1 -2 -3]]
2nd Input array :
 [[ 4  5  6]
 [-4 -5 -6]]
Output stacked array :
 [[ 1  2  3  4  5  6]
 [-1 -2 -3 -4 -5 -6]]
```

3. Following is the answer:

```
Z = np.arange(10)
np.add.reduce(Z)
```

4. Following is the answer:

```
# Delete the rows with labels 0,1,5
data = data.drop([0,1,2], axis=0)
# Delete the first five rows using iloc selector
data = data.iloc[5:,]
#to delete the column
del df.column_name
```

5. Following is the answer:

```
df.to_csv("file_name.csv",index=False, sep=",")
```

6. **Not a number** (NaN), such as a null value. Within pandas, a missing value is denoted by NaN.

7. Following is the answer:

```
df.drop_duplicates()
```

8. Following is the answer:

```
from matplotlib.pyplot import figure
figure(num=None, figsize=(8, 6), dpi=80, facecolor='w',
edgecolor='k')
```

9. Matplotlib, Plotly, and Seaborn.

Chapter 18, MySQL and SQLite Database Administrations

1. To store the data in rows and columns, and perform the different operations easily and faster.
2. In the database, CRUD means (Create, Read, Update, Delete).
3. Yes, here's an example:

```
MySQLdb.connect('remote_ip', 'username', 'password', 'databasename')
```

4. Yes.
5. **DDL** stands for **Data Definition Language**. It is used to define data structures. For example, with SQL, it would be instructions such as create table, alter table. **DML** stands for **Data Manipulation Language**. It is used to manipulate the data itself. For example, with SQL, it would be instructions such as insert, update, and delete.

Other Books You May Enjoy

If you enjoyed this book, you may be interested in these other books by Packt:

PowerShell Core for Linux Administrators Cookbook
Prashanth Jayaram, Ram Iyer

ISBN: 978-1-78913-723-1

- Leverage the object model of the shell, which is based on .NET Core
- Administer computers locally as well as remotely using PowerShell over OpenSSH
- Get to grips with advanced concepts of PowerShell functions
- Use PowerShell for administration on the cloud
- Know the best practices pertaining to PowerShell scripts and functions
- Exploit the cross-platform capabilities of PowerShell to manage scheduled jobs, Docker containers and SQL Databases

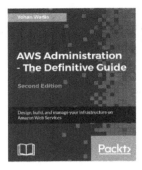

AWS Administration - The Definitive Guide - Second Edition
Yohan Wadia

ISBN: 978-1-78847-879-3

- Take an in-depth look at what's new with AWS, along with how to effectively manage and automate your EC2 infrastructure with AWS Systems Manager
- Deploy and scale your applications with ease using AWS Elastic Beanstalk and Amazon Elastic File System
- Secure and govern your environments using AWS CloudTrail, AWS Config, and AWS Shield
- Learn the DevOps way using a combination of AWS CodeCommit, AWS CodeDeploy, and AWS CodePipeline
- Run big data analytics and workloads using Amazon EMR and Amazon Redshift
- Learn to back up and safeguard your data using AWS Data Pipeline
- Get started with the Internet of Things using AWS IoT and AWS Greengrass

Leave a review - let other readers know what you think

Please share your thoughts on this book with others by leaving a review on the site that you bought it from. If you purchased the book from Amazon, please leave us an honest review on this book's Amazon page. This is vital so that other potential readers can see and use your unbiased opinion to make purchasing decisions, we can understand what our customers think about our products, and our authors can see your feedback on the title that they have worked with Packt to create. It will only take a few minutes of your time, but is valuable to other potential customers, our authors, and Packt. Thank you!

Index